WOMEN IN HIGHER EDUCATION

Changes and Challenges

Edited by
LYNNE B. WELCH

New York
Westport, Connecticut
London

Library of Congress Cataloging-in-Publication Data

Women in higher education : changes and challenges / edited by Lynne
   B. Welch.
      p.   cm.
   Based on papers from the First International Conference for Women
in Higher Education held in El Paso, Texas in January of 1988.
   Includes bibliographical references (p.   ).
   ISBN 0-275-93208-7 (alk. paper)
   1. Women college teachers—United States. 2. Women college
administrators—United States. 3. Mentors in the professions—
United States. 4. Sex discrimination in education—United States.
I. Welch, Lynne B. II. International Conference for Women in Higher
Education (1st : 1988   :   El Paso, Tex.)
LB2332.3.W67   1990
378'.0082—dc20   89-29669

Library of Congress Catalog Card Number: 89-29669
ISBN: 0-275-93208-7

First published in 1990

Praeger Publishers, One Madison Avenue, New York, NY 10010
An imprint of Greenwood Publishing Group, Inc.

Printed in the United States of America

∞

The paper used in this book complies with the
Permanent Paper Standard issued by the National
Information Standards Organization (Z39.48-1984).

10 9 8 7 6 5 4 3 2 1

Contents

Tables and Figures

TABLES

FIGURES

Acknowledgments

I want to acknowledge the assistance of Drs. Rita Landino, Donna Thompson and Jeannette Ludwig for reviewing the individual chapters of this book for their use at the First International Conference for Women in Higher Education held in El Paso, Texas, in January of 1988. Dr. Doreene Alexander gave me valuable assistance and encouragement in the editing and production of this book. The authors are pleased to have an opportunity to share their research and experience with others who are interested in the changes and challenges facing women in higher education today.

SECTION ONE

WOMEN IN HIGHER EDUCATION

Issues that deal with women who work in institutions of higher education are many and varied. In this section such issues as promotion and tenure for women, collaboration both within and without the university, communication styles and aspirations of college women are addressed.

The difficulty of combining motherhood and promotion tenure is explored by Hensel. She found that women in her study who had babies did not encounter difficulties in achieving tenure.

Landino and Welch describe a framework for supporting women in the university environment. Successful strategies are described and examples are given which demonstrate efforts at collaboration and networking in one university setting.

Walker and Kuk followed a group of young college women for ten years to determine whether or not their opinions about life-styles and careers changed. They identify that it is the difficulty in combining a career and managing a household that is the problem, not combining a career and a marriage.

1

Maternity, Promotion, and Tenure: Are They Compatible?

Nancy Hensel

PROBLEMS OF MATERNITY

For the first time in American history there are more women in the labor force than out of it. Recent surveys indicate that three out of five women with children under six are working outside the home and approximately 50 percent of new mothers return to work before their babies are a year old (EPC, 1985).

While most women work because of economic necessity, the importance of work extends beyond the income it provides. Women like being part of the world of work outside the home. Work increases their self-confidence, feelings of independence, autonomy, and powerfulness.

Managing a home, career, and being an effective parent is difficult. While women's roles and their expectations for their lives have changed, social policy has not. The social support system for women's new role is not yet in place. For many American women, the dual roles of worker and mother are overwhelming; some are opting for full-time motherhood; others are choosing full-time careers and foregoing motherhood.

Tillie Olsen (1978) discusses the difficulties women have when they try to combine motherhood and writing. Very few women who were successful writers, she said, were also mothers. Being a mother means being constantly interruptible and continually responsive to the needs of someone else. It is very difficult to develop the concentration necessary to write when one must be readily accessible to children.

In 1897 Charlotte Gilman Perkins wrote,

We have so arranged life that a man may have a house, a family, love, companion-
ship, domesticity and fatherhood and yet remain an active citizen of age and country. We have so arranged life, on the other hand, that a woman must "choose"; she
must either live alone, unloved, uncompanied, uncared for, homeless, childless,
with her work in the world for sole consolation; or give up world service for the
joys of love, motherhood, and domestic service. (Perkins, 1906, p. 496).

Many women are not finding the choices any less difficult now than they
were almost one hundred years ago.

Certainly women do work and have children but the evidence is clear
that, for women, having children is a detriment to a successful career, while
for men it can have a positive effect. Aside from the question of fairness to
women, one might ask what difference does it make whether women writers or women executives have children. Tillie Olsen (1978) argues that the
silences in literature are the lack of the mother's perspective in the work of
women writers. While there are many good women writers, Olsen believes
that there may have been profound understandings of human life that are
absent in literature because so few women wrote from the mother's point
of view. Marilyn Loden (1986) believes that the feminine perspective is
similarly important in business. The same thing could be true in other fields
as well. Would a biologist who is also a mother ask different research questions from a biologist who is not a mother? Or a sociologist, historian, or
psychologist?

STRESS OF DUAL ROLES

Women experience intense feelings of guilt when they feel they are not adequately fulfilling their maternal role. On the other hand, they also experience frustration and guilt when they feel they are not spending enough
time on their work. As a society, we expect women to be good mothers; if
they are also good in their work, that is an added benefit. We expect men to
be good in their careers but we seldom talk about paternal neglect as a result of spending too much time at the office.

Joining the work force doesn't mean women relinquish their home responsibilities. Women with full-time jobs work an average of 70 hours per
week, 35 of those hours are spent doing housework and taking care of children. Men spend an average of seven hours per week working in the home
(Ratner, 1980). Work outside the home is not a liberating experience for
most women; rather it is an increased burden. The stress of managing work
and a family leads to emotional and physical fatigue.

An academic career ought to lend itself to combining motherhood and
work. The hours are flexible, the job is reasonably autonomous, and for

many faculty there is time off during the summer and holidays. Recently, however, the *Chronicle of Higher Education* (MacMillan, 1987) reported an increase of stress among male and female professors. Academic careers are increasingly stressful because the competition is tougher than it used to be; the pay is low; resources for research and travel are tight; and mobility is lessened. Academic careers are especially difficult for women because women assume the major responsibilities for raising a family. Women faculty may be competing against men who have more traditional wives to take care of the home and children. In many ways an academic career is like that of a writer because one needs uninterrupted time to think, read, plan research, and engage in technical writing.

Women have a difficult time in the work force because it has not sufficiently adjusted to accommodate the special needs of women. Just as the school calendar year reflects our Christian, agricultural heritage, the world of work reflects the male dominance in society. Women are different from men and the differences constantly impact upon their work. The basic area of difference is that women, rather than men, bear children. The career cycle has not adjusted to allow time for childbearing. Farber (1977), for example, speculated that the pay differential between men and women faculty is caused in part by the time women take off from their work to have children. Farber found that women of childbearing age earned less than men in comparable positions and were promoted less frequently. When childbearing enters the picture, the conflict between work and femaleness becomes most intense.

Women face tremendous difficulties when they try to combine family and career. Wendy Williams testified in 1977 at the Senate hearings on the Pregnancy Disability Act that "it is fair to say that most of the disadvantages imposed on women, in the work force and elsewhere, derive from the central reality of the capacity of women to become pregnant and the real and supposed implications of this reality" (Williams, 1977, p. 123).

MATERNITY LEGISLATION

Legislatively, the issue of pregnancy and work was first recognized in 1946 when the Federal Railroad Unemployment Insurance Act was passed. This act provided temporary disability insurance for pregnant women. It also provided 16½ weeks maternity leave (Kamerman, 1983). Until 1974, however, pregnant teachers were still forced to leave their jobs without pay in the fourth or fifth month of pregnancy in order to protect children from the sight of a conspicuously pregnant woman (Kamerman, 1983).

During the Kennedy administration (Kennedy's wife was one of the few first ladies to be pregnant while in the White House), the President's Commission on the Status of Women studied the types of protection needed for women and concluded that labor standards should benefit men as well as

women, especially if women would be placed at a disadvantage otherwise. They also concluded that women should receive six months of maternity leave without loss of reemployment and seniority rights. Unfortunately, the Commission's recommendations were not acted upon (Kamerman, 1983).

Ten years later the Equal Economic Opportunity Commission (EEOC) issued guidelines stating that pregnancy should be considered like any other temporary health disability. The Supreme Court, however, did not see it the same way. In 1975, in *Gilbert* v. *General Electric*, the court ruled that the exclusion of pregnancy from disability benefits did not discriminate against women. They concluded that since women were covered for like disabilities to men, the fact that only women could be affected by pregnancy did not constitute sex discrimination (Little, 1985).

In reaction to the Gilbert decision Congress passed the Pregnancy Disability Act (PDA), an amendment to Title VII, which states that discrimination based on pregnancy, childbirth, and related medical conditions or abortion is illegal. Women cannot be fired because of pregnancy nor can an employer refuse to hire a pregnant woman. She is also guaranteed reinstatement after childbirth, and she accrues retirement benefits and accumulates seniority. The thrust of the PDA is that pregnant women must be treated in the same manner as other applicants or employees. If an employer provides disability leave, the same leave needs to be provided for pregnancy (Hewlett, 1986). The law does not require an employer to provide maternity leave. If a company does provide maternity leave, however, it must provide the same benefits for men. California and a few other states have enacted legislation that requires employers to provide minimum maternity leave. But there is no provision for paid leave. The California law was recently challenged by California Federal Bank and other California employers on the basis that it was discriminatory since only women had to be provided with maternity leave. Maria Johnston, deputy attorney general for California said, "Since men never lose their jobs due to pregnancy disability, the state statute does not grant preferential treatment to women. It simply guarantees equality for all workers" (Savage, 1986). The National Organization for Women (N.O.W.) filed a brief with the Supreme Court protesting what they thought could be interpreted as protective legislation (California Federal, 1985). N.O.W.'s position was that the state law granted preferential treatment to women and they felt that employers would react by not hiring women (California Federal, 1985). The court found that the California law was not in conflict with the Pregnancy Disability Act and that it was designed to allow women to have families and continue to work (Savage, 1986).

In 1986 Representative Patricia Schroeder introduced the Parental and Medical Leave Act, H.R. 925. If the bill had passed, it would have required all private and public employers with five or more employees to provide up to four months' parental leave with job security, and up to six months

medical disability leave with job security. Paid leaves are not required (H.R. 925, 1986).

While the Schroeder bill would be an improvement over the present law, it still does not assure U.S. women the benefits that their counterparts in other developed Western countries enjoy. The United States ranks at the bottom of the list when it comes to childbirth policies (Bernstein, 1987). Our present laws are really not concerned with the welfare of children and families, but rather only with the medical condition of the mother. Even this concern is limited because we do not provide national health care for pregnant women.

SURVEY

In 1987 a brief ten-item questionnaire was sent to the Affirmative Action Officers of 57 small, private liberal arts colleges. The colleges were chosen from the National Directory of Colleges and Universities and were selected on the basis of geographic distribution and similarity to the University of Redlands in size, type of college, and tuition costs. Sixteen schools returned the questionnaire. The results are fairly easy to report since most colleges said they treated pregnancy just like any other disability and made no special provisions for maternity. Only two of the responding colleges provided benefits beyond the minimum legally required. One institution provided a one-semester combined childbearing and child rearing leave. The faculty member could teach a three-course load for one semester and receive two-thirds pay for the year. Health and life insurance would be continued as would the TIA-CREF benefit, adjusted for the rate of pay. The continuation of benefits is especially important to a young family. Some institutions were not so generous. One institution indicated that insurance benefits were continued for the month in which the leave started and would resume again the month the employee returned to work. The employee could pay for the benefits while on leave. The only other institution that provided additional maternity benefits gave the employee a choice between a semester leave at one-half pay or a temporary reduction in work load. The reduced work load could include one-half of the employee's regular duties (one course and advising) or a temporary leave during the semester of delivery. The work load reduction would be at full pay. This same institution offered a child care leave of up to one year without pay for either parent.

Only one college surveyed has a policy of stopping the tenure clock for women who give birth. The clock is stopped only if it is deemed necessary and is done by mutual agreement of the faculty member and the administration. A second institution indicated it could stop the tenure clock if it appeared necessary, although it did not have a specific policy.

Fifty-four women faculty members from 13 responding institutions had babies in the last five years. Of these 54 women, only one failed to return to

work after childbirth and one did not achieve tenure. These statistics are significant in two ways. First of all, they indicate that nearly every professional woman will continue with her work even after having children. It also raises the main question of this chapter which is whether childbearing and child rearing really are detrimental to professional advancement.

Sylvia Hewlett (1986) discloses that she did not get tenure at Barnard and attributes that decision in part to the difficulties she experienced in having children and maintaining a professional career. She also states that between 1973 and 1984 four Barnard women assistant professors in the economics department were turned down for tenure. Within a 13-year period the department has gone from a 100 percent female senior faculty to only 25 percent. This is occurring in a period when we are supposedly interested in bringing more women into the academic profession. Alice Rossi (Sandler, 1981) pointed out earlier that women are not as likely to earn tenure as men. Etaugh (1984) and Menges and Exum (1984) also concluded that women are less frequently tenured than their male counterparts. Farber (1977) found the sex differential in awarding tenure was most pronounced during the childbearing years. The number of women in higher faculty ranks is significantly less than the number of men. Currently, almost 33 percent of the pool of Ph.D. candidates is female and about 25 percent of the junior faculty is female. However, a 1982–83 AAUP survey found that there are still very few women in the senior ranks. At Harvard only 4.2 percent of the full professors are women; at Princeton it is 3.2 percent, at Stanford 2.6 percent, and at Yale 3.9 percent (Hewlett, 1986).

At the University of Redlands in 1987 there were 26 women faculty and 85 men faculty. Of this number, 15 women and 65 men were married, and 11 women and 50 men had children. Forty-seven men and ten women were full professors, while nine women and eleven men were assistant professors.

While the statistics from the survey do not indicate that women who have babies encounter difficulties achieving tenure, the results may be a bit skewed because of the type of institution surveyed. All institutions were small and presumably the faculty knew one another relatively well and were aware of each other's relative productivity. At this type of institution, it is possible for a personnel committee to take individual circumstances into consideration in awarding tenure. A woman who is perceived as capable and productive with the exception of the time surrounding her childbearing period might be awarded tenure at a smaller institution whereas she might not at a larger institution. Also, smaller institutions tend to emphasize teaching more than research and publishing in awarding tenure and promotion. Teaching is least likely to be affected by childbearing as opposed to research and writing.

Another difference may be the more intense competition at the larger university. Hochschild (1975) has said that "the classic profile of the aca-

demic career is cut to the image of the traditional man with his traditional wife" (p. 49). She believes that academic women have a difficult time achieving the same professional recognition in a university community because they are competing not just against men, but with the "head of a small branch industry" (p. 49). Women do not have a wife at home who will handle housekeeping and child care responsibilities. Nor do they have a wife who devotes a significant portion of her time to her mate's career. If a woman is married, it is likely that her husband has a career of his own and has little time to support his wife's career. Even men who have working wives are at an advantage over professional women because their wives are more likely to be working at nonprofessional or less competitive jobs. It is said that a professorship is a two-person career. When a woman is in the position, it is a one-person career and the one person may be psychologically divided between home and career.

SOLUTIONS

What can be done and what should be done? Neither laws nor policies will make everyone equally successful. However, laws and the structure of work can provide each individual with an equal opportunity or an equal shot at success. For women, this means being able to choose. Gender equity is essentially the liberty to choose. It also means that the choices made by women must be viable. Gender equity is different from racial equity. Skin color is the only difference between blacks and whites and public policy should be blind to this difference. With gender, however, the differences are significant and we do not wish to ignore them in many aspects of our social structure. The essential difference is that women have the capacity to bear children. This capacity is both their special privilege and their special burden. Gender policy cannot be neutral to the differences between men and women. Women need laws and policies that take into consideration their childbearing capacity if they are truly to have the equal liberty of choice.

We must begin to look at what we are doing to families, women, and children by our efforts to maintain gender-neutral policies. Childbearing does not just effect women and it is not just a women's issue. It is a social issue. Ensuring the successful development of children is no longer an individual issue. It is an issue for society as a whole.

The following are general suggestions for the maternity dilemma:

1. We should add mothers to the protected class of citizens for the purpose of affirmative action. This would allow our national government to develop policies that give preferential treatment to mothers without jeopardizing their employment opportunities. If we placed a premium on employing mothers, they would become a desirable category and employment practices would necessarily ad-

just to their special needs. If it helps in our understanding of this concept, we can view working mothers as veterans. We give preferential treatment to veterans because they have performed a service to their country; certainly bearing and rearing children is equally as important as serving in the armed forces. Producing children is as necessary to our country as defense. Or we could look at mothers as handicapped. Currently, the law treats pregnancy as a temporary disability. Children, however, do not go away when pregnancy is over and many mothers would probably agree that children are a disadvantage to success in one's career.

2. We need a national health care package that will provide prenatal, childbirth, and postnatal care for all mothers and their children. The United States is one of the lowest ranking countries in the world in terms of infant mortality.

3. We need to provide paid childbearing leave for all employed women. Women should not have to make the choice of working or having children. Families should not have their income decline at the very time when they need added income to support a new member of the family.

4. We need a national policy for paid child care leave. The payment ought to be directly to families and allow them the option of choosing which parent would like to stay home and care for the baby or provide child care if both wish to return to work. It ought to be the role of government to support families in the different types of life-styles they choose rather than to advocate or support one particular life-style. Although child development research indicates that infants need a consistent, loving care giver, there is no clear evidence that the care giver must be the biological or psychological parent.

5. Maternity and child care leaves must be job protected with no loss of seniority rights or benefits.

Solutions specific to universities are:

1. Universities need to look at the effect of maternity on women faculty. Personnel policies should provide a means to stop the tenure clock for women who bear children prior to receiving tenure.

2. If a woman chooses to return to work immediately after childbirth, she should still be given the option of stopping the tenure clock for a one-year period.

3. Ways of providing alternate work schedules during the first six months after childbirth should be explored.

REFERENCES

Bernstein, H. (1987, January 21). Maternity leave should be a priority. *Los Angeles Times.*

California Federal Savings and Loan v. *Guerra.* (1985). Brief amicae of the National Organization for Women.

Economic Policy Council. (1985, December). Work and family in the United States: A policy initiative. *Economic Policy Council of UNA-USA.*

Etaugh, C. (1984). Women faculty and administrators in higher education: Changes in their status since 1972. In *Strategies and Attitudes: Women in Educational Administration*, Farrent, P. (Ed.). Washington, D.C.

Farber, S. (1977). The earnings and promotion of women faculty: Comment. *American Economic Review*, 67, 199–206.

Hewlett, S. (1986). *A Lesser Life: The Myth of Women's Liberation in America*. New York: William Morrow.

Hochschild, A. R. (1975). Inside the clockwork of male careers. In *Women and the Power to Change*, Howe, F. (Ed.). New York: McGraw-Hill.

House of Representatives Bill 925. (1986, February).

Kamerman, S. B., et al. (1983). *Maternity Policies and Working Women*. New York: Columbia University.

Little, C. (1985). Mother load or overload. *Journal of International Law and Politics*, 17, 717–749.

Loden, M. (1986). *Feminine Leadership or How to Succeed in Business without Becoming One of the Boys*. New York: Times Books.

MacMillan, L. (1987, February 4). Job related tension and anxiety taking a toll among employees in academe's stress factories. *Chronicle of Higher Education*.

Menges, R. J., and Exum, W. H. (1984). Barriers to the progress of women and minority faculty. *Journal of Higher Education*, 54, (2).

Olsen, T. (1978). *Silences*. New York: Delacorte.

Perkins, C. G. (1906). The passing of matrimony. *Harper's Bazaar*, 40, 496.

Ratner, R. S. (1980). *Equal Employment Policy for Women*. Philadelphia, PA: Temple University.

Sandler, B. (1981). Strategies for eliminating sex discrimination: Times that try men's souls. In *Sex Discrimination in Higher Education*, Farley, J. (ed.). Ithaca, NY: New York State School of Industrial Relations, Cornell University.

Savage, D. (1986, September 24). Pregnancy on the job tests. *Los Angeles Times*.

Williams, W. (1977). *On Discrimination on the Basis of Pregnancy: Report on U.S. Senate Hearings*. Washington, DC: U.S. Government Printing Office.

2

Supporting Women in the University Environment Through Collaboration and Networking

Rita Landino
Lynne B. Welch

Professional women have tried different strategies to warm up the chilly professional climate they experience as faculty and administrators on campus (Project on the Status of Women, 1986). This chilly climate is the result of relatively low numbers of women on campus, particularly in positions of power. Most campuses have yet to achieve the critical mass of women necessary to allow the easy mix of men and women found in "painless networking" (Green, 1982, p. 19). Therefore, planned strategies are necessary.

The authors were instrumental in developing a network of women at a large, comprehensive northeastern state university. We came together out of a need for mutual support and collaboration to improve the atmosphere for women at the university.

THEORETICAL BACKGROUND

Networking has been documented as an important dimension of women's advancement into the traditionally male power structure (Kanter, 1980; Green, 1982; Swoboda & Millar, 1986). Networking has been called an effective substitute for the missing mentors available to women on campus (Kanter, 1980). Moreover, networking has been described as a more effective and less risky model of mentoring for women than the dependent one-to-one grooming model common among men on campus (Swoboda & Millar, 1986).

An effective network provides access to power and resources, creating a bridge to the center of the system (Green, 1982). Consequently, two key ingredients in effective networks are supportive peer groups and access to established leaders. Moreover, networks work most effectively for women who already have some access to power; such women are the ones most motivated to come together for access, knowledge, and support (Green, 1982).

One of the advantages of the network-as-mentor model is the degree to which it fosters what Swoboda and Millar (1986) call "self-reliance," and what Bandura calls "self-efficacy" (1977, 1986). A woman learns the system and how to navigate around its barriers from colleagues acting as role models and verbally encouraging her, as any mentor would. But in contrast with the dependency inherent in the mentor relationship, a woman involved in a collegial network can feel efficacious about her own accomplishments, which are fostered by the supportive environment of the network.

In developing our women's network, the authors implemented a number of the steps outlined by Swoboda and Millar (1986), especially those involving selection and communication: Seek out other women colleagues, invite key women on campus to join, include all levels of the power hierarchy, include different role models and leadership styles, recommend women for jobs and other key assignments, share personal expertise, learn to give and accept criticism and tolerate differences in opinion and style.

In planning for organizational change, we identified several critical elements in the university environment, as described by change theorists such as Lewin (1958) and Lippitt (1973). Our goal was to "warm" the chilly climate for women on campus, the result of tension between the women's community on campus and the predominately male administrative power structure. Change was induced by decreasing the tension between the two systems. The actions of one system, the women's network, affected those of another, the administrative power structure, to the extent that the boundaries between the two systems became permeable. The Women's Commission became a vital driving force in facilitating change. A critical restraining force was the inertia built into the university hierarchy and the fear of changing the status quo.

THE NETWORK

The women's network consisted of women faculty, managers, administrators, staff, and students. The broad representation of women in the university was one of the critical factors in improving the climate for professional women on campus. Because our members were involved in virtually all aspects of university life, we were able to stay on top of the formal and informal information flow.

Our network used two primary mechanisms, one formal and the other informal. Our formal mechanism was the Women's Commission, which had been started several years before, but was at the time of network development more or less "limping" along. The informal mechanisms consisted of lunches, hallway conversations, and telephone calls between various commission members.

The Women's Commission met on a regular basis to identify specific problems, share relevant knowledge, gather additional information, and propose solutions. In the process, we kept our focus on the central issue: gaining access to the power and resources of the administrative power structure to reduce the chilly climate for women on campus.

The commission slowly became a vital force within the university. Personal contact with key women in leadership roles who represented a variety of groups on campus was one element that ensured our success. Another key component was the participation of high-ranking and respected faculty, both male and female: the dean of students, the president of the clerical union, program heads, and division directors. Thus, we had input from all levels of the hierarchy. Students played many important roles in the commission. They tended to be upper division or nontraditional female students who were interested in women's issues. As in Green's model (1986), the commission attracted people who already have some access to the power structure.

Another critical element in the success of the commission was the leadership of the authors: one a well-respected faculty member and counselor, and the other an academic dean. Critical to the commission's success was having the chair be a member highly placed in the decision-making process of the university administration. Her involvement on key decision-making bodies of the university enabled her to keep track of all the major happenings in the university and to affect policy that was sensitive to the needs of women. Moreover, her position in the administration allowed the commission to keep important linkages with decision makers.

Once we identified our need, we identified strategies to meet those needs. We developed subgroups of women who were interested in each of the particular areas of need. Then we discussed the general direction that each subgroup would take and shared information about the appropriate strategy to gather the background information needed. We identified both the key administrators and the individual responsible for touching base with them. Our contact was generally someone who worked closely with them or someone who knew them well. We met on a regular basis to give feedback, make suggestions, and generally keep informed. We evaluated our progress and direction on a regular basis, using our goals as the basis for the evaluatory process.

AREAS OF CHANGE

Using the Women's Commission as the change agent, we identified certain issues on which to focus. Among them were the Women's Center, child care on campus, and sexual harassment.

Women's Center

Begun in 1980, the Women's Center was organized as a collaborative effort of members of two departments within Student Affairs, the Counseling Center, and Health Services, and the academic Department of Social Work. The organizing effort was a grass roots effort, using the Women's Commission as an umbrella under which to operate. As conceived, the Women's Center was an on-campus training site for student interns from social work, journalism, and counseling education. The three women faculty members who spearheaded the movement to start the center acted as supervisors for the student interns. Over the years the center became less of a training site and more of a service agency staffed by student volunteers with faculty advisers.

We established the need for the center through a survey of women student needs conducted by the Women's Commission. In 1980 those needs were for programming and information, and supportive services such as individual peer counseling, support groups for returning women students, and referral services. The primary need, however, was for a pregnancy testing service that was low in cost, confidential, and readily accessible on campus. The Women's Center set up services to respond to each of those needs. In time, those specific needs broadened to include lobbying for expanded health services on campus, providing support for women reporting sexual harassment, and counseling support for victims of sexual assault.

Using personal negotiating skills to obtain university support, we obtained space from the medical director of health services and the support of the dean of students. University funding came in the form of access to campus copying services, telephone service, and staffing with work-study students. Programming funds were secured from graduate and resident student boards.

The Women's Commission acted as an advisory board for the Women's Center, securing a more central location for the center and providing important political strength for the center when it became a low priority during a volatile time of change in the university's administration. The center's viability was insured by the continuing dialogue of the commission's chair, who was the only woman in upper management, and the new dean of students, who was committed to a healthy women's center.

The potential of the collaborative model is illustrated by a proposal for an expanded Women's Center. Under the sponsorship of the Women's

Commission, we obtained the support of the dean of students. Architectural planning for an expanded center has been completed, and program funding has been secured from the graduate student governing board. The Women's Commission has renewed this initiative by committing itself to obtaining a paid director for the Women's Center.

Child Care

For a number of years the university operated a child development center as a training site for education students, answering some of the needs for child care on campus in the process. But beginning in 1984 the Women's Commission began a concerted effort to increase child care services for both students and employees at a location on or near campus. A subcommittee of the commission established the need for increased child care services through surveys conducted both in 1984 and 1985. In addition, the subcommittee consulted with community and campus-based day care operations in the area. But child care was not an important university priority at the time.

Finally, in 1986 these planning efforts were encouraged by an initiative from the central office governing the university system. The Women's Commission was asked to develop a master plan for child care services on campus. Planning efforts moved to the administrative level; representatives from the Women's Commission served on that planning task force. With the hiring of a director and three staff members, on campus child care services began during the 1988–89 academic year.

Sexual Harassment

An ad hoc group of faculty and administrators, together with the affirmative action officer, met over a period of three years to write a document establishing a university policy about sexual harassment and procedures to handle sexual harassment complaints. The Women's Commission monitored the document's development and facilitated the approval process. Sensitive negotiations between the administration and faculty governing bodies and employee unions were necessary.

Once approved, the document needed to be interpreted to both employees and students. The Women's Commission spearheaded the educational effort by publishing an explanatory brochure and holding workshops to sensitize the university community to the meaning of sexual harassment in its overt form and in its more subtle forms, such as the chilly classroom climate for women students.

Together with the Women's Center, the Women's Commission set up two-person support teams to consult with women registering complaints of sexual harassment. Composed of a faculty member and a student, the team

provides the woman information about the complaint procedures and support during the complaint process.

Sexual harassment in its most violent form as sexual assault became the focus of a broader form of networking into the larger community. Representatives from all of the colleges in the greater metropolitan area have formed a consortium to share information about programming and develop more effective response services. A more important reason for collaborating in a network is to reduce the stigma and guilt that sexual assault brings to a campus community.

EVALUATION

Our collaborative and networking model has been successful for a number of reasons. The open structure and powerful coordinator of the Women's Commission increase communication both within the women's network and with the administration. The broad base of interest and support represented in the commission ensures that commission initiatives and strategies will be supported by the different constituencies represented in the women's community. The commission seeks to work within the university structure. Moreover, many of the commission's values are shared by the administration. Consequently, the administration can support the commission by linking with it.

Open Communication

Communication within the women's network is facilitated by the Women's Commission's open structure. The commission has become the voice of women in the university, but it has never become a closed system. It is open to all women in the university community; it addresses the needs of women as they are brought to the commission's attention. This openness in structure and agenda keeps communication open within the women's network at the university. Such openness serves to promote cooperation and reduce competitiveness within the women's network.

On the administrative side, communication between the commission and the administration is enhanced by the presence of a dean or senior faculty member at the helm of the commission.

Broad-Based Support

When specific issues are brought to the Women's Commission, they are quickly placed into the larger context of the university community because of the broad base of interests represented on the commission.

Currently the commission includes representatives from the student body, faculty, student affairs, library staff, middle management, top man-

agement, clerical staff, the campus ministry, and men interested in women's concerns.

Interests represented on the commission include the Women's Center,
the Women's Studies program, women in management, union issues and
career mobility, equity issues on campus, child care for students and employees, women's health services, and sexual harassment.

Administrative Links

Certainly the commission's credibility and effectiveness are enhanced by
its coordination by a woman dean. The obvious connection with the university's top management serves to forge collaborative links between the
women's community and the university administration.

Because of these links, administrators—both individually and collectively—are more likely to support commission initiatives. Similarly, commission programming and initiatives are more likely to mesh with
university initiatives. Therefore, there is high probability of maximum fit
between commission and university interests.

FUTURE DIRECTIONS

The most recent indication of the commission's success is the recognition of
the commission as a presidential advisory commission. Future goals include a more formal orientation for new women professionals on campus,
identification of women worthy of meritorius recognition by both campus
and community bodies, continued research into issues of gender equity on
campus, and continued advocacy for more tangible administrative support
of the Women's Center.

The beauty of this collaborative and networking model is that it can
continue to operate successfully despite personnel changes. The Women's
Commission was established as a presidential committee in 1972 and has
survived three presidents and one acting president. In addition, the commission has been led by at least seven different people over the past 15
years. Over the years the mission of the commission has changed and its
effectiveness has wavered. The collaborative and networking model we
have developed with the Women's Commission as its heart has proved to
be very effective.

In the current climate of conservative attitudes about women in higher
education it is difficult for many women in higher education to feel efficacious about their studies and work. Our networking model supports
women by giving them opportunities to see their ideas develop into successful performance accomplishments and the opportunity to see women
role models and mentors demonstrate the kind of behavior that results in
rewards in the university environment. Moving from the individual per-

spective to the larger campus community, the networking model provides the women's community with access to information, power, and support so that women are able actually to change their campus environment.

REFERENCES

Bandura, A. (1977). Self-efficacy: Toward a unifying theory of behavioral change. *Psychological Review,* 84, 191–215.

———. (1986). *Social Foundations of Thought and Action.* Englewood Cliffs, NJ: Prentice-Hall.

Green, M. F. (1982). A Washington perspective on women and networking: The power and the pitfalls. *Journal of NAWDAC,* 46(3), 17–21.

Kanter, R. M. (1980). Quality of life and work behavior in academic life. *National Forum: Phi Kappa Phi Journal,* 15(4), 35–38.

Lewin, K. (1958). Group decision and social change. In Maccoby, E. (ed.), *Readings on Social Psychology,* 3d. ed. New York: Holt, Rinehart and Winston.

Lippitt, R. (1973). *Visualizing change: Model building and the change process.* LaJolla, CA: University Associates, Inc.

Project on the Status and Education of Women. (1986). *The Campus Climate Revisited: Chilly for Women Faculty, Administrators, and Graduate Students.* Washington, DC: Association of American Colleges.

Swoboda, M. J., and Millar, S. B. (1986). Networking and mentoring: Career strategy of women in academic administration. *Journal of NAWDAC,* 50(1), 8–13.

3

Aspirations, Choices, Realities: College Women Ten Years Later

Alice A. Walker
Linda Kuk

Many current reports on the attitudes and aspirations of women refer to a return to a more conservative attitude by young women of today (e.g., Weeks & Botkin, 1987). A second theme that frequently emerges is the assumption of college women that issues of discrimination have been resolved and the world will be their oyster (e.g., Travis, 1976). A third theme that has appeared frequently in both the popular and professional literature is whether women can "have it all"—career, marriage, and family. In fact, today the question more often is not *"whether* they can do both" but *"how* to do both" and at what costs (Yogev, 1982; Perum & Bielby, 1981).

This chapter will examine these issues based on the results of a longitudinal study of career development of a group of women that was begun during their freshman year in college.

METHODS

Sample and Procedure

During the 1978–79 academic year, 113 freshman women participated in a career exploration demonstration project. A group of approximately 70 was mentored by female faculty during their freshman year and also participated in a career exploration course. The remainder were in a control

group. At that time data were gathered on their career aspirations, attitudes toward the status of women, and level of self-esteem. In the fall of 1987, five years after they should have graduated, a follow-up to the original study was conducted, gathering information on their current careers and life-styles, and again administering the same surveys of attitudinal and self-esteem measures that they filled out as freshmen. Of the 113 surveys mailed, seven were returned as undeliverable. Forty-seven women responded and 45 of the completed responses were usable for analysis.

Measures

Respondents completed the Coopersmith Self-Esteem Inventory (SEI), the short version of the Attitude Toward Women Scale (AWS) developed by Spence and Helmreich (1973) and a 35-item survey, Occupational Status of Women Scale (OCCST) which specifically looks at women and work. All three of these scales had been filled out by the respondents when they were freshmen. The respondents also completed an eight-page life-style questionnaire that asked a series of questions with regard to their current life-style. These questions specifically focused on issues of education, employment and career, child rearing, friendships and activities, and general life experiences.

LIFE-STYLE CHOICES—A PROFILE OF
THE PARTICIPANTS

While in college, these women majored in 23 different areas of study. Currently, 23 (52%) of these women have obtained or are in the process of obtaining graduate degrees. All but nine of the women are currently employed in full-time occupations or are pursuing graduate study in a specific occupational area. For purposes of this study, respondents were divided by occupation into four categories: (a) Nontraditional, (b) Traditional Female, hereafter referred to as Female, (c) Gender Neutral, hereafter referred to as Neutral, (d) Homemakers. Thirteen women were included in the Nontraditional group, 16 women in Female, seven women in Neutral and the nine women employed half-time or less and not enrolled in graduate school on a full-time basis were classified Homemaker.

Employment

The majority of women in the study (82.2%) do not believe they have experienced any disadvantages or advantages in pursuing their education or their career because they are women. Seventy-nine percent (31 of 45) of the

women are satisfied or extremely satisfied with their work situation. They view themselves as quite successful.

The things that please them the most about their work are intrinsic factors including challenge of work, autonomy, job responsibility, and relationships on the job and with clients. Difficulties encountered with people they work with and for, not being paid enough of a salary, and having to work too many hours were cited as the things that bother them the most about work. Generally, they felt their treatment as a worker had been at least equal to that accorded men. Of those who felt they had not received equal treatment, salary was most frequently cited as the area of inequality.

Personal Lives

The women indicated that they were reasonably satisfied with the way they allocated time between career and family. The majority of women (82.2%) appear to have some form of significant relationship. The women in significant relationships stated they were happy and felt the nicest things about their relationships were the open communication and supportive nature of the relationship.

Outside of employment averaging 45.5 hours per week, the women generally spend the greatest amount of time with their significant other, averaging 32 hours per week for the Nontraditional and Female groups and 20.5 hours per week for the Neutral and Homemaker groups. Only the Homemakers, who spend an average of 120 hours per week in child care and 42 hours per week in homemaking, do *not* spend the highest percentage of nonwork time with their significant other. Nontraditionals, Females, and Neutrals as a group average no time in child care, since only two women outside of the Homemakers have children.

Lack of time was a critical issue for women from all of the groups. The issues of time for self, time for friends, and time for social activities were most common. Only six (13%) felt they are really doing what they want. Ironically, those employed full-time would like more time for nonwork-related activities (i.e. family, friends and education) while those not employed (the Homemakers) overwhelmingly would like more time to pursue career activity.

Issues related to participation in household activities are of concern to all four groups; however, satisfaction varied among the groups. Nontraditionals appear to have the highest level of satisfaction and the Homemakers have the least amount of satisfaction with two-thirds of the women indicating they were not satisfied with the assistance received.

Accomplishments and Goals

The most frequently stated personal goal at the end of college across and within each of the four groups was the desire to have a significant relationship, followed by a desire to have a family, to be independent, and to relocate geographically. In citing their accomplishments to date, career accomplishments were the most frequently stated by all groups. With regard to future aspirations, the focus was on having a career and a significant relationship simultaneously.

Mentoring

One of the original goals of the project in 1978 was to focus on mentoring relationships for women. Within the group ten years later, 53.3 percent of the women indicated that they had not had a mentor at any time in their lives. Of the women who stated they had mentors, eleven had male mentors and eight had female mentors. A variety of responses were given regarding ways the mentors had influenced them.

Attitudinal Measures

Coopersmith Self-Esteem Inventory (SEI)

The mean score on the SEI for the respondents as freshmen was 19.5 and in the follow-up the mean was 21.4.

Examination of the individual items showed the women increased in confidence in themselves as individuals. For example, as freshmen, 18 percent of the sample agreed with the statement, "I often wish I were someone else." Now, only one woman agreed with this statement. Similarly, 37 percent of the freshmen agreed with the statement, "There are lots of things about myself I'd change if I could," but only 13 percent currently agreed with the statement. Several other items reflected similar changes. On two items there were reversals of percentages that are interesting. As freshmen, 22 percent agreed with the statement, "It's pretty tough to be me." Currently 38 percent agreed with that statement. Similarly, 10 percent of the freshmen agreed with the statement, "My family expects too much of me." Currently 20 percent agreed with that statement (see Table 3.1 for comparative data on selected items).

Attitude Toward Women Scale (AWS)

The AWS, developed by Spence and Helmreich (1972), is a widely used scale that taps the roles, behavior, and attitudes that people feel are appropriate or inappropriate for women. Currently, the respondents are more

Table 3.1
Coopersmith Self-Esteem Inventory

Item	Agreement	
	Fall, 1978	Fall, 1987
1. I often wish I were someone else.	17.9%	2.2%
2. There are lots of things about myself I'd change if I could.	37.5	13.3
3. My family expects too much of me.	9.8	20.0
4. It's pretty tough to be me.	22.8	37.8

likely to agree that a "woman should be as free as a man to propose marriage" (93.3% versus 79.8% as freshmen), and that "economic and social freedom is worth far more to women than acceptance of the ideal of femininity which has been set up by men" (75.6% versus 66.3% as freshmen). Currently they are also *less likely* to agree that "swearing and obscenity are more repulsive in the speech of a woman than a man" (24.4% versus 56.7% as freshmen) and that "intoxication among women is worse than intoxication among men" (6.7% versus 24% as freshmen). Two other items show large shifts over the past ten years. Currently, respondents are less likely to agree that "a woman should not expect to go to exactly the same places or have quite the same freedom of action as men" (4.4% versus 28.8% as freshmen) and that "there are many jobs in which men should be given preference over women in being hired or promoted" (2.2% versus 15.4% as freshmen) (see Table 3.2 for comparative data on selected items).

Occupational Status of Women Scale (OCCST)

The OCCST, in contrast to the AWS scale, focuses only on attitudes and behaviors related to the world of work. Again, there is a significant change (p<.01) toward a more realistic view of the workplace.

An examination of individual items shows that the respondents have a more positive view of women's competencies and aspirations. However, this is accompanied by a more negative view of opportunities for women. For example, no one agreed that "in general, women are less able than men" whereas as freshmen 10 percent agreed with the statement. Similarly, only 9.1 percent agreed that "deep down, most women don't want equality" whereas as freshmen 26.6 percent agreed. Currently, only one woman agreed that "it is acceptable for women to work to supplement family income; it is unrealistic for them to expect meaningful implementation of

Table 3.2
Attitude Toward Women Scale*

Item	Agreement	
	Fall, 1978	Fall, 1987
1. Swearing and obscenity are more repulsive in the speech of a woman than a man.	56.7%	24.4%
2. Economic and social freedom is worth far more to women than acceptance of the ideal of femininity which has been set up by men.	66.3	75.6
3. A woman should be as free as a man to propose marriage.	79.8	93.3
4. A woman should not expect to go exactly the same places or have quite the same freedom of action as men.	28.8	4.4
5. Intoxication among women is worse than Intoxication among men.	24.0	6.7

*Selected Items

vocational self concepts" whereas as freshmen 18.5 percent agreed. However, 30 percent of the respondents agreed that "the discrepancy between salaries received by men and women for doing the same work is increasing," 81.8% agreed that "in spite of legislation which makes it illegal to do so, many companies continue to restrict opportunities for women," 82 percent agreed that "in order to succeed in a field traditionally considered a man's domain, women must surpass men in both ambition and intelligence," and 25 percent agreed that "in the foreseeable future, women will fill only very limited leadership roles in work settings." All of these percentages are higher than they were when the women were freshmen. One other item of interest is that 68.9 percent agreed that "working women feel guilty about being away from their homes and children" compared to 55 percent as freshmen (see Table 3.3 for comparative data on selected items).

DISCUSSION

As adults, the women clearly are liberal in their views regarding educational, vocational, and political opportunities. The data are consistent with those of McKinney (1987) who did a partial replication of the Spence and Helmreich research using the AWS.

The data reported here is longitudinal and shows an increase in liberal attitudes, which is consistent with the McKinney findings.

Table 3.3
Occupational Status of Women*

Item	Agreement	
	Fall, 1978	Fall, 1987
1. In spite of legislation which makes it illegal to do so, many companies continue to restrict opportunities for women.	83.5%	81.8%
2. In the foreseeable future, women will fill only very limited leadership roles in work setting.	14.7	25.0
3. Working women feel guilty about being away from their homes and children.	55.0	68.9
4. In order to succeed in a field usually considered a man's domain, women must surpass men in ambition and intelligence.	67.9	82.2
5. Deep down most women don't want equality.	67.0	56.8
6. The discrepancy between salaries received by men and women for doing the same work is increasing.	26.9	30.0
7. It is acceptable for women to work to supplement income; it is unrealistic for them to expect meaningful implementation of vocational self-concepts.	18.5	2.3

*Selected Items

Bardwick and Douvan (1975, p. 351), in discussing young women's choices today, state, "Both the work and the housewife roles are romanticized, since romanticism is enhanced when reality does not intrude." To some extent the women in this study give credence to this analysis. Those employed full-time would like more time for family and friends, those who are homemakers would like more time to pursue career activities.

This study also give support to Yogev's (1982) contention that there is little evidence to support the view that participation in the work force is a potential threat to marriage and family because of conflicts, role blur, and marital dissatisfaction. The women in this study emerge as confident, goal-oriented young women who are involved in significant relationships and thus far seem to be fairly successful in combining career and relationships. It appears that the real issue is not combining career and relationship, but

rather combining career and managing a household. The addition of children, especially more than one, compounds the problem.

These findings appear to corroborate the findings of many reports that men are not assuming an equal share of the household responsibilities, including child care. Thus, the only group that appears satisfied with the equity in managing household responsibility was the Nontraditionals. This may be related to the choice of significant other rather than actual differences among the women themselves.

Whether these women can successfully combine career and family is yet to be seen. A majority of those employed full-time have expressed a desire to have children but thus far have postponed child rearing. However, since they are now in their late twenties, it is an issue that will become more pressing in the near future. Since those who are employed full-time already indicate they wish they had more time for themselves, how they and their significant others deal with the additional pressure of children will be an important issue.

REFERENCES

Bardwick, J. M., and Douvan, E. (1975). Ambivalence: The socialization of women. In Muuss, R. E. (Ed.), *Adolescent Behavior and Society: A Book of Readings* (2nd Ed.) (34–353). New York: Random House.

McKinney, K. (1987). Age and gender differences in college students' attitudes toward women: A replication and extension. *Sex Roles*, 17, 353–358.

Perum, J., and Bielby, D. (1981). Towards a model of female occupational behavior: A human development approach. *Psychology of Women Quarterly*, 6, 234–252.

Spence, J., and Helmreich, R. (1973). The attitudes towards women scale: An objective instrument to measure attitudes toward the rights and roles of women in contemporary society. *JSAS Catalog of Selected Documents in Psychology*, 2, 66.

Spence, J., et al. (1973). A short version of the attitudes toward women scale (AWS). *Bulletin of the Psychonomic Society*, 2, 219–220.

Travis, C. (1976). Women's liberation among two samples of young women. *Psychology of Women Quarterly*, 1, 189–199.

Weeks, M. O., and Botkin, D. R. (1987). A longitudinal study of the marriage role expectations of college women: 1961–1984. *Sex Roles*, 17, 49–58.

Yogev, S. (1982). Happiness in dual-career couples: changing values. *Sex Roles*, 8, 593–606.

SECTION TWO

WOMEN IN THEIR DISCIPLINES

This section provides a unique look at several of the disciplines in higher education and their unique contributions to the body of knowledge and life of the university.

Frangione describes the rich history of dance in America, and looks at its symbolic language as both a means of communication and an art form. She predicts that dance will reform and change the manner in which we communicate in the future.

The impact of women in the engineering work force is explored by Anil and Runjani Saigal. The difficulty of female entry and acceptance into engineering is pointed out graphically by their study, which shows that male engineers believe that female engineers have lower ability. The need for societal change is identified by the researchers.

The Impostor Phenomenon in theology today is identified and discussed by Range, who believes that organized religion makes women clergy feel and believe that they are imposters. The dominant forces that have contributed to a purely male view of religion and God are emphasized with several effective consciousness-raising examples.

Messmer compares the tenure rates of nursing faculty and other university faculty to discover that nursing faculty are not as "ten-

ured in" as other university faculties. She explores some of the possible factors that may have contributed to this discrepancy.

The study of deity provides Rannells with a vehicle by which to explore how women can be empowered. She uses goddesses and creative learning experiences to help women integrate their conscious and unconscious beliefs and feelings about womanhood.

4

The Bodies of Change: Dance and Women in Higher Education

Danna Frangione

Fifty years ago, a small group of zealots clad in highwater tights and armed with minimal degrees and Martha Graham exercises set out to make a difference. Their dreams for changing the landscape of education were naive and heroic. They wanted America to dance. They wanted each individual to learn the most basic truths—personal and universal—from the revealing discipline of art. They wanted to change the world.

It hasn't happened all at once. The pioneers in dance education espoused a rich system of training not easily understood in philosophy, method, or product. Often called aesthetic or barefoot dancers, these ladies (for they were and still are predominantly women) fought to give my generation a place to work in higher education. I mean that in the most concrete sense. Their time was spent gaining territorial space—studios, barres, mirrors—a *place* in which to house dance. And, with unparalleled diligence, these frontierswomen built programs, class by class, then worried endlessly over the ebb and flow of that curricular evolvement. They worked to gain academic recognition, indeed any recognition, in the face of an enduring, albeit benevolent, prejudice that limited growth even as it protected jobs. Viewed as primarily service personnel whose role was to train young ladies in poise, posture, and deportment, our tentative emergence into the current academic arena was delayed, disorganized, and agonizing.

Dance education entered college life through physical education, migrating from that uneasy home to theater or music and back again. But in phys-

ical education the pioneers fought a constant battle for acknowledgment of dance as a performing art and of dance educators as more than coaches for the muscularly aware. In theater, where art is understood or at least recognized, they were pressured by the exigencies of box office demands.

Wherever they landed, they were inundated with the types of bizarre requests that often accompany fundamental misunderstanding. Dance educators were asked to produce work for any event or organization remotely related to movement, ranging from rather logical requests for musical theater choreography to service that signifies a more subtle reasoning such as choreography for syncro-swim teams, half-time entertainment, graduation exercises, and outdoor garden fêtes. And, because our art is embracing or perhaps because gaining exposure was requisite to survival in academe, the pioneers produced gladly, even at the expense of individual careers or artistic sensibilities.

The early pioneers were missionaries; on and off campus, outreach programs were legion. Dance educators joined a variety of public school colleagues in the "spreading of the word of the dance" in cafeterias across the country. I was one of the kids they reached, discovering time, space, force—and myself—while dodging fallen corndogs and jujubes.

Today I work in one of the hundreds of college dance programs nationwide. I, like my colleagues, continue to learn from the pioneers and their legacy. But we owe the next generation a new legacy. We owe tomorrow's dance educators and those professional dancers whom we now train on college campuses social, political, and economic power just as the pioneers owed us mirrors, barres, and safe dance floors. In the 1700s, Americans employed dancing masters to teach their children the social graces, for dancing, as Agnes de Mille so aptly states, was "the way to get on." Our professional concerns for the next generation and those who follow must be interdisciplinary in scope and political at heart so that the future dancers and dance educators possess "the way to get on" in society.

Now I believe that dance educators are basically apolitical, functioning uneasily in academe. We would rather be dancing than attending meetings, choreographing instead of doing quantitative research. Our intense sense of physical discipline leaves us impatient with "playing the game" for funds and power. But more and more I am becoming aware of my involvement in an environment that has rendered dance educators and the dance artists we train powerless. And, at the same time, we are collectively, paradoxically, reinforcing that powerlessness.

A friend of mine describes our conceptual location as the "ghetto of academe"—low rank, low pay, low power, high visibility. Its signposts are everywhere, ranging from the broadly professional to the deeply personal. Professionally, we have awakened in the 1980s to find ourselves immersed—and sinking—in a dance education crisis we are ill-prepared to meet. For example, in the face of a twenty-year dance and fitness boom,

dance educators are engaged in bitter skirmishes for promotion and tenure and are often left fighting for program retention with curricular expediency. Most of us reside at the bottom rung of the academic ladder and do not yet receive official load time for choreography, performance, touring— basic recognition of our artistry. Although our department chairs are often male, the rank and file are overwhelmingly female. And though we have made some forays beyond the studio door into the laboratory, we are still perceived as fundamentally nonacademic and primarily cocurricular. Higher education has grown to embrace us but the perceptual base upon which that embrace stands sometimes seems askew. Over the years, I have too often been asked, "Oh, do you teach disco dancing, flashdancing, dirty dancing?"

Dance is a dynamic balance. Yet dancers often lead terribly unbalanced personal and professional lives. As dancers coming to grips with tremendous conflict, we are only just beginning to realize that our lives must have balance and quality. We have believed for far too long in the Western concept of the artist as an individual outside of society who must somehow "pay dues" to create art. And, in academe, perhaps we have also believed our bad press, best exemplified by a quote from an anonymous chancellor: "Promotion? Maybe. But tenuring a dancer is out of the question; they just get old and wear out."

These perceptions are deeply entwined in our cultural view of movement and the body, its value and its purpose. What was in primitive times homeopathic ritual is today a pattern of cultural excess. For dance today is big business. Products are literally dancing into our homes—from jazzy spark plugs to tap dancing laxatives to ballerina Cynthia Gregory asking, "Do you know me?" On music video, the world has become an explosive mixture of the visual, the aural, and the physical. Dress a model like a dancer, wet her down and film her from odd angles and you have a gold mine in erotic aerobics. America is being assaulted and seduced by what is most current and what is most current in dance—or at least a fantasy of dance.

The fantasy extends to the body. The female dance form designed by George Balanchine and nurtured by a culture obsessed with thinness is an interesting vision: long limbs, tiny head on a long slender neck, no breasts, no hips. Not a single secondary sexual characteristic in sight and slimming over time, all the time. Famed principal ballerina Alexandra Danilova throughout her 30-year career maintained an "ideal" 5'5", 112-pound frame. This androgynous body says dance (translation: sex) and is highly useful in the marketplace.

We've become the ideal! So, one would think that such a trend would bode well for the profession of dance, giving it a certain legitimacy that comes with American popularity and eradicates some of the prejudices and myths about the field. We've all heard the talk about dancers, our very own cultural bias, which is a long time dying.

Female dancers, for instance, embody the ranges and extremes of sexuality. They are the romantic ethereal virgins of fragile beauty, the eternal prepubescent little girls with a hint of the attraction perceptible in the unattainable. Or they are the "back-street ballerinas," the bump and grind hootchy-kootchy girls who strut it all on "Solid Gold." Or they are barefoot dancers, Isadora Duncan–style, given to passionate declarations, children out of wedlock, and socialist tendencies. In any case they are . . . different. I know what my parents said: "A dancer?! But dear, you're smart; you could do something useful! How will you earn a living? How will you ever find a husband?"

Which brings us to the male dancer. Booted off the ballet stage in the Romantic era, they returned slowly as porters, toting ballerinas across the stage. George Balanchine, who guided American dance tastes for almost 50 years, has stated, "Ballet is woman. She is queen. Men are consorts." Perhaps the men got a little too close to the queen for it is the unhappy image of the gay dancer that still haunts the profession today. It has been a vicious cycle in America. Not only did dance somehow seem to attract the "suspiciously undergendered," but association with the profession could somehow emasculate.

There is a point to be made here. Dance as an industry does have the uncanny ability to emasculate or eliminate personal power even as it produces the strong, flexible bodies that symbolize independence. Here is a profession that assigns the title "boys" and "girls" to full-grown men and women. This profession acknowledges physical abuse and glorifies a body image that normally signifies starvation. With a life-style that has earned them the name "gypsies," dancers remain locked in a tightly encapsulated world that fosters dependency, passivity, and obedience. Even "taking class," the dancers' daily ritual, is all too often an exercise in movement and conceptual replication and not artistic interpretation. We are excellent mimics; we do as we are told.

Much has been written recently about the abuses of the dance industry. With its traditional methods, the profession appears from the outside almost medieval in its lack of protection for the artists who remain the living repositories of our ongoing culture. The exposure of problems touches us all because it affects every level of dance in this country from the corner ballet school to the college major program to the New York City Ballet. The patterns of dance training—good and bad—are formed in the emotional and physical memories of dancers long before the age of consent. There is no standard to be met, no certification without which one cannot teach, no review board for abusive practices—no real parameters.

We tell our students that dance is the most fundamental of the art forms, the mother of the arts, a basic human need. We urge them to seek and express human values. Yet we have not shown them (and, in fact, we have failed to find for ourselves) the way to integrate into the very society about

which we move. Whether perceived as the victims of a wicked ballet master or martyrs to high art, we remain external.

We do belong. The dance of the twenty-first century will include a seed of militantness born from the emerging recognition of dancers as members of a group of individuals whose working realm will serve as a primary force for change in society. The time has come to use the power of dance and the arts to effect change beyond the studio door. We have a multitude of tools at our disposal. M. C. Richards (1973) wrote in *The Crossing Point*: "People are hungering and thirsting after experience that feels true to them on the inside." People find in movement a fundamental truth; only that which is deeply felt can change us, shape us, make us whole. It is time for dancers to use the positive tools of our trade to help ourselves and those who must lead us into the next century.

Let's examine the tools dancers possess:

1. We possess a symbolic language that has the power to affect the total viewer in a kinesthetically contagious way: homeopathic ritual power to motivate individuals and lead groups.

2. We have at our disposal a verbal language that is rich in both the practical and metaphorical. In an art form passed from generation to generation in primarily the oral tradition, we've had to be incisive and imaginative in our technical language. Our classroom language is designed to appeal to both the right and left hemispheres, promoting critical analysis and creative insight, and fostering an integration of intelligence domains.

3. Our art form is multichanneled, appealing to all the organs of perception. It is also an art form of successive perception, changing in space through time. As dancers, we use these attributes to guide the viewers through an illusionary world of our own making, tailoring reality and expressing the inexpressible.

4. We possess the power to help individuals channel physicality into personal meaning, guiding them toward transcendent experiences.

5. Perhaps most importantly, we serve as the repositories of our most basic cultural heritage. "Man's whole body records his emotional thinking" (Todd, 1937) and dance records, reflects, and predicts universal human values.

Isadora Duncan (1928) wrote:

I see America dancing, beautiful and strong, with one foot poised on the highest point of the Rockies, her two hands stretched out from the Atlantic to the Pacific, her fine head tossed to the sky . . . dancing the language of our pioneers.

Are her dreams and those of the founding dance educators so naive and farfetched? Not at all. We meet the criteria set forth by Eisner (1983), Maslow (1962), and others as critical to a fully functioning individual, including:

1. Multiple forms of literacy;
2. personal autonomy;
3. creative, insightful questioning within the context of a shifting environment;
4. integration of mind and body;
5. ability to fuse concreteness with abstractness; and
6. a deep, open affection for life and learning.

Unfortunately, dance education has traditionally been relegated to the fringe area of curriculum decision making and indeed resides at the last outpost of arts education in America. We are the also-rans. In apologies for arts education, after plugs for music, drama and art comes "and the like"— that's us. Ignored even as physical education for youngsters in *A Nation at Risk* (USDE, 1983), there is a call for changes that may herald a new age of creativity in society with an integrated course of study including language, art, cultural heritage, societal issues, and personal identity.

Some scholars (Bennis and Nanus, 1985, p. 13) believe that "we are approaching a major turning point in history . . . where some new height of vision is sought, where some fundamental redefinitions are required, where our table of values will have to be reviewed." Massive change is frightening. Sanford Reitman (1986, p. 143) contends that fear—a paralysis of will—has already prompted us to lose faith in our American frontier ability to take risks and solve problems; the old tools just don't work. He writes: "The future has at last caught up with us and we are stupefied by its terrifying demands for radical restructuring of our personal lives and institutional organization."

Dance, the arts and ritual must fill the space generated by that fear. That space is our domain and has been our territory and our strength since primitive times. In preliterate societies, art was a communal source of expression, a way of life encompassing dance, music, drama, ritual, and, yes, science and technology, knitting together the fabric of society. Before such a word existed, art ritualized the ineffable and gave meaning to that which is not easily understood or controlled. Jamake Highwater (1978, p. 18) contends that art also provides us with visions of the future. Dance, he writes, gives us the "capacity to awaken imagery within us, to compound mystery, and to illuminate the unknown without reducing it to the commonplace."

The self-conscious view of art in Western society reflects a worldview that is narrow, static, and ill-suited to serve a changing society. In every aspect of our culture, our old views are evolving to include the ambiguous as we rediscover the nonrational as a source of knowledge and understanding. Already the distinction between body and spirit, animate and inanimate, are blurring as research delves into robotics, bionics, and neurobiology. Our scientific rationalism has delivered us into a world

where we can no longer depend on our coveted beliefs in absolute reality, truth with a capital "T" and linear time. Gone is the comfort of a cosmic egotism that guarantees superiority and centrality. Our world is adapting to a new, fast-paced, nonverbal, and highly visual mode. This scientism of our own devising is forcing us into a new grey area, beyond rationalism, beyond humanism—perhaps to creativism.

Those of us in the arts may already have the key to this future. With interdisciplinary cooperation and research, we can reenter the culture as leaders and leave behind our current status as external, conservative mirrors of societal change. Four elements are pivotal to our leadership potential in the next century and warrant examination: historical congruence, socialization, marketing and language.

We can no longer afford to devalue or accept devaluation of our work in academe or society. Besides, it's just not necessary. *Wall Street Journal* analyst Peter Drucker (1982) has predicted that creativity, innovation, and insight will be the most valuable commodities of the twenty-first century. Leadership will fall to those who can most effectively communicate creative vision. But will those leaders be artists? As training in science and technology widens to include laboratory experience in the creative process, critical thinking, and mind/body perception, will the instructors be artists or will they be members of a new profession—like ethical aesthetics—due to our inability to see our moment of historical congruence and align ourselves to fill a void with information we already have available in our "laboratories." As artists and educators, we have everything to gain by placing our profession on the cutting edge of research and much to lose if we delay.

Peters and Waterman (1982, p. 261) contend that business, not art, is developing the most integrated means of providing society with its ritual needs. Businesses, they write, "have become sort of mother institutions," creating a socializing web of symbols, myths, and legends. Marketing the "technology of foolishness" (Peters and Waterman, 1982, p. 62), business is institutionalizing improvisation and creative risk-taking.

Science, too, has entered the artist's realm. Researchers are currently seeking ways to define and reproduce creative vision using chemical enhancement (Gallagher, 1986) and pattern visualization (Brandt, 1986). In ways uniquely American, business and technology are investigating the mechanisms of insight and marketing emerging concepts—the concepts of art.

Again, while we stand defending ourselves, the mainstream has adopted our ideas! Perhaps dance needs an element of entrepreneurship combined with the serious assessment needed by all minority groups. Hofferek (1986) contends that minority groups are subject to internal barriers to success that may be just as destructive as external bias. Perhaps artists, by investigating such barriers as self-hatred, tokenism, and internal devalua-

tion, will find that we have untapped acceptance, marketability, and influence in the academic workplace and in society.

In order to dovetail and subsequently influence societal values, we must socialize students into the profession, training artists to share common goals and urging them to demand their rights. First, we might use marketing techniques to predict the future leaders of our culture and target the education of those individuals to include an arts education that is integrated and pervasive. Further, we might recruit "political animals" into our ranks. We know from our own youth that there is a time in life when we are inherently politically active, when questioning can lead to questing. No longer passive, our knowledgeable, politically savvy artists will not overthrow their art forms—they will accomplish what my generation has not done. They will provide a future where moral education will accompany aesthetic education. Our power base is already established. Industrial growth in this country now means cultural growth. Robert D. Stern (1981, p. 38), representing Alcoa Industries, admonishes dancers not to ask for money "hat in hand, head bowed, as if you were asking for charity. Ask for money, yes, but remember that you deserve it. In the business world of scratch-my-back-and-I'll-scratch-yours, you hold some important cards, you are operating from a power base of your own . . . the dance world offers a commodity of immense value. It is precious. Valuable. Irreplaceable."

For most people, the creative process is a mysterious force, couched in obtuse language and guarded by eccentrics. Artistic ideas and evocative language need not be foreign to the public. On the contrary, the creative process should be a communal phenomenon, a societal responsibility and a personal right. In order to effect change, to become academically and culturally viable, we must reveal our process as inherently and generically human, expose the creative process to scrutiny through both qualitative and quantitative methods and establish a clear, interdisciplinary language accessible to the layperson.

As artists and teachers, we have the power to galvanize education into a new awareness of the strength and scope of the arts. As a culture and as artists, we stand to gain far more than academic equality for a small group. Now may very well be a time of historical congruence as we begin to explore creativity as a force for change. Let's take back into our ranks the real artists—all of us.

REFERENCES

Associated Press–Washington. (1986, November 2). *Report indicts colleges on degree-mill charge.* 19, 47, 1.

Bennis, W., and Nanus, B. (1985). *Leaders: The Strategies for Taking Charge.* New York: Harper & Row.

Brandt, R. (1986). On creativity and thinking skills: A conversation with David Perkins. *Educational Leadership, 41,* 8.

Drucker, P. (1982, February 2). *The Wall Street Journal.*

Duncan, I. (1928). *The Art of Dance.* New York: Holt, Rinehart and Winston.

Eisner, E. (1983). The kinds of schools we need. *Educational Leadership, 41,* 8.

Gallagher, W. (1986, August). The looming menace of designer drugs. *Discover, 7,* 8.

Highwater, J. (1978). *Dance: Rituals of Experience.* New York: A and W.

Hofferek, M. (1986). *Going Forth: Women's Leadership Issues in Higher Education and Physical Education.* Princeton, NJ: Princeton Book.

Maslow, A. (1962). *Toward a Psychology of Being.* New York: D. Van Nostrand.

Peters, T., and Waterman, R. (1982). *In Search of Excellence.* San Francisco, CA: Jossey-Bass.

Reitman, S. (1986, Winter). Daring to make teaching an art. *The Education Forum, 50,* 2.

Richards, M. C. (1973). *The Crossing Point.* Middletown, CT: Wesleyan University.

Stern, R. (1981, October). Viewpoint: Industry's need for dance. *Dancemagazine, 4,* 3.

Todd, M. (1937). *The Thinking Body.* New York: Dance Horizons.

USDE: National Commission on Excellence in Education. (1983). *A Nation at Risk: The Imperative for Educational Reform, a Report of the Nation and the Secretary of Education.* Washington, DC: U.S. Government Printing Office.

5

Professional Prejudices Against Women Engineers

Anil Saigal
Ranjani Saigal

While engineering itself has existed as a profession for a very long time, women entered this profession only during the turn of this century. It was during World War II, when the engineering industry lost a significant part of its male work force to the battlefields, that women were encouraged to enter the engineering profession. Ever since then, women have been proving their worth in every aspect of this challenging profession.

The changing face of the engineering field over the past few years has made it very attractive for women to become a part of this male-dominated profession. With the advent of electronics and sophisticated computers, engineering has become a field that challenges the intellect rather than the physique of the individual.

The impact of this change has clearly been felt both by industry and educational institutions. The number of women opting for engineering programs has significantly increased both in terms of their absolute numbers and as a percentage of the total number of students graduating in these disciplines. Many engineering schools in the United States have been able to maintain their standards and even improve upon them as a result of the larger pool of qualified women high school graduates interested in engineering studies.

Current estimates of the percentage of women engineers in this country range from 5 percent (National Science Foundation) to 7 percent (Commission on Professionals in Science and Technology) of the estimated 1.6 to 1.7

million engineers (Colborn, 1987). This represents a tenfold increase from 1972, when women engineers accounted for only 0.8 percent of the 1.1 million engineers. The Engineering Manpower Commission reports that women received about 15 percent of undergraduate degrees last year, compared with 4.9 in 1977 and 1.35 in 1971. Advanced degrees awarded to women have also more than doubled.

PROBLEMS FACED BY WOMEN ENGINEERS TODAY

Even though the statistics presented above are quite impressive, entering the engineering profession and building a successful career still remain a difficult task for women. Studies have reported that career counselors and academic advisers often discourage young women entering nontraditional fields, such as engineering (Whatley, 1985). Many people are still of the opinion that women go to engineering schools for the purpose of finding a spouse rather than to prepare for a career. There is also the ever-persisting fear that a woman's career will cause problems and interfere with her family life.

Apart from these factors, the workplace itself poses problems for women. Various studies indicate that there is a tendency to rate women as less effective than their male counterparts. Also, the quality of their work is underrated in performance evaluation, particularly in male-dominated jobs. A study conducted by the University of New Orleans found that women with masculine characteristics are most likely to be promoted ("Women Workers," 1986). Women engineers are not exceptions. Studies such as these show that there is a significant prejudice against women in the professional world.

There are a number of organizations that have made an attempt to deal with some of these problems. The Society of Women Engineers, through the volunteer efforts of its members, plays a leadership role in providing career guidance to young women, serving as a support network for women engineers, and informing young women and their parents as visible proof that it is possible for women to have a successful engineering career and still be effective wives and mothers. However, according to a report prepared by the female graduate students and research staff in the Laboratory for Computer Science and Artificial Intelligence Laboratory at MIT (1983), women engineers encounter additional problems that unfairly limit their academic, professional, and personal growth as compared to men ("Barriers," 1983). Some of the problems specifically mentioned are:

- general feeling among men that women are underqualified
- expectations of women that are different from expectations of men
- uncomfortable social atmospheres
- assessing women's commitment to a professional career

In order to provide an effective solution to any problem, we should first be able to identify clearly the specifics of the problem. In this chapter we attempt to get a better understanding of many of the issues confronting a woman in the engineering profession today.

METHODOLOGY OF THE STUDY

In order to obtain an insight into the problems faced by working women engineers, a survey was conducted. First, specific issues related to their problems were identified and a set of questions framed dealing with these issues. The issues highlighted through these questions were:

- ability of women engineers in comparison to male engineers
- success of women being attributed to their luck and their being a minority
- ease or difficulty in finding jobs on the basis of the fact that they are women
- assignment of routine and less challenging jobs to women engineers at entry level compared to their male counterparts
- retardation caused in the progress of young women engineers due to lack of role models in the form of senior women engineers
- proof of success requiring more evidence from women as compared to men
- need for women engineers to work harder for promotions and other professional recognitions compared to men with comparable qualifications
- lesser reward to women engineers compared to men for the same degree of professional achievements.

First, the responses to these questions were obtained from male engineers. These responses were analyzed and correlated to the background information obtained as part of the survey (Saigal, 1987). The questions related to background information dealt with:

- educational qualifications
- the number of engineers of opposite sex working in their department
- the number of years association with their counterparts
- the level of interaction with their counterparts—supervisor, colleague, or subordinate.

The same set of questions was then sent to women engineers for their responses. The women engineers surveyed work for various kinds of organizations including Digital Equipment Corporation, Wang Laboratories, Arthur D. Little, Tufts University, and others. In all, there were 66 female and 207 male responses to the 100 and 250 questionnaires mailed respectively. This chapter summarizes the responses obtained from women engi-

neers and those obtained earlier from their male counterparts, compares the responses and draws certain conclusions therefrom.

ANALYSIS OF THE SURVEY

Table 5.1 summarizes and compares the responses to various questions dealing with issues related to women engineers. Even though 27 percent of male engineers believe that women have lower ability than men and 16 percent attribute women's success to luck and their being a minority, *not one woman engineer felt the same.* This goes on to show that indeed there is a feeling among male engineers that women have lower ability. However, both men (37 percent) and women engineers (36 percent) agree that it is

Table 5.1
Survey Analysis

Question	Percentage of respondants with positive response	
	Women	Men
The ability of women engineers is less as compared to men	0	27
Women's success is more due to luck and her being a minority than her efforts and skill	0	16
It is easier for women engineers to find jobs just because they are women	36	37
Entry level women engineers are generally assigned routine and less challenging jobs as compared to their male counterparts	60	33
The lack of role models in the form of senior women engineers seriously hampers the progress of young women engineers	68	33
Proof of success requires more evidence from women as compared to men	81	50
Women engineers have to work harder for promotions as compared to men with comparable qualifications	86	58
For similar success, the rewards are greater for men than for women	80	43

somewhat easier for women engineers to find jobs just because they are women. This may be due to the incentives provided by the government to various organizations to hire minorities and women, and the establishment of Equal Opportunities and Affirmative Action Offices.

Thirty-three percent of male engineers and 60 percent of women engineers believe that entry level women engineers are generally assigned routine and less challenging jobs as opposed to their male counterparts. This in part may be due to the feeling that women engineers have lower ability. If in fact this is the reason, many organizations may be underutilizing their female engineers' services.

Sixty-eight percent of women engineers tend to believe that the lack of role models in the form of senior women engineers seriously hampers their progress while only 33 percent of male engineers felt the same. A few male engineers mentioned that young women engineers should try to use male engineers as role models. However, the fact remains that women engineers felt that they tend to relate better to women engineers than to male engineers.

The last three questions substantiate some of the professional prejudices women engineers face at work. As shown in Table 5.1, 81 percent of women engineers as compared to 50 percent of the male engineers surveyed agree that women have to provide more evidence than men as proof of success. Not only that, 80 percent of women engineers and 43 percent of male engineers felt that for similar success the rewards are greater for men than women. Based on the above discussion, it should come as no surprise that 86 percent of women engineers and 58 percent of male engineers surveyed believe that women have to work much harder for promotions as compared to men with comparable qualifications.

CONCLUSIONS

These surveys indicate the existence of an overall prejudice against women engineers even in today's society. A majority of the women engineers and a significant percentage of the male engineers covered by the survey strongly believe that women engineers have to work much harder not only to prove their ability and the quality of their work but also to gain respect that they deserve from their male counterparts in the engineering profession.

So it is clearly seen that women do find the workplace less friendly as opposed to their male counterparts specifically in a male-dominated profession such as engineering. Even though women engineers have come a long way since the early years, they have far to go before they will indisputably be accepted as professional engineers of the highest quality. The U.S. government, the Society of Women Engineers and other organizations have been working toward changing the scenario for professional women. But what is needed is a societal change in attitudes toward women. Probably

time is the best instrument to bring about such a change, which will help make the engineering industry suitable for everyone, men and women.

REFERENCES

Barriers to equality in academia: Women in computer science at MIT. Report to MIT Computer Science and Artificial Intelligence Department. (1983, February). Cambridge, MA: MIT.

Colborn, K. (1987, February). What's changed and what hasn't. *Graduating Engineer.*

Saigal, A. (1987, December). Women engineers: An insight into their problems. *Engineering Education.*

Whatley, S. K. (1985, January/February). President's column. *U.S. Woman Engineer,* 2.

Women workers don't get their due. (1986, August 13). *USA Today,* D1.

6

The IP (Impostor Phenomenon) and Women in Theology

Joan A. Range

When Pauline Clance's book, *The Impostor Phenomenon,* was published in 1985, she did an invaluable service for many people, men and women alike, but a truly unique service to women in theology. She named the feeling that many of us experience who try to function in a predominantly male world and in an exclusively male tradition, that is, theology. Naming something, as we are told in the Bible, is a way of controlling it. Because we have *felt* like impostors, women, by naming that feeling, are able to deal with it and are liberated for the task of making theology our home turf and not a foreign land.

Let me explain how Clance describes the IP (Clance 1985). While it is by no means restricted to women, it can afflict women more frequently than men, especially in areas or disciplines which have been (as most have been) and still are (as theology certainly is) dominated by men.

When I heard one of our graduate students say the following I knew that the IP was alive and well among us women theologians or aspiring theologians. Marilyn said that when one of her classes began, she felt that all the men had been "born speaking Greek" and she couldn't even recognize the alphabet. Another one recounted the fact that one of her fellow students told her that women pick "really different topics" to write their papers on from the other students, "others," of course, meaning men.

Clance gives a test in her book that reveals how deeply a person can be afflicted by the IP. Let me name a few of the statements by which you can

grade yourself: "I can give the impression that I am more competent than I am," or "I tend to remember the incidents in which I have not done my best more than those times I have done my best," or "Sometimes I'm afraid others will discover how much knowledge or ability I really lack," or "If I receive a great deal of praise and recognition for something I've accomplished, I tend to discount the importance of what I've done" (Clance 1985, 19). And so on. A rather dreary, but true, list of the doubts a person may have who suspects she is an impostor and will someday be found out.

Bernice Sandler, director of the Project on the Status and Education of Women, reflects the same kind of phenomenon when she speaks of the "chilly climate" of the academic world for women, whether they be students, faculty, administrators, or staff (Sandler & Hall, 1986). Her work documents the obstacles and difficulties that academia imposes on women.

What can be done about this foreign world that should be our native land, this chilly world in which we cannot become comfortable and warm as in our own homes amid family and friends?

My particular discipline is theology and it poses special difficulties for someone suffering from IP. There are the obvious difficulties: the male theological tradition, the related ecclesiastical structures, the language. Then there is the more powerful, subtle difficulty, that is, the pervasive influence of 4000 years of patriarchy (Lerner 1986), including an understanding of a patriarchal God. This enormous patriarchal tradition is as strong now as ever and is even somewhat stronger today in certain areas because it senses a threat coming from the excluded but now educated ones, the women.

The question that my chapter addresses, then, is: How does a woman become a full-fledged citizen in this strange land? Some would ask: Does she even want to become one? How does she warm that chilly climate that marginalizes her, to mix a metaphor, and refuses her the warmth and comfort of the family hearth with its household gods?

I will address this question by briefly reviewing some work that is presently being done by women and suggest some points that need to be borne in mind as we continue the work of feminist theology.

BIBLICAL THEOLOGY

For Christians a central, foundational area for building any kind of theology is the study of the Scriptures, not only the Hebrew Scriptures, but also the Christian Old Testament, and the New Testament, the writings of the first Christian generations. Certainly these texts have supported the male-dominated view of a woman's role, a woman's place, over the centuries of the Judeo-Christian tradition. What has been done to correct this one-sided development?

One of the more daring scholars in this field is Elisabeth Schüssler Fiorenza. With a very carefully worked out methodology, she understands,

evaluates, and then substitutes a theory of what feminists need to do in order to make the Scriptures a source of liberation for women rather than *the* source of oppression (Fiorenza 1983). For when women think, as we have for centuries, that God ordains our subordinate role, there can be no question about what our role is and our obligation to accept it. Fiorenza has done outstanding work to uncover the activity of women during the life of Jesus and of the early Church, thus giving women a "usable past" (Russell 1974). The lack of evidence about women in leadership positions, for example, as preachers, prophets, and leaders of prayer, has discouraged many feminist scholars to the point where they no longer see any hope within the Christian tradition for the liberation of humanity from the formidable grip of this patriarchal religion. How, then, with this kind of traditional presumption regarding the subordination of women, does Fiorenza proceed?

Her main insight has to do with the past, the biblical past, and its role in teaching us about the meaning of revelation. Rather than beginning with the teachings of the Bible about what it means to be an image of God (Old Testament) and a child of God (New Testament), Fiorenza begins with women's experience. Where do women feel the oppression with which patriarchal Christianity has burdened us through the ages? Where are the messages in the Scriptures that liberate all of us? There are surely the latter, as women have historically experienced Christianity and as women experience it today. How then do we get at these texts?

Fiorenza spells out the task of biblical scholars for interpreting the Bible as a liberating revelation for women. We need a feminist hermeneutics:

A feminist critical interpretation begins with a *hermeneutics of suspicion* rather than with a hermeneutics of consent and affirmation. It develops a *hermeneutic of proclamation* rather than a hermeneutics of historical factualness, because the Bible still functions as Holy Scripture in Christian communities today. Rather than reducing the liberating impulse of the Bible to a feminist principle or one feminist biblical tradition, it develops a *hermeneutics of remembrance* that moves from biblical texts about women to the reconstruction of women's history. Finally, this model moves from a hermeneutics of disinterested distance to a *hermeneutics of creative actualization* that involves the church of women in the imaginative articulation of women's biblical story and its ongoing history and community. (Fiorenza 1984, 15)

To this thick, rich, hermeneutical task must be added, of course, the task of translating and even rewriting, as Fiorenza recommends, some biblical stories in order for women to claim as liberating the revelation of the God of the Christian religion. This task has begun already with the work of such scholars as Phyllis Tribble (Tribble 1978), Virginia Mollenkott (Mollenkott

1977, 1983), and Carol Ochs (Ochs 1977), to name only a few American biblical scholars.

HISTORICAL THEOLOGY

History, the record of human existence, was always made by women and men; it certainly would not have occurred, could not have happened, without the participation of women. Yet, it was written by men, about men, and from the perspective of patriarchy. By history, I mean the broadest meaning of that word, the entire human past that was recorded. Since it was written as it has been, women do not seem to have had a past. We have no common memory that identifies us except the one that has been given us by patriarchy. The records women *have* left are only now being discovered and properly interpreted. These feminist historians, women and men, have been sensitized to the enormity of the gap in the human past which the lack of women's history reveals.

Although these gaps are being filled by the endeavors of various feminists, this is not a sufficient redress for the human race and its future. "Adding women," as Gerda Lerner writes, is not sufficient because the entire historical perspective is patriarchal (Lerner 1986). The same interpretive vision is at work. By adding women, of course, the vision encompasses more of the human past. This shift, helpful as it is, is not revolutionary. Feminism is revolutionary and when it occurs, the inevitable earthquake will realign the human terrain, fill the gaps, and present us with a new earth and a new heaven.

Some of the most important questions in theology, then, are the basic anthropological ones: What is a human being? What is human nature? What is a man, a woman? Are they equally human? Until this century, the theoretical answers were "no": Women are not equally human. Men are superior in humanity and women are inferior. To use more theological terms, did the Creator create women inferior? Or, to put it another way, is God sexist? As incredible as that question may sound, we must take it seriously because to understand women's role as determined by God underlies the Judeo-Christian position regarding women and how this tradition interprets revelation.

God, of course, is *not* sexist, no more than God is racist or anti-Semitic or prejudiced in any way against God's own creation. That kind of limitation is impossible for the reality we intend when we use the word *God*. History has shown us the inappropriateness, to understate the matter, of the principle of racism, that God created some races naturally inferior to others, or of anti-Semitism, that God rejected one people and accepted another in its place.

Can feminists show as clearly that God is not sexist? Can we show that sexism, the subordination of women to men, is *historical*, just as other

theories of "natural" subordination or inferiority have proved to be un-
founded in nature? Gerda Lerner's work, *The Creation of Patriarchy,* sets
about doing just that.

Women have become subordinate to men because of history and culture,
not because of nature. To maintain on principle that this subordination is
the will of God is to blame the Creator for the activity of the creature. The
subordination of women *happened* and, just like other human errors, can be
overcome. If one believes that the Creator does not will the subordination
of women, no more than the Transcendent One wills the inferiority of
other races and people because they are naturally inferior or unacceptable,
then the obligation to work for the liberation of women becomes a requirement of justice and one that the Judeo-Christian tradition must engage in if
it is to be true to *its* own nature.

As a result of this historical development, (the subordination of women) the major
metaphors and symbols of Western civilization incorporated the assumption of female subordination and inferiority. With the Bible's fallen Eve and Aristotle's
woman as mutilated male, we see the emergence of two symbolic constructs which
assert and assume the existence of two different kinds of human beings—the male
and the female—different in their essence, their function, and their potential. This
metaphoric construct, the "inferior and not quite completed female," became embedded in every major explanatory system in such a way as to take on the life and
force of actuality. On the unexamined assumption that this stereotype represented
reality, institutions denied women equal rights and access to privileges, educational deprivation for women became justified and, given the sanctity of tradition
and patriarchal dominance for millenia, they appeared justified and natural. For
patriarchally organized society, this symbolic construct represented an essential in-
gredient in the order and structure of civilization. (Lerner 1986, 211)

Most Christian churches today sense some kind of obligational justice to
undo the results of the centuries of oppression from which women still suffer. How far that obligation goes, what the vision is that propels it, only
time will tell. We know that the vision of feminism is truly a revolutionary
vision and will stand patriarchal churches on their respective heads when
the truth hits home.

ICONOGRAPHIC TRADITION

Another source for reading women's history is iconography. Christian
iconography, both East and West, is a rich and beautiful source for feminist
historians to study (Miles 1985). Sometimes a jolt to one's consciousness
can cause one to see, to look at it and its meaning in a new way.

I experienced such a jolt last year during my sabbatical when I had an
opportunity to spend a semester in La Paz, Bolivia, doing research on
women who live in conditions of extreme poverty. There was a group of

women, called *desocupadas*, unemployed women, whom the city employed for road and street building in the barrios. The city paid them for this hard work by giving them food which it itself had gotten free. Every Wednesday after their third and last workday of the week, one of the women, Ceferina, would invite the others to come to her house for some time of relaxation, prayer, and tea. About 20 women would come each week.

Besides joining these women on Wednesdays, I had the opportunity to interview most of them individually. Toward the end of my stay I wanted to do something for them. These Bolivian women, I had found, were fine women, rich in their courage and goodness. The natural beauty they live in, the grandeur of the Andes, is breathtaking. But their houses and neighborhoods are dreadful. So, I bought a large and rather nice reproduction of *The Last Supper* and installed it in their meeting room. When I looked at the picture and then at the women I knew immediately that there was something missing. There were no women or children in the picture.

I found it impossible to give it to the women without pointing out to them this unforgivable omission. It made no sense to describe that scene unless I pointed out whom the artist had omitted: the mothers, wives, and children of the well-known participants.

Earlier on in that same year, the sisters I was living with in La Paz had celebrated the Thursday of Holy Week, Maundy Thursday, by having what is called the Seder Supper, a reenactment, to some extent, of the meal that Jesus would have had with his friends on the night before his death. We had invited the church caretaker, his wife, and children, to share the meal with us.

During the course of the meal we had the usual, unexpected events that happen when a family eats together. Hilda, the mother, had a baby at her breast and whenever he became restless she would give him her breast. The three-year-old daughter got caught sliding down between the stacked pillows on her chair and the back of the chair. When I rescued her, everyone laughed. The meal continued with the customary dialogue between the father and one of the children recalling the meaning of that night for the Hebrew people as they were liberated from Egypt and the transformed understanding of the meal for Christians.

As the action of the Seder progressed, it became clear to me that what we were experiencing must have been the way it had originally happened. It was a family meal. The absence of women and children from the painting I had given to the desocupadas was wrong. The Last Supper could not have happened the way our iconographic tradition had depicted it. Yet Christian artists reflected that tradition and it had subsequently shaped our understanding for centuries about who was present at the Last Supper, to whom Jesus addressed the words the Gospels recount, and, then, to whom the church has understood those words were addressed—only men.

Another experience of the same kind gave me another jolt. Toward the

end of my stay I wanted to give each of the women individually something beautiful to express my thanks to them for their generous cooperation in my work. I had found some rather nice reproductions of Mary, something beautiful for their poor, small, crowded homes. I gave them to them on *El Dia de la Madre*, the Bolivian Mother's Day. As before, I found myself realizing that the traditional picture of Mary was inadequate and, before I could give it to the women, I had to explain it.

The picture of the Virgin Mary was that of a beautiful young woman. The reality of the Bolivian woman was that most of them had lost many of their teeth, their faces were lined by the hardness of their lives, and they were exhausted from their hard work. I realized that Mary probably looked more like them than like the beautiful, young maiden in the picture. "For every child a tooth" is a common saying in the Andes. There is no way a woman living in conditions of extreme poverty can replace in her body the nutrients which pregnancy and lactation deplete. The state of those women's bodies is so *real*, reflecting the toll their daily lives take, especially the care of their children, that I found myself apologizing for the appearance of Mary in the picture.

She, too, grew old, I told the women, just as all women do. She probably had lost some of her teeth, just as all child-bearing women who are poor do, and her face must have showed the hard conditions of her life just as their faces did. She, too, grew old and died just as all women grow old and die.

I had never before thought of any of what I was explaining to the women. But I realized that I had to say it; it was true. My brief acquaintance with them showed me the inadequacies of the iconographic tradition regarding women that had developed in Western Christianity and which shapes our understanding in a profoundly deep way. This formation is even stronger in the understanding of illiterate people, and most of these women were illiterate, they had never had the opportunity to become literate.

The influence of iconography on the developing consciousness of people cannot be underestimated, whether it is Michelangelo's depiction of God's creation of *man* and the role of Eve in the fall of man, or the artistic depiction of the Last Supper, or of Mary, whom virginity, according to legend, kept forever young.

Perhaps these inadequacies and distortions are apparent to more women than I realize, but I suspect not. The images that form our minds of the events of Christian history shape our understanding of what happened, who participated in the events, and what roles they played. I realized, because of the insights I had received from these Bolivian women, the inadequacies of this tradition for women.

Margaret Miles has done some excellent work on the interpretation of religious art. Her book, *Image as Insight*, is groundbreaking, I believe, in this

task for feminist scholars. Much more needs to be done to read accurately the source that art is on the formation of the Western Christian mentality and so of theology, in order to liberate us to see and understand what is there and what is missing and to redress this imbalance.

SOME POINTS TO REMEMBER AS THE FEMINIST THEOLOGICAL TASK CONTINUES

The most debilitating result of patriarchy is the way it has divided women against themselves. It is very hard for women to discern this division and work against it. This division renders women as a group less powerful (if not actually impotent) than we could be as we work to abolish the weak state in which we live within patriarchy. Lerner says:

Men take their place in the class hierarchy based on their occupations or on their father's social status. Their class position may be expressed by the usual outward sign—clothing, residential location, ornaments or their absence. For women . . . class distinctions are based on their relationship—or absence of such—to a man who protects them, and on their sexual activities. The division of women into "respectable women," who are protected by their men, and "disreputable women," who are out in the street unprotected by men and free to sell their services, has been the basic class division for women. It has marked off the limited privileges of upper-class women against the economic and sexual oppression of lower-class women and has divided women one from the other. Historically, it has impeded cross-class alliances among women and obstructed the formation of feminist consciousness. (Lerner 1986, 139)

As Lerner observed, these divisions include those caused by socio-economic factors (poor women vs. richer women, good mothers vs. lazy mothers, good occupations vs. menial work); religious factors (prostitutes vs. respectable women, women who want abortions vs. women who condemn them, women who have too many children vs. women who responsibly plan their families); racial and class factors (women who save for the future vs. women who use food stamps, bag ladies and homeless women vs. women who are solid citizens, women of the dominant race vs. other kinds of women, women who are well educated vs. women who drop out, women who are ambitious vs. women who are lazy, lesbian women vs. straight women, pagan women vs. women of monotheistic religions, etc.).

These divisions come from our pervasively patriarchal world. It is very difficult to understand them intellectually much less to feel their divisive effects emotionally. It is not necessary to agree with the alternative groups to overcome this division. But an awareness of how patriarchy divides us from each other is the first step toward eliminating these differences as

causes of division among us. As examples of the power of some of these categories to divide, I will use the issues of abortion and lesbianism.

Positions on these issues derive from strong beliefs, strong value systems, and gender definitions that are among the deepest culturally. As a result, women have not been able to meet as sisters when these issues are introduced. To speak of reproductive rights and compulsory heterosexuality is to hoist red flags that participants either cannot or will not ignore. A breakdown of the possibility for encounter and dialogue ensues, and women see each other as enemies.

The issues of abortion and lesbianism have been given to women by patriarchy. They are symptoms of a terrible disease, one which will not be cured by treating only the symptoms. As a matter of fact, the disease worsens when only the symptoms are treated. Women wind up wasting human life and tolerating destructive relationships because patriarchy tells them that men know what is right about human sexuality and our culture controls women's reproductive powers through its ethics and laws. This tradition teaches women what the relationships between two women may and may not be and labels the relationships it cannot accept as unnatural and deviant.

As long as we let these issues, as well as the many others I noted above, be defined by patriarchy, women will never be able to hear each other and understand the suffering women experience because of the definitions these issues have. The debilitating divisions continue and human liberation retreats yet again from realization. The present theological explanation of women's concerns reflects only the patriarchal vision of what it means to be human, to be good, to be a sinner, to be forgiven, to be loved, and to love.

Another important point for feminists to remember in doing theological work is the understanding of God. The work that some are doing regarding a past in which there was worship of a goddess and in which priestesses functioned is important, I believe. This work can shake our imaginations loose for creative alternatives for worship today. It can point out inadequacies in monotheistic religions that portray only a masculine, father god. The limitations put on the Transcendent One by theologians of monotheism must be uncovered and redressed and some feminist theologians do that. Mary Daly pioneered work like this (Daly 1973).

Some of their work is energized by anger, it seems, and is, therefore, discounted by "objective" theologians. But anger can be very effective. "First," said the gentleman who hit his stubborn mule on the head, "you have to get its attention." Anger can do that. When we recall revolutionary movements, anger was a result of experience, it needed expression, and could mobilize people. The discovery of grave injustices requires it. Anger is not pleasant nor are we, women or men, well prepared to deal with it constructively. But we may not ignore it. Angry feminist theologians must be heard;

we must hear each other. The passions that run among feminists is an enormous source of energy and we need to utilize it. That's hard work, but it is such a rich resource for engaging in any discipline. Theology, therefore, can also be energized and enriched by the anger of women.

The theology of God is, of course, foundational in any faith as well as its anthropology. So this is true for the Judeo-Christian tradition. Our theological tradition recognizes as far back as biblical times that the first and last sin of the human race is idolatry; to make God into our own image. Patriarchy has been guilty of this; the God of the Judeo-Christian tradition is the Great Patriarch, the God who demands, threatens, punishes, and holds grudges. Realization of the inadequacy of this image of God must function strongly among feminist theologians until it is equally recognized by all other theologians. When women know that we, equally, are created in the image of God, that we are daughters, not sons, of God—when a woman can recognize herself in the revelation that the Transcendent One made of its own reality, in her body as well as in her spirit, in the mighty acts of God as well as in the teachings of God, in the guidance whereby we human beings strive to live as children of this God and to work to bring about the reign of this God—then we will feel like and indeed be full citizens, neither strangers nor impostors in this ongoing conversation we call theology. The climate will be warm and invigorating for women as well as for men.

There are more insights that feminist theologians need to experience, more concepts that should be borne in mind. I would like to suggest only one more because it enlightened me very much. Feminists must be able to recognize as their sisters women who live in conditions of poverty, whether these women be among us here in the United States or be women of the Third World. I say this because I experienced the enlightenment that comes from being among women we call poor and was so deeply enriched by them. Their lives, their personalities, their hopes and dreams, their sorrows and joys have helped me recognize so much in the theological tradition that reflects patriarchy. They have been my teachers. The creative power that springs from dialogue with them is enormous. Without that power the issues that feminist theologians deal with are greatly reduced in significance for the discipline of theology. Just as churches today lack credibility when they do not build up those whose lives are weighed down by injustice, even while their teachings exhort their members to work for it, so feminist theologians will lack credibility when the issues we deal with represent our lives only and not the lives of our sisters who are even more oppressed than we are. Sisterhood includes every woman, not only those of us who are educated, who will never be poor, and who receive respect and recognition because of what we accomplish. Surely theology must deal with survival issues; salvation is that or it is nothing, a luxury not many people can afford to engage in. To recognize in the survival issues of the poor the proper ter-

rain of theology is to become a theologian of reality in the family of humanity—not an impostor, but a genuine, card-carrying theologian.

Finally, within this process and struggle, feminist theologians need to model their conviction of peacemaking. Our discourse must manifest our commitment to peace. This challenge is especially difficult for those of us who are so angry and who have earned the right to our anger. But if feminist theology is to be the revolution it purports to be—the use of violence, even linguistically, and the application of power, the pressure which forces instead of the persuasion which frees—it must not mimic the strategies of theological and ecclesiastical leadership that so often are contrary to the revolutionary ideals of feminism. Integrity is essential to any enterprise of feminism and so of theology as well.

REFERENCES

Clance, P. (1985). *The Impostor Phenomenon*. Atlanta, GA: Peachtree.

Daly, M. (1973). *Beyond God the Father*. Boston, MA: Beacon.

Fiorenza, E. (1983). *In Memory of Her: A Feminist Theological Reconstruction of Christian Origins*. New York: Crossroads.

———. (1984). *Bread Not Stone: The Challenge of Feminist Biblical Interpretations*. Boston, MA: Beacon.

Lerner, Gerda. (1986). *The Creation of Patriarchy*. New York: Oxford University Press.

Miles, M. (1985). *Image as insight: Visual Understanding in Western Christianity and Secular Culture*. Boston, MA: Beacon.

Mollenkott, V. (1977). *Women, Men and the Bible*. Nashville, TN: Abingdon.

———. (1983). *The Divine Feminine: The Biblical Imagery of God as Feminine*. New York: Crossroads.

Ochs, C. (1977). *Behind the Sex of God: Toward a New Consciousness—Transcending Matriarchy and Patriarchy*. Boston, MA: Beacon.

Russell, L. (1974). *Human Liberation in a Feminist Perspective—A Theology*. Philadelphia, PA: Westminster.

Sandler, B., and Hall, R. (1986). *The Campus Climate Revisited: Chilly for Women Faculty, Administrators, and Graduate Students*. Washington, DC: Association of American Colleges.

Tribble, P. (1978). *The Rhetoric of Sexuality*. Philadelphia, PA: Fortress.

7

Factors Affecting the Granting of Tenure in Schools of Nursing

Patricia R. Messmer

The literature (Moloney, 1986; Murphy, 1985; Aydelotte, 1985; Conway, 1983; Henry, 1981) indicates that nursing faculty are struggling to meet the standards of tenure while trying to fulfill all the obligations imposed by being both excellent academicians and professional practitioners. The purpose of this chapter is to examine the factors involved in tenure decisions. Deans from 139 National Leagues for Nursing (NLN) schools of nursing offering both accredited baccalaureate and masters degree granting programs were surveyed for a profile of tenure practices. The survey requested data on the deans' perceptions of their institutions' tenure practices and information on individual faculty members considered for tenure. The response rate was 97 percent with 135 of the 139 deans completing the questionnaires. However, only 133 responses were included in the data analysis since tenure was not offered by two of the schools.

This study concluded that there are legitimately three broad areas of tenure criteria: teaching, research, and service. The demographic data indicated that tenure was a widely accepted practice in nursing programs although 6 percent of the institutions reported a quota system and 30 percent reported informal guidelines for limiting the number of tenured faculty. Many schools may continue to restrict the number of tenured faculty members due to the decreasing enrollment in schools of nursing and the increasing emphasis on cost containment.

ACADEMIC RANK ACCEPTED FOR TENURE

Of the institutions reported in this study, virtually all institutions accepted associate professor rank for tenure while a few more than half (54%) accepted the assistant professor rank for tenure. This suggested that the assistant professor rank for nursing faculty was accepted for tenure in the university setting only half as often. In a subanalysis of schools of nursing with doctoral programs, 34 percent of those programs accepted the assistant professor rank for tenure. This finding indicates a trend toward accepting the higher rank of the associate professor as more doctoral programs are developed. In most disciplines, one proves oneself as assistant professor and tenure is granted as one is promoted to associate professor rank. Nursing, as an emerging profession, is considered a neophyte within the university and may lag behind in its application of the tenure guidelines.

ACADEMIC QUALIFICATIONS ACCEPTED FOR TENURE

In this study, 61 percent of the universities and colleges required a doctoral degree in nursing or in a related field for tenure. In the schools not requiring a doctorate, many indicated that their criteria were changing to a doctoral requirement. In a subanalysis of the schools with doctoral programs, 78 percent accepted the doctorate degree for tenure, which indicates a trend for nursing programs to accept the doctorate for tenure. In other disciplines, a faculty member is required to possess a doctorate prior to accepting an academic position in order to have credibility for teaching and conducting research that is accepted in prestigious professional journals. The former prevailing lack of a doctorate among nursing faculty indicates that nursing now strives to upgrade its professional standards.

NONTENURE TRACK

This study revealed 94 nursing schools (70.7%) had nontenure track positions. Employment in nontenure track positions may present a problem for faculty members applying for a tenure track position, since only 23 schools (17%) allowed faculty to apply for a tenure track position from a nontenure track position. In most cases, faculty had to first apply for a tenure track position and then could be accepted only if there was a position available in the tenure track. There appears to be a definite trend toward the nontenure track position, since this position has been one mechanism used to hire nursing faculty not qualified for tenure. Some deans felt that the provision of a nontenure track was beneficial for nursing faculty members who needed additional time to acquire the necessary credentials and to establish a publishing record. A mechanism must be provided for mobility in and out of the tenure system if the nontenure track is utilized.

TENURED NURSING FACULTY COMPARED TO TENURED FACULTY IN THE UNIVERSITY

There was a higher proportion of tenured university faculty than tenured nursing faculty in the university. This finding indicates that nursing faculty members are not as "tenured in" as are other disciplines. The lower proportion of tenured nursing faculty, compared to the proportion of tenured faculty in the university at large, may indicate that nursing faculties do not possess the necessary academic credentials for tenure or a general misunderstanding of nursing as a profession.

RELATIVE IMPORTANCE OF TENURE CRITERIA

The three broad areas of teaching, research, and service were subdivided into 26 academic activities. The academic activities related to teaching were rated as significantly more important than the academic activities related to research and service. The academic activities related to research were rated as significantly more important than the academic activities related to service.

Teaching

In the principal components analysis, evaluations of clinical and classroom performance along with chairman, peer, and student evaluations shared the same commonalities, representing consistency for evaluating teaching effectiveness. Deans' evaluations did not share the same commonalities indicating that deans' ratings are not always consistent with the other evaluative measures. The dean's evaluation, from an institutional perspective, may represent a separate composite of the faculty's overall performance. Peer evaluation was considered less important as a factor in tenure decisions than evaluations by chairperson or dean.

In the chi-square analyses there was no significant relationship between the amount of classroom, x^2 (2, $N = 348$) = 3.75, $p > .05$, and clinical teaching load, x^2 (2, $N = 320$) = .98, $p > .05$, and faculty attainment of tenure. The amount of clinical teaching load or classroom teaching load did not have an impact on faculty being considered for tenure. Faculty members' management of their time appeared more important than where the time is spent.

In the chi-square analyses, there was no significant relationship between teaching at the graduate, x^2 (1, $N = 403$) = 3.01, $p > .05$, or undergraduate x^2 (1, $N = 401$) = .03, $p > .05$, level and the attainment of tenure. This indicates that both graduate and undergraduate faculty members are able to attain tenure, but teaching at the graduate level alone does not guarantee the attainment of tenure. However, in the discriminant analysis, teaching at the

graduate level, $F(5,243) = 20.65, p < .05$, was a predictor for attaining tenure. Faculties at the graduate level are interacting with peers and graduate students who are involved with research projects. Teaching at the graduate level requires necessary credentials for the higher theoretical knowledge and abstract conceptualization. Graduate faculty may have a lower student ratio and lower credit load assignment than undergraduate faculty. Many deans reported having faculty members teach both graduate and undergraduate classes; thus, inequities in teaching load may be resolved.

Faculty members rated as having a high quality of teaching were more likely to attain tenure than those having a medium or low quality of teaching. The discriminant analysis found that quality of teaching, $F(1,247) = 54.72, p < .05$, was one of the best predictors of attaining tenure.

A higher number of deans indicated that teaching as rank ordered had a higher priority in tenure decisions than research and service. However, in a subanalysis of programs that offered doctoral degrees, a higher number of deans indicated that research as rank ordered had a higher priority in tenure decisions than teaching and service. Research is a major component of the faculty role in institutions granting masters and doctoral programs. Many of the deans commented that research is becoming a more significant and critical factor in attainment of tenure while quality teaching continues to be expected.

Research

In the principal components analysis, the academic activities related to evaluation of research found that there were commonalities between funded research, nonfunded research, publications related to research, publications in professional journals, publications in refereed journals, publications in nonrefereed journals, papers at professional meetings, books published, junior authorships, and chapters in books. Those academic activities appear to be good indicators for evaluating research with the exception of chapters in books and junior authorship. Research productivity as validated by shared authorship may be difficult to measure.

Audiovisuals, initially thought to be an aspect of the research/scholarly component, were found to be related more to the dimension of professional and university service than to research. This indicated that most deans did not consider developing audiovisuals to be a research or scholarly activity. The value of audiovisuals was only recognized by a few deans who indicated that faculty should be rewarded if the audiovisuals were marketable.

There was a significant relationship between the presence of funded research, funded projects, and publications in refereed journals and faculty attainment of tenure. There was no significant relationship between the

presence of publications in nonrefereed journals and books and faculty attainment of tenure. However, publications, $F(6,242) = 17.70$, $p < .05$, and authorship of books, $F(4,244) = 24.72$, $p < .05$, were predictors for attaining tenure in the discriminant analysis.

Faculty having a high quality research were more likely to attain tenure than faculty having medium or low quality research. The discriminant analysis indicated that the dean's rating of the quality of research, $F(2, 246) = 40.59$, $p < .05$, was one of the best predictors of attaining tenure.

Service

This study found that deans in a rank order indicated that service was the least important criterion in tenure decisions among teaching, research, and service in all analyses. Faculty may place a low priority on the service component, if they must devote a great deal of time to research or scholarly activity in order to attain tenure. This low priority on service from the deans' perspective ought to have an effect on how nursing faculty spend their time. It is important for faculty to be selective in the type and amount of service involvement and to be mentored, since overinvolvement or the wrong type of service activity may be detrimental to attainment of tenure.

However, service was still far from unimportant, especially in the dean's perception of quality of service. Faculty members with higher degree of involvement in service activities were more likely to attain tenure than faculty having a medium or low degree of service. Thus, it is helpful for individuals being considered for tenure to have significant involvement in professional, community, and university service to attain tenure. The discriminant analysis indicated that quality of service, $F(3,245) = 30.75$, $p < .05$, and involvement in professional associations, $F(7,241) = 15.59$, $p < .05$, were significant predictors for attainment of tenure.

SUMMARY

This research indicates that there is an associative relationship between tenure criteria and attainment of tenure. This study indicated that nursing faculty members are expected to achieve excellence in teaching, research, and service for attainment of tenure. The process of tenure is working in that nursing faculty members are promoted and retained who are intelligent, active, involved, and productive. Nursing faculties must be professional and strive for excellence in teaching, research, and service while being careful of the priorities. As the number of doctoral programs increases and norms reflect an increased emphasis on research, financial support and release time should be provided to facilitate the requirements for research and publication. Orientation for new faculty members should include advice on improving quality of teaching, guidance for professional

recognition of research, and recommending that involvement in profession, community, and university service be highly visible. Tenure criteria must be clearly defined and available and nursing faculty should be made aware of the specific tenure criteria including both written and unwritten expectations. Nursing faculty members should be advised of the tenure process at their time of appointment and provisions should be implemented for the mentoring of nontenured faculty on standards for tenure and promotion. Neither the institution nor faculty benefits when faculty members become cognizant of the fact that they can be employed at an institution but cannot be retained if they do not meet the tenure criteria.

REFERENCES

Aydelotte, M. (1985). Approaches to conjoining nursing education and practice. In J. McCloskey & H. Grace, (Eds.), *Current Issues in Nursing.* Boston, MA: Blackwell Scientific Publications.

Conway, M. (1983). The administrative process as dialectic. In M. Conway & O. Andruskiw (Eds.), *Administrative Theory and Practice.* Norwalk, CT: Appleton Century Croft.

Henry, J. (1981). Nursing and tenure. *Nursing Outlook, 29.*

Moloney, M. (1986). *Professionalization of Nursing.* Philadelphia, PA: J. B. Lippincott.

Murphy, M. (1985). A descriptive study of faculty tenure in baccalaureate and graduate programs in nursing. *Journal of Professional Nursing, 1.*

8

Empowerment: An Example from Women's Studies

Jean Saul Rannells

An empowering experience is one in which a woman gains an increased sense of power and autonomy. Empowerment represents a new understanding of her power. Such experiences of empowerment are important to the self-understanding of women for the energy, autonomy, and affirmation they give to women. Too often women allow others to determine who they are, what they will do, how they will speak and act. In this manner, women's lives have been ignored, devalued, and diminished throughout the centuries.

One area of our lives where empowerment can occur is in learning experiences. These are happenings, events, activities in which we acquire a skill, knowledge, and/or attitudes. Classes, courses, workshops, reading, discussing, writing, viewing, hearing, tasting—all are potential learning experiences. These learning experiences can be designed in many ways and can include many different topics, activities, attitudes, and possibilities for learning. We design activities for our own learning and participate in the design of experiences for the learning of others. As we create these experiences, we can use specific learning activities to facilitate the experience of empowerment.

As women ourselves, and as women who work with women, we want to maximize our experience of empowerment for three reasons. First, we want to counteract the heritage of disempowerment and silence that women have lived. Second, we want to claim for ourselves all the skills, talents, and

enjoyment of life that is there for us. Each of these has a place in the process of empowerment and will be evident in the example below. The third
reason for studying empowerment is its relationship to the process of
individuation which comes from the psychology of Carl Jung. Individuation is the lifelong process of development of consciousness, a unique process of self-development (self-actualization) for each person (Jacobi, 1967).
Empowerment is one aspect of individuation.

INDIVIDUATION AS A THEORETICAL FRAMEWORK

It will be helpful to examine this concept of individuation which has so
much to offer educators for the understanding of the learning process of
the individual.

First, individuation is wholistic: it encompasses all areas of the individual's
growth—the spiritual and the intellectual, the emotional and the relational, the
"feminine" and the "masculine," the conscious and the unconscious. (Jacobi, 1967)

Second, individuation recognizes that symbols and archetypes are integral in the individual's self-development. While unique in their manifestation to individuals, the images, the archetypes, have a timeless quality
which offers connecting points with other persons (and cultures) in the
individuation journey (Jung, 1982; Jacobi, 1967).

Third, individuation is a process within which the individual comes to
see herself as a unique person, differentiated from the rest of the community. There are similarities among individuals, to be sure; yet, only as
one sees herself or himself as a distinct psychic entity will the wholeness
and integration of self be achieved (Rannells, 1986a; Ulanov, 1971;
Whitmont, 1984).

Some scholars have criticized Jung's ideas as male-based and therefore
inappropriate to describe the psychic development of women (Goldenberg,
1979). Others have affirmed the power and clarity of archetypes and metaphors associated with individuation. Instead, Pratt (1981, 1985) and Lauter
(1985) propose a "re-visioning" of the symbols from a feminist perspective
for the illumination of women's growth. This research supports the latter
point of view.

WHAT IS EMPOWERMENT?

Empowerment is a new affirmation of one's self-worth. It is increased confidence in one's power but it is at a much deeper level than awareness. It
represents a resounding "I AM" spoken deep in one's being. Within this utterance is the implicit "I am . . . and I can do . . ." although action may not be

the result or even contemplated in the affirmation. When empowered, a woman has an increased sense of power and autonomy.

This sense of empowerment may be expressed in three ways:

1. As an experience arising from within. One feels within one's self that she has the power to believe and act in a desired manner. A woman might say, "I was renewed with the knowledge that my sexuality was beautiful and desirable."

2. As an expression of emotional strength. One feels ardent, strong, forceful, intense. It is a deep acceptance of self. A woman might say, "All of a sudden I just knew that I was able to handle those end-of-the-year decisions."

3. As an expression of zest and vitality. A woman might say, "I leave the class feeling full of energy and power."

Empowerment represents the ability and capacity inherent within the woman to act, respond independently and autonomously. It is not conferred from an exterior source or authority (Rannells, 1986b).

HOW IS EMPOWERMENT INVESTIGATED?

The concept of empowerment was investigated in research with 16 women who participated in a women's studies class, "Women and Mythology" at a large Midwestern university. The women were 19 to 43 years old. The purpose of the class was to explore classical and feminist interpretations of certain Greek and pre-Greek myths and to examine their influence on the lives of contemporary women. Both the content of the course and the teaching methodology encouraged students' reflections on their everyday life experiences. Research data were gathered from an in-depth interview with each of the women, a journal that each kept, a written paper and a creative project of the student's choice.

Content analysis methods were used with the written documents to determine the presence of the concept of empowerment in the statements of the women. Two coders (women) read the materials to determine whether each segment of writing was evidence that the writer was communicating this sense of empowerment. Not all women did give such evidence. The number of incidents coded "Empowerment" in the interviews ranged from zero (four women) to eight (two women), with a mean of two.

HOW IS EMPOWERMENT MANIFESTED IN THE CONTEXT OF LEARNING?

As has been shown in the definition and examples, empowerment arises from within the individual as an expression of an inner state newly felt as power, or vitality, or strength. As such, empowerment appears to be the result of an interaction between an unconscious element of one's experience

and a conscious experience. It is as if a present experience calls to mind something in the unconscious; when conscious, this "old" material can be integrated with the "new," creating the energy of empowerment. For example, Kris, one of the women in the course, had a very difficult semester because of academic pressure and decisions. At the end of the semester she said about her experience, "I'm growing. The last time I felt so powerful, I was alone in Europe. It's come back to me! Oh, how I love myself!" Now that is empowerment! It came as a result of her awareness in the present of a connection between her feelings in the current experience of the class and her feelings when in Europe. Kris has a new sense of herself as a powerful woman.

There were three particular student activities in the class that gave evidence of experiences of empowerment—writing, creative projects, and shared women's experience. These and similar experiences are often available to us outside of the classroom as well; thus it is important for women to understand the possibilities for empowerment within these activities.

WRITING

Students were asked to keep a personal journal of their reactions and responses to the themes of the readings and class discussions. They were also asked to write a paper which included a personal response to the topic. The key point is that writing a personal response to a theme helps the woman engage the unconscious and conscious in a dialogue, thus gaining a new perspective on the concern. This can happen in many different ways. Here is one example.

Kris had a very negative experience in another class and she chose to write a paper about it. She thought that writing the paper would help her think through the situation and suggest alternative responses to the event; it would be a healing process. The event was a slide presentation of science technology in Hawaii into which the male professor had interjected beach scenes of women to "spice it up." Kris reacted with extreme anger and embarrassment. She felt this presentation portrayed women as sex objects and personally felt diminished and devalued as a woman. Yet, as she reflected upon the event, Kris realized that she had identified with these stereotypic images of women, denying women power and value as women. This perception is what she wanted to change.

The dialogue between the conscious and unconscious is obvious in Kris's actions. The slide show had evoked anger and embarrassment in her conscious being. These emotions welled up from her unconscious from internalized norms that the self now found constricting and destructive. A new self-concept of Kris and women in general as powerful and positive was being integrated.

Kris claimed the power of change for herself in two ways—intellectually

and affectively. Writing the paper documented the intellectual process of understanding the learning. Kris dealt with the affective process through the drama of storytelling; she told and mimed a story of women's power to the class. "By telling stories (in my supportive group of women), I can use my own voice, hear my own worth and literally feel the bondings between me and my community . . . creating connections and empowerment and new consciousness." In summary, it was through the process of writing the paper that Kris identified and transformed experiences in her past and present into a positive self-image. She then created a symbol (storytelling) of the transformation of her image of women.

CREATIVE PROJECT

For this assignment students were to express an idea from the course through a medium such as poetry, drama, or artwork. As an example, consider Diane, an art student specializing in pottery. She read of Athena and Hephaestus who created artworks for the Greeks. Hephaestus showed his work only when it was perfect; Athena encouraged people to watch her work. Diane realized she valued Athena's outlook on sharing art; yet she, like Hephaestus, shared only "completed" work. For the project, she chose to work in oils because she was uncomfortable with oil painting and wanted to gain practice sharing with others the tender and vulnerable aspects of her work as an artist. Working in an uncomfortable medium and sharing it with the class allowed her to try out new behaviors and attitudes.

Diane was attracted to the work habits of Athena and Hephaestus; these also generated an attentiveness to her own unconscious and enabled her to examine and come to a new understanding of herself as an artist. She could (and would) share her work-in-progress. At another level, it is interesting to note the actual picture Diane chose to paint—three images of Athena creating, breathing life into, and celebrating a new being. In her painting Diane represented what was happening to herself and what she was doing for herself. She was creating, breathing life into, and celebrating her new being, her empowerment as an artist. The appreciative response of the class to the powerful portraits of Athena was also empowering for Diane.

SHARED WOMEN'S EXPERIENCE

The value of women's experience was a fundamental one for the class. For instance, readings by women authors were used extensively. Ann expressed her interest in and appreciation of one of the assigned readings about and by a woman. "What this author has discovered is a quest that is both peculiarly female and also one followed by other women. This book tells me my ideas are legitimate, because other people have the same ideas, and they are good ideas." Ann was especially interested in the spiritual

journey, so the reading would be calculated to appeal to her; however, it took on added strength, since it was written by a woman and identified elements of the journey that Ann experienced as very similar to her own. "I just felt that I could have written it, that I already knew it. I could say, 'Oh, I know that!' It was very powerful for me."

In addition, the community spirit which developed in the class helped Kris in her search for new understanding of women's power. She said, "We're all women and all have different messages about what's negative about us and things that aren't respected in us as women . . . just being able to identify these things in other women and see them and react to them very positively and notice them in yourself. It's really a wonderful feeling. I get a lot of good stuff from being in the group . . . which really helped." Women talking about their experiences enabled Kris to look at herself in a new way. She found the process affirming to her in her struggle to reshape her own image of herself and women.

DO DEITY IMAGES ENHANCE POWER?

There is another aspect of the course that provided the opportunity for empowerment. Since the course dealt with mythology, women studied the activities and attitudes of the goddesses. The deities were important symbols for women's progress in individuation and empowerment. The deity was seen not as a worship object, but as a symbol; in other words, Athena was a symbol for Diane of the artist's growth through sharing her artistic process. Women identify with an attribute of the deity and see themselves in a new way (Bolen, 1984; Pratt, 1985). For example, Artemis, a Greek goddess revered for her life in the outdoors and for her skill as a huntress, was a symbol for Ann. Ann loved canoeing and backpacking and had spent many meaningful vacations in this way. Yet, she also believed these were not "women's activities," thus diminishing part of herself. When she learned of Artemis, a deity honored for her being-in-the-woods, Ann was able to reevaluate her self-understanding as a canoeist and backpacker.

Another example comes from Cathy and her attraction to the myth of Inanna. Inanna was a Sumerian goddess who made a journey into and from the underworld to learn the meaning of life and death. (This story was written about 2500 years before the birth of Christ.) Cathy was the victim of incest and her recognition and efforts to deal with that trauma felt to her like a journey into the underworld. She claimed the myths of Inanna as tools for her reflection on this journey of descent and ascent.

The goddesses became role models for the women. They were manifestations of the attributes and attitudes the women wanted to work on in themselves—for Ann it was value and enjoyment as an outdoorswoman, for Cathy it was reflective growth and learning from the death-rebirth met-

aphor for her dealing with incest. For other women the symbols were inner peace, strength, nurturing, assertiveness, and decision making.

SUMMARY

The research and excerpts from narrative data presented here suggest three findings for educators. First, empowerment is an important process in women's self-understanding and development of consciousness. Second, learning experiences can be designed to enhance empowerment. These activities include writing, creative projects, and shared women's experiences. Third, the symbols represented by deity images (i.e., skill outdoors or journeying into the underworld for growth) can contribute to the empowerment of women.

The theoretical framework of individuation from Jungian psychology supports this evidence in two ways. Empowerment is manifested through a dialogue between the conscious and unconscious, the self uses symbols of past and present experiences integrating them into new understanding of self and world. Classroom activities act as stimuli for the process. Jacobi states that "writing, painting, sculpting, modelling, dancing, etc. help to activate the psychic depths, to maintain the vital contact between conscious and unconscious contents and to express the emerging symbols in plastic form" (1965, p. 58). Educators attentive to the self-actualization process through empowerment will utilize class activities to enhance the process.

REFERENCES

Bolen, J. S. (1984). *Goddesses in Everyone: A New Psychology of Women*. San Francisco: Harper & Row.

Goldenberg, N. R. (1979). *Changing of the Gods: Feminism and the End of Traditional Religions*. Boston, MA: Beacon.

Jacobi, J. (1965). *The Way of Individuation*. New York: Harcourt, Brace and World.

Jung, C. G. (1982). *Aspects of the Feminine* (R. C. F. Hull, Trans.). Princeton, NJ: Princeton University Press.

Lauter, E. (1985). Visual images of women: A test case for the theory of archetypes. In Lauter, E., & Tupprecht, C. S. (Eds.). *Feminist Archetypal Theory: Interdisciplinary Re-visions of Jungian Thought*. Knoxville: University of Tennessee Press.

Pratt, A. (1981). *Archetypal Patterns in Women's Fiction*. Bloomington: Indiana University Press.

———. (1985). Spinning among fields: Jung, Frye, Levi-Strauss. In Lauter, E. & Rupprecht, C. S. (Eds.). *Feminist Archetypal Theory*. Knoxville: University of Tennessee Press.

Rannells, J. S. (1986a). "Women's learning: A perspective from Jungian psychology," *Proceedings of the 1986 Adult Education Research Conference*. Syracuse, NY: Syracuse University.

————. (1986b). *The Individuation of Women Through the Study of Deity Images: Learning from a Jungian Perspective.* Doctoral dissertation. University of Wisconsin–Madison. 1986.

Ulanov, A. B. (1971). *The Feminine in Jungian Psychology and In Christian Theology.* Evanston, IL: Northwestern Press.

Whitmont, E. C. (1984). *Return of the Goddess.* New York: Crossword.

SECTION THREE

WOMEN AND THEIR WORK

Women have many complex roles to juggle if they should be also pursuing an education or a career. Several of the factors that affect women and their work are explored by the authors in this section.

Seeborg reaffirms the fact that women in the United States still have the primary responsibility for the management of the home and child care. In a study of dual-career households, she found that the women spend more time than their husbands on almost all household chores, and that men significantly underestimate the amount of time that their wives spend on these household chores.

The thesis that instead of supporting women, the media have become oppressive of women in general and working women in particular is discussed by Jussawalla. Many examples to support her view are given from current magazines and newspapers. Jussawalla believes that the media pit women against each other in an unhealthy way.

The differences between communication styles of women and men in higher education are identified by Case. She makes recommendations to women who wish to be "heard" by male academic counterparts. The examples and advice are readily applicable to the business world.

Commuter marriages—a twentieth century phenomenon—are rapidly becoming a part of everyday life for many working couples.

Hileman discusses some of the advantages and disadvantages of these commuter marriages, which she believes is the latest in new sociological trends.

The attitudes of people toward women as managers—in this case Hispanic women—are studied by Payne and Hoffman. While ethnicity did not play as big a role as the researchers anticipated, males were more strongly biased against women as managers than were the women surveyed.

Division of Labor in Two-Career Faculty Households

Irmtraud Streker Seeborg

Statistics published as recently as 1986 show female faculty members' annual income to be 76.7 percent that of male faculty members' income at colleges and universities (Mellor, 1986). Possible reasons for this include discrimination, concentration of women in certain disciplines such as nursing or home economics which may generally pay less, or late entry into the field; there is also the possibility that women are paid less because they spend more time in lower ranks (assistant professor level) than men. A recently conducted study of ten midwestern universities shows that women are disproportionately concentrated in lower ranks (Ball State University, 1987) and also frequently have more years at the assistant level than men.

One reason why women remain in the assistant rank longer may be their smaller number of publications. Ferber and Green (1982) found "that articles published is the largest contributing factor to academic rank, but that sex is also a significant factor." A study by Diamond (1986) shows the influence citations have on faculty salaries. Diamond argues that citations can be used as a measure of quality and quantity of faculty productivity and affect both salary and promotion decisions; gender is not considered in this study.

An important factor affecting research productivity is time. All else being equal, the person who has more time to devote to research and writing will be able to produce a larger number of articles or place articles in more highly regarded and selective journals, thus increasing chances for salary

increases and promotions. In the dual-career family, that time may not be as readily available to the faculty spouse as in a family with a wife who is not employed outside the home, or for a single faculty member without children, since the demands of traditional housekeeping and child care activities increase for each spouse, decreasing time available for research activities.

A question of interest in this context is who performs the household chores in a dual-career family when one or both spouses are faculty members. Studies of dual-career households in general have shown that men still spend only a small portion of their time doing household chores, although that seems to be changing. Even when the husband is unemployed, he does much less work in the household than a wife who works full-time (Barrett, 1984).

Studies regarding the division of household tasks have used several methods. One basic distinction is between studies which are strictly descriptive and those which attempt to explain the division of labor based on some theoretical framework.

One type of descriptive study surveys women and asks whether tasks are shared in their households. For example, a 1984 survey of 722 female executives indicates that in less than 10 percent of the households, men take responsibility for laundry, meal planning and preparation, or child care (Rogan, 1984). A more recent survey (Baron, 1987) of 1712 women in nontraditional roles indicates that over 50 percent of the respondents' husbands help with child care and household chores (with the exception of laundry, which still seems to be "women's work"). However, in a survey of this kind, it is difficult to assess how much time each spouse actually spends—helping with child care could be anything from watching the children on Saturday morning to taking full responsibility on a regular basis.

For the question considered in this chapter, namely, how much time does each spouse actually spend doing work in the home, studies that look at the actual time spent are more relevant. Geerken and Gove (1983) studied the allocation of time between job, housework, relaxation, and sleep for 849 respondents and found that in working-wife families, wives spent about 2.5 times as much time on housework as men and, consequently, had less time to spend on relaxation (or, in the case of the faculty member, research). This study included families with and without children.

There are articles in popular magazines praising "the new husband" who takes an equal share in all household-related tasks (see, for example, Weil, 1986; Weil, 1985; Barthel, 1985). But the fact that these husbands are singled out for praise may indicate that they are the exception rather than the rule.

More theoretically oriented studies attempt to explain task sharing by looking at a number of explanatory variables. Becker (1981) has provided a detailed theoretical discussion of household task sharing. He considers

stocks of human capital and the value of that human capital in the market as a determinant of allocation of time to household and market tasks. In many dual-career households, the market wage for both spouses may be comparable which makes the allocation of time to household tasks equally attractive (or unattractive) for both partners. This would be especially true for faculty couples who start their careers with relatively equal human capital endowment.

Bird, Bird, and Scruggs (1984) conducted an empirical study attempting to explain family task sharing. They developed seven task groups through factor analysis: meal preparation, child care, maintenance and repair, management of family activities, financial management, cleaning, and lawn and garden. In a sample of 166 couples where one spouse is a university administrator, they find that individual or family income is the most significant independent variable for meal preparation, cleaning, and lawn and garden tasks, with an increase in the wife's income leading to increased sharing; child care tasks are shared in two-career families. A husband's more egalitarian sex role orientation (husband as coprovider and coparent rather than provider and head) significantly increases his sharing in many tasks.

However, one might expect some differences in two-career faculty households. For example, teachers in colleges and universities (and, to some extent, even in elementary and secondary schools) have more flexibility than those employed in a business setting with fixed hours and often required overtime. Thus, it should be possible in a faculty household (here defined as one in which at least one spouse holds a teaching position) to share household tasks more equally. In addition, in a two-faculty household, both spouses are more likely to have an understanding of the other spouse's needs in terms of research and preparation time and, thus, may be more willing to share in tasks equally to give each partner the opportunity to perform to the best of his/her ability. Where spouses are in related areas, collaborative research is also a possibility, which would again imply increased sharing.

The present study was designed to answer both descriptive and explanatory questions for a specialized group of households: those in which at least one spouse holds a university teaching position. Questions to be explored include

1. How are household tasks distributed in two-career faculty households?

2. Do spouses perceive each partner's contribution to total household labor correctly, or do husbands see themselves sharing more equally than the actual times reported warrant?

3. To what extent can allocation of time spent on household tasks between husband and wife be explained by variables such as age, education, income, and the availability of household help?

4. In households where both spouses teach, do partners share more evenly than in other households?

5. In households where only one spouse teaches, does the spouse with the teaching job assume a larger share of the household tasks?

METHOD

In the spring of 1985, a mail survey was conducted among faculty members at a midwestern university. Questionnaires were sent out and returned by campus mail.

Subjects

The sampling frame for the survey was a list of all faculty members by department. Information on marital status was obtained from departmental secretaries, and a survey was sent to every second married faculty member on the list. Thus, all departments were included in the mailing.

The questionnaires were sent to 350 faculty members, and 101 usable questionnaires were returned. For reasons of confidentiality the department name was not asked on the survey; thus, it is not possible to ascertain whether all academic disciplines are represented in the actual sample. A tabulation of yearly income indicates that all salary levels are fairly represented in the sample. The age distribution of husbands and wives covers the full spectrum (26 to 73 years) with an average of 44 years for males and 43 years for females which is typical for the university. It is, of course, not possible to judge from the available data whether there is a response bias with respect to division of household tasks.

Instrument

Each couple received three questionnaires—one to be filled out by the husband, one by the wife, and a household questionnaire to be filled out by either. The questions on the husband and wife questionnaire were identical except for the word "husband" or "wife." For example, the husband questionnaire contained the question: "How much time does your wife spend . . ." and the corresponding question on the "wife" questionnaire was "How much time does your husband spend. . . ."

Questions related to the number of hours spent by the respondent on household tasks such as child care, laundry, meal preparation and cleanup, housekeeping, grocery shopping, lawn care; the number of hours spent by the respondent's spouse on those same activities; and the respondent's perceptions of the influence of income on the distribution of household tasks.

The household questionnaire asked for information on variables that might affect the total amount of work to be done, such as number of chil-

dren, availability of household help, and whether the couple lived in a house or apartment and had responsibility for lawn care.

Variables

The dependent variables in this chapter are based on responses to the following questions: "How many hours do you routinely spend doing each of the following family-related tasks in a typical week?," followed by a list of tasks, and "How many hours would you guess your husband (wife) spends doing each of the following family-related tasks in a typical week?," followed by the same list of tasks. The tasks are similar to those used in other studies (e.g., Bird, Bird, and Scruggs, 1984); they include child care, laundry, meal preparation and cleanup, housekeeping, food shopping, budgeting, and lawn care.

Since time spent (in absolute terms) varies from family to family, and the focus of the chapter is on allocation of household labor between husband and wife, the dependent variable used in the analysis is the difference between the time spent on each task by wife and husband (self-report data).

Independent variables and their definitions are listed in Table 9.1.

Table 9.1
Independent Variables

AGEM	Husband's age (years)
AGEW	Wife's age (years)
NOCH	Number of children living at home
EDUCM	Husband's education (years of schooling)
EDUCW	Wife's education (years of schooling)
INCDIF	Husband's income minus wife's income
HHH	Availability of household help (housecleaner and/or cleaning service, number of hours per week)
HCHLD	Availability of child care services (in-house, at sitter's house, or daycare center, number of hours per week)
FLEX	Dummy variable, 1 if both spouses teach, 0 otherwise
WFLEX	Dummy variable, 1 if wife teaches, husband does not

RESULTS

Table 9.2 shows the difference in time spent per week by husband and wife on the seven household tasks listed. A positive difference indicates that the wife spends more time at this task. The data indicate that tasks are divided along traditional lines in these couples: wives spend significantly more time than husbands (at the .01 level) on child care, laundry, meal preparation, housekeeping, and food shopping; husbands spend significantly more time with lawn care.

Table 9.2
Time Spent on Household Tasks: Differences Between Wife and Husband

Task	Time (Hrs) Difference	T-Value
Child Care[a]	1.2	3.52*
Laundry	2.5	8.74**
Meal preparation/cleanup	3.3	7.58**
Housekeeping	2.0	6.34**
Food shopping	0.8	3.27*
Budgeting	-0.3	-0.99
Lawn care	-1.8	-5.74**

a   only couples with children under 18 years of age are included.

*   significant at the .01 level

** significant at the .001 level

All time estimates are based on self-reports. It is possible that self-reports are not always realistic. To the extent that husbands (or wives) would systematically over- (or under-) report the times they spend, the estimated differences would not be accurate. Respondents were also asked to estimate the time the other spouse spent on household tasks. We can, therefore, compare the self-report data to the perception of time spent as reported by the spouse of the respondent.

There are large differences in perception with respect to husbands' and wives' reported times. Table 9.3 compares husbands' and wives' perceptions of time spent on the seven tasks.

Table 9.3
Difference (Hours) Between Time Reported and Time Perceived by Other Spouse

Task	Wife's Actual Time Minus Time Perceived by Husband	Husband's Actual Time minus Time Perceived by Wife
Child care	.96 (3.44, **)	.65 (2.45, *)
Laundry	.57 (2.96, *)	-.68 (-5.35, ***)
Meal Preparation	2.67 (14.13, ***)	.89 (3.97, ***)
Housekeeping	.78 (3.76, **)	.07
Food shopping	-.39 (-2.93, *)	-.38 (-3.42, **)
Budgeting	-.59 (-6.30, ***)	-.29
Lawn care	-.18 (-1.01)	.47 (2.23, .03)

* significant at .01

** significant at .001

*** significant at .0005

Husbands significantly underestimate the time wives spend on child care, laundry, meal preparation, and housekeeping, but overestimate the time spent on food shopping. The most dramatic difference is on meal preparation where wives report 1.6 times as many hours as husbands estimate.

Wives underestimate the time husbands spend on child care, meal preparation, and lawn care, but overestimate the time spent on laundry and food shopping. Generally, the wives' estimates are closer to the times reported than the husbands' estimates. On balance, wives spend almost four hours more a week than husbands' estimates whereas wives only underestimate husbands' time by 45 minutes.

In an attempt to understand the situation better, a multiple regression analysis was conducted with time spent by wives minus time spent by husbands as the dependent variable. At first, a simple model with demographic variables (husband and wife's age, husband and wife's education, number of children) as explanatory variables was analyzed. None of these variables explains much of the difference; the only model that approaches significance is one with time spent for a combination of chores (laundry, housekeeping, meal preparation, and shopping) as dependent variable. The variable with the most explanatory power in almost all cases is wife's years of schooling: the higher educational attainment, the smaller the difference in time spent. This is consistent with Becker's (1981) time allocation model.

Table 9.4
Difference in Time Spent: Regression Results—Expanded Equation

Task	Multiple R	Significance F[a]	"Best" Variables[b]
Child Care	.25	.001	HHH (.001), Wife's schooling (.04)
Laundry	.17	.001	NOCH (.001)
Meal preparation	.13	.01	HHH (.02), INCDIF (.05)
Housekeeping	.20	.001	HHH (.005), INCDIF (.01)
Grocery shopping	.37	.000	NOCH (.0001), INCDIF (.01), Wife's age (.02)
Budgeting	No variables entered		
Lawn care	No variables entered		
Chores	.26	.001	NOCH (.01), INCDIF (.02), HHH (.05)

[a]Refers to entire equation
[b]Significance of t-value in parentheses

More interesting results come from a larger regression model that includes as additional independent variables the amount of household help available (HHH) and the availability of child care (HCHLD) plus the difference in income between husband and wife (INCDIF). Table 9.4 shows multiple R and the variables which entered the equation in a stepwise regression for each of the dependent variables.

For those tasks where the availability of household help is a significant predictor, it always increases the difference in time spent—in other words, the "help" applies to the husband whereas the wife's load is not reduced by outside help. Income difference and number of children are also positively related with the difference in time spent. The effect of wife's schooling remains unchanged: as wife's schooling increases, the difference lessens.

Although all members of the sample were dual-career couples with one spouse a faculty member, not all were two-faculty couples. When one partner has a more flexible schedule than the other (e.g., teaching versus a management position in industry), one would expect, all other things being equal, that the teaching spouse would spend more time on household tasks. On the other hand, if both spouses teach, then the difference in time spent should narrow. Table 9.5 shows the results of a regression model including the two flexibility variables FLEX and WFLEX (see Table 9.5).

Table 9.5
Difference in Time Spent: Flexibility Model

Task	Multiple R	Significance F	"Best" Explanatory Variables
Child Care	.13	.02	FLEX (.02)
Laundry	.18	.001	NOCH (.001)
Meal preparation	No variables entered equation		
Housekeeping	.20	.002	WFLEX(.05), INCDIF (.03). NOCH (.04)
Grocery shopping	.22	.0001	NOCH (.0003), INCDIF (.03)
Budgeting	No variables entered equation		
Lawn care	No variables entered equation		
Chores	.23	.0002	NOCH (.001), INCDIF (.01)

DISCUSSION

The method used here is an improvement over surveys asking whether the husband shares in household tasks in two ways: actual time spent is obtained that gives a more objective measure than amount of sharing, and input from both husband and wife was solicited that should lead to less biased results.

As can be seen from the reported results, wives in the faculty sample still spend more time than husbands on most household-related activities. This may to some extent be due to the husband's lack of knowledge of the actual time required to perform certain tasks, as exemplified by the underestimation of times shown in Table 9.5. Consistent with other results reported in the literature, husbands don't do laundry.

One positive finding is that husbands seem to be more willing to help when there are children in the household. This is apparent both in the smaller difference in time spent and in the effect of number of children in several of the regression equations. Children may be the main hindrance to a faculty member's research productivity since children's needs cannot be postponed in favor of deadlines, as is the case with housekeeping or laundry. Thus, a supportive spouse is especially important for a faculty member with children.

The results of this study may not be typical for areas of the country outside of the Midwest. Also, the large differences in time reported by one spouse and estimated by the other casts some doubt on the accuracy of the results. Thus, a similar study using diary data over a period of several weeks would give more accurate data; however, it might be difficult to find a large number of faculty members willing to participate.

SUMMARY

A survey of 101 faculty members at a midwestern university was conducted to estimate the amount of sharing of household tasks in dual-career faculty households. It was found that wives spend more time than husbands on almost all household tasks listed (with the exception of lawn care and budgeting); that husbands underestimate significantly how much time wives spend on household tasks, whereas wives' estimates of their husbands' contributions are fairly accurate; that wife's years of schooling and the difference in income are the most important personal variables explaining differences in time spent; and that household tasks are shared more equally in households where both husband and wife hold teaching positions.

REFERENCES

Barrett, Karen. (1984, June). Two-career couples: How they do it. *MS,* pp. 39–42, 111, 114.

Baron, Alma S. (1987). Working partners: Career-committed mothers and their husbands. *Business Horizons,* pp. 45–50.

Barthel, Diane. (1985, November). When husbands and wives try working together. *Working Woman,* pp. 54–56.

Becker, Gary S. (1981). *A Treatise on the Family.* Cambridge, MA: Harvard University Press, chapter 2.

Bird, Gloria W., Bird, Gerald A., and Scruggs, Marguerite. (1984). Determinants of family task sharing: A study of husbands and wives. *Journal of Marriage and the Family,* 46 (2), pp. 345–355.

Ball State University (1987). BSU salary study for MAC schools. (Analytical Studies and Planning Office). Muncie, IN.

Diamond, Arthur M. Jr. (1986). What is a citation worth? *The Journal of Human Resources,* 21 (2), pp. 200–215.

Ferber, Marianne A., and Green, Carole A. (1982). Traditional or reverse sex discrimination? A case study of a large public university. *Industrial and Labor Relations Review,* 35 (4), pp. 550–564.

Geerken, Michael, and Gove, Walter R. (1983). *At Home and at Work: The Family's Allocation of Labor.* Beverly Hills, CA: Sage Publications.

Mellor, Earl F. (1986). Weekly earnings in 1985: A look at more than 200 occupations. *Monthly Labor Review,* 109 (9), pp. 28–32.

Rogan, Helen. (1984, October 30). Executive women find it difficult to balance demands of job, home. *The Wall Street Journal,* pp. 33, 35.

Weil, Denie S. (1986, June). Husbands who star in supporting roles. *Working Woman,* pp. 114–116.

Weil, Denie. (1985, July). Real-life supercouples. *Working Woman,* pp. 60–63.

10

Mothers, Work, and the Media: How Women Don't Support Other Women

Feroza Jussawalla

Recently, a syndicated newspaper columnist, Anna Quindlen (1987) of *The New York Times* divided the world of women into two groups: single women who work and mothers. Her taxonomy did not include women like me: working mothers. The mothers in her column were discussing how they would love to "chuck it all": their baking of brownies and waiting for the children to come home from school. The baby boomer working corporate woman was amazed: she would rather have stayed home with children. But what about the mother who does not have the option to stay home with the children, the mother increasingly under attack by the media, from *Newsweek* to the daily newspapers' Ann Landers and Dear Abby columns? The working mother is accused of leaving her children in day care, thereby robbing them of the pleasures of playing with neighborhood children in the neighborhood's park. She is accused of relying too much on her stay-at-home neighbor but also of making this mother feel inferior. The working mother is today's whipping boy. While it seems perfectly natural to accept discrimination from institutions and male colleagues, the new phenomenon is an attack from the media directed specifically, it seems, at working mothers—an attack often written and produced by women.

This women's attack on women perpetuates another evil—it pits "working mothers" against mothers in general and makes networking support systems impossible. In the light of feminism and the call for sisterhood, this

phenomenon is particularly distressing. And, it is not men so much as other women who do not provide the support systems necessary for women to "do their job" in this complex world. Working mothers in particular need support to do the job of both sending out articles or preparing business reports for publication and making sure that the apple juice is devoured by the constipated toddler, as well as mopping it up from the kitchen floor.

The image the media perpetrate of the "working mother" makes it impossible for women to establish real-life networks. The image is largely that of a "tycoon." One example is the idea of the working mother as propagated by the magazine of that name, *Working Mother* (1987). With a circulation of 2.5 million, their description of their readership, the "working mother" is as follows: "aged 34, 81.6% employed with a household income of $40,500," interested in buying "self improvement," "career guidance," "jewelry and beauty aids" (p. 152). This profile has damaging effects on the morale of stay-at-home mothers who feel they do not indulge in jewelry and beauty aids. It also has damaging effects on the morale of working mothers not at the top of the corporate ladder and unable to afford "jewelry and beauty aids."

And so it is that instead of providing a supportive network for women, the women of the women's media have become the oppressors of women in general and working women in particular. While the effects of these media portrayals are psychologically damaging to women, they also create the unhealthy atmosphere that surrounds women—they create the women bosses who think you should be able to do everything, the husbands who can't understand why you cannot look like or be like the "working mother" image in magazines, the mother-in-law who insists that you should go out and support yourself and questions why her son should support you when there are at least 25 million female workers in the U.S. married with children (*Infographics*, 1987) who work and support marriages, and the next door neighbor who resents you because you work. Let us take a look at how the media is destructive to a network of women supporting women.

First of all, *all* of us know and realize that the "media" are all around us and often determine the way we think. Without having done any readership surveys, we know instinctively that the medium that is most influential in women's thinking is the grocery store women's magazine. And the vast array of perspectives is mind-boggling—from *Cosmopolitan* to *Ms.*, from *Working Mother* to *Glamour*. I have already noted that *Working Mother* has a circulation of 2.5 million—*Cosmopolitan* has 10 million (*Nightline*, 1988). These magazines are influential just in the numbers that they reach. And the women writing for these magazines added to the newspapers on currently fashionable women's issues, prey upon the entire readership's consciousness.

A stereotypical image of working women is impressed on the minds of women who don't work reinforcing the image of working mothers as self-

ish women working for material gain. On Friday, November 20, 1987, for instance, the *Las Cruces Sun-News*[1] ran a special on working mothers. The undertone of the entire special was that mothers who work are "stressed out," and that the children suffer. In an earlier issue on Sunday, July 26, 1987, in a special box headed "Christian parents are aided by faith," a woman journalist, Kristie Jones, quoted a network organizer as saying, "Just because you work doesn't mean that your children are going to turn out bad. It's not impossible" (p. 2C). The *Sun-News* is a good example of a small town newspaper that typifies the attitudes of middle America. The implicit meaning conveyed to middle America then is that children will "turn out bad" if they have working mothers. So, the image of the working mother is that of someone who doesn't care about her children or the children who come in contact with her children, of a woman who is self-centered, who only wants to dress well and wishes to escape the responsibility of baking snacks for her child's preschool class.

With this image impressed upon them, women who stay home rarely wish to help the working mother or even to recognize her merits. They write endless letters to Ann Landers complaining about the mothers who go off to work and expect that their children returning from school to an empty home will be solaced by the stay-at-home neighbor. Recently, a conflict like this arose in a babysitting co-op that I belong to. Invited to participate by another mother who works full-time in a hospital, I eagerly looked forward to the egalitarian co-operative principle with equal share for all and the idealized feminist principle of rotating leadership. However, most of the volunteering for the tasks of the co-op, interestingly, is done by the working mothers in the group—organizing Christmas parties, phone committees, and so on. At a recent meeting when no one volunteered for the phone committee, two working mothers did: myself and a school teacher. In the middle of exam week the high school teacher had attempted twice to get hold of a nonworking mother to inform her of the co-op's Christmas party where children would be receiving presents. The nonworking mother's daughter was in the *Nutcracker* and had rehearsals to attend. Every time the high school teacher called in the evening, no one was home. The enraged nonworking mother called the chairwoman of the group, also a nonworking mother, who called both members of the phone committee with accusations about how working parents don't care about children and their feelings and the generalization that working parents had trouble meeting the responsibilities related to children. She would find replacements. After two hours of calling to find replacements she called the offending phone committee members. None of the nonworking mothers would volunteer. They were too busy with duplicate bridge, Christmas fairs, and so on.

Now, it has been debated and established that all mothers are working mothers. And certainly our experiences show that getting the house all or-

ganized and orderly is as difficult as organizing the accounts of a client or running a program. We all know what it takes to get the laundry done, the dishes washed, the baby cleaned. So is my term "working mother" spurious? Not at all. The working mother often does all this and more. But, then think of the mother who brings her sick toddler to preschool, despite repeated protests, because she could not miss her bridge game or her sorority luncheon. Of course in today's economy only 17 percent of all families make up the traditional white, middle-class pattern, and yet the voices of the women in traditional homemaker roles are loud enough to fuel the controversy continuously. In the light of such encounters, perhaps a new term needs to be coined for the mother who does not have working responsibilities outside the home—very often the mother who refuses to provide the supportive network society must provide for those women who must work outside the home.

Take for instance the question we all refer to as the question of "Choice," an issue often raised by the nonworking mother who claims she has made her choice to downgrade her standard of living to raise her children. In the Valentine (February 1987) issue of *Working Mother,* Olivia Burke attempts in her editorial to make a case for the following: "Rather than occupy opposing camps, we all need to work together to make it possible for each woman to make choices from an array of options . . . " (p. 8). But note the rhetoric of her opening paragraph:

Over the course of the last nine years, during which I've worked full time, I've encountered a fair amount of resentment from mothers who do not work outside the home. But no matter how much they hinted at the welfare of my children, I often had the feeling that these women were not primarily expressing disapproval of my parenting abilities. Instead, they seemed on the defensive—to have assumed some implicit disapproval on my part of their choice to remain at home. (p. 8)

To describe the nonworking mother as being on the defensive is simply to put her on the offensive thus marking choices with a societal imprimatur. Olivia Burke quotes a mother writing in to *The New York Times* who addresses this issue as follows:

Choices in our lives are not simply our choices. What choices we make are subject to the scrutiny of society. Someone out there passes judgement on women's lives and we are not able to escape that judgement. (p. 8)

The very addressing of women's questions over and over again in the media gives them a prominence that indeed puts all of us on the defensive.

It is interesting just in passing to note as a comparative touchstone that the question of choice is not one that is raised either in the Third World countries or in the European countries. "Choice," like the influence of the

media, is the result of an advanced capitalist society's affluence. No one asks the women coolies in India why they choose to work. I myself was raised in a joint family system by a mother who had an extremely successful career. But no one questioned her choice—Indians are used to women working in all different levels. In my school days, all my classmates had working mothers. Vaseema's mother was an attorney, Sanju's mother was an ob-gyn, Masuma's mother was a legislator, and so on. At the other end of the economic spectrum, my *ayah* (or nanny) was a working mother. In my son's preschool class of 14, he is the only deprived child with a full-time working mother and, as he puts it, doubly deprived because he's the only child without two mommies and two daddies! What is important is that where the pressures of the media and the myths perpetrated by the media are absent, women are much more likely to be able to form and maintain supportive networks. In India, for instance, while one woman goes to work she can count on a sister-in-law or a mother-in-law to provide the necessary support with household responsibilities. Most of the time it is necessity that forces these women out to work at all class levels; and the employment, where and when available, is according to skills and ability and these could range from the strength to carry bricks to the ability to obtain a Ph.D. It is interesting to note that in countries that we stereotypically think of as not having made advances in women's rights supportive networks for women seem to be most available. In a wonderful descriptive passage, Raja Rao in his *Kanthapura* (1984) tells of how women pooled their resources in the political struggle for independence. As they marched in the forefront of the resistance movement, women either left their children with each other taking turns in the care of children, or sometimes left them with the men or sometimes all the able-bodied had to leave the children with those not strong enough or young enough to undertake long marches. The common goal is often lost sight of in our more self-centered defensiveness—a defensiveness that results from the inadequacies we feel we have in the face of what we assume the other person has.

Also, where the media make more accurate portrayals and where the organized women's efforts are more realistic in attempting to obtain a common goal for women at large, women seem to cause less grief for each other. Take the European media for instance—and the fact that we know that in Europe greater advances in child care and maternity leave policies have taken place. Legal & General, the life assurance company, reported that "wives work 92 hours a week, labour to the value of £19,253 a year (approximately $30,000). Legal & General used employment agencies' fees to find out what it would cost to get a housewife's work (as shopper, waitress, window cleaner, nurse, driver, cleaner, cook and childminder) done by someone else" (p. 1A). The answer was £370 a week! The figure is the price of 38 hours a week looking after children (£133), 10 hours spent driving (£36), 18 hours in the kitchen (£99.75), 11 hours cleanup (£33), and so on.

Such a media report is likely to have a vastly different psychological impact on women in general and on husbands and mothers-in-law.

On the contrary, look at the U.S. media's treatment of women. The first stage of course is dealing with the childbirth experience. Women's media from *Ms.* (1984) magazine's "Giving Birth in America" issue to *Glamour's* (1985) "Cesarian Controversy" issue all believe that women should be denied the technological advances we afford to all other life-saving situations. Being truly liberated and "macha," as it were, means to have a premature baby delivered "naturally" in a subway station on the way to work rather than sending for an ambulance and going to intensive care. What is more, having "bonded" with the baby for a half hour, the baby should be placed in the hands of the nearest wet nurse en route to a board meeting. Gloria Steinem seems to believe that the cesarian is a male genitalist plot developed by male genitalist gynecologists. Contrarily, the whole natural childbirth movement seems rather like a "masculist" plot for the further oppression of women that says "be superwoman at home and in the workplace and then don the Madonna image in childbirth to satisfy our egos." Why are women and women's magazines perpetrating this plot? As a feminist, I believe in women's rights to procure good medical care and rights to equal opportunity to take advantage of technological advances. More and more women are beginning to feel this way. Here is a response to *Glamour's* cesarian issue published in the May 1985 issue.

I am sick and tired of reading articles that make someone feel guilty for having a c-section. I am a mother of a six-month-old daughter delivered by cesarian section. My operation was necessary to save my life and my daughter's, because she was breech, in fetal distress, and my cervix could not dilate. I seriously doubt that a greedy doctor or an impatient hospital staff is relevant when an emergency occurs, and I doubt that a birthing center or a home delivery would have prevented these complications. Whatever kind of delivery is done, the most important point is that the child's health be top priority.

Once the baby is born, the media, it seems, raise the question of "quality time." "Parenting," the "quality of time you spend with your child," and the "quality" of your own time are supposed to be important prerogatives obtainable through "time management"! But then, to Olivia Burke (1987, March), editor of *Working Mother*, quality time is a "myth" / a "Hollywood cliche." She tells us that in trying to create quality time, we're only overscheduling the kids and losing spontaneity! Such a clamor of conflicting viewpoints preys on the working mother's consciousness.

The "hottest trend" in all of this is the "quality" of your time, which inevitably in the women's media means "romance" or "glamour." The ideal to aspire for is that of Kim Alexis and her baby. Even *Cosmopolitan* ("When Mothers Work," 1986), that supposedly last antifeminist bastion, perpetu-

ates the myth of "having it all": romance, sex, the six-figure salary, and rosy-cheeked children.

The most ironic twist of feminism and the new liberated women's media is the celebration of men. Would a woman, if she chose to stay home, rate an article about the "house mommy"? Would she be the hero of the 1980s? When Larry McMurtry said, on The University of Texas at El Paso campus in the spring of 1987, that he had used his Guggenheim fellowship largely running after a two-year-old toddler, he received a round of applause. If a woman said that, the Guggenheim would never award another fellowship to a woman. It's like the Doonesbury cartoon:

Rick, you know what would happen if those thoughts were written by a woman? Such a diary couldn't be published from a woman. It'd be banal.

But you're a man . . . so you change one dirty diaper and it's a literary event.

And so our extreme feminism leads us back to the age of men. Men are to be celebrated and never criticized. According to Niki Scott, picking a husband's tie would label a woman a "nurturer," something she cannot do because "if we are in charge of our own safety and self-esteem, we can allow others to think, feel or do whatever they need to think, feel or do." Valentine's Day issues of women's magazines advocate treating husbands/boyfriends to vacations in the Bahamas. In being able to show men that we can provide for them and are independent women, we take one step back. We are to do everything for men. And in our competition to keep men comfortable and happy, we must not support other women.

But then, Niki Scott tells us that "men do not want working wives." Why not? Because one "two-person career" is bound to be more successful. Eric Zeucey's (1987) note of envy expressed indeed in what one would expect to be an enlightened journal, *The Chronicle of Higher Education,* is as follows:

My old colleague George (who has a wife who stays home and does the housework), liberated from responsibility for the day to day affairs of his own life is an academic ratebuster. The institutions that employ us have always assumed that a professor's job description describes a two-person career and as long as even a minority of professors continue to enjoy the fruits of the oppression of women, our employers will continue to assume so. (p. 104)

Prof. Zeucey feels sorry for himself as a "superdaddy" who feels the burden of "time involved in doing domestic chores, . . . noticing, caring, planning." Note the language of "superdaddy." Should he vacuum the rug or reread his students' essay exams? Ironically and interestingly, the male Prof. Zeucey, the "superdaddy," can express this and maybe even get brownie points on his merit evaluations for the *Chronicle* viewpoint essay. What if a *working* mother had written that article?

Mr. Eric Zeucey fantasizes thus about the perfect personnel committee: "Members sit around a seminar table waiting quietly as the candidate is ushered in. 'Mr. Smith,' the chairwoman begins, 'You indicate here on your vita that you have two children age 2 and 5. And that you've also published two books in the past three years.' Mr. Smith smiles, broadly, pleased that his diligence and dedication have been noticed. 'How,' asks the chairwoman, 'do you explain that?'" (p. 104). Unfortunately, I don't think Ms. Smith can be substituted for Mr. Smith in the scenario that Eric Zeucey creates. In fact, Ms. Smith would be found to be at fault, even if she chose not to interrupt her career, for not being dedicated enough as she produced children instead of more books. And, it would be an all-women panel that would find fault with her.

How does all this affect us as women in higher education? In the opening chapters of her devastating book, *A Lesser Life: The Myth of Women's Liberation in America,* Sylvia Ann Hewlett (1986) describes her experiences as a beginning tenure-track professor of economics at Barnard College: miscarriages resultant from the pressures of tenure-review panels, phone calls from male colleagues requesting absence from meetings rather than bring her child to a crucial meeting in the light of a babysitting crisis, and a note from a feminist colleague that read, "Dear Prof. Hewlett, I would like to point out that we at Barnard, are not running a creche, but a college" (p. 22). This is what Hewlett writes:

In the wake of my childbearing experiences, I decided to form a committee with other junior faculty women to press for the adoption of a maternity policy at Barnard College. . . . Our biggest surprise was to find that the feminists on the faculty disapproved of maternity policies. . . . Barnard College is one of the few elite colleges to have an undergraduate major in women's studies and there is a powerful group of feminist scholars on the faculty who teach in this program. In our naivete, we thought that all this emphasis on women's rights and feminist values had to translate into concrete support for the working mothers on the faculty. It did not.

Many of my feminist colleagues did not have children and were not enthusiastic about families. Indeed, one of them publicly accused me of trying to get a "free-ride" when I spoke out at a meeting for a college maternity policy. Didn't I understand that if women wanted equality with men, they could not ask for special privileges? (pp. 31–32)

Women conditioned by the media not to support each other placed in the defensive position of being "mothers" or "non-mothers," working women, or nonworking women continue to prey on each other. Women administrators are perceived as not supporting women's professional careers. In return, women who should support women administrators and who should take pride in the success of their female colleagues do not. They feel instead that male bosses, out of sheer defensiveness, can be more supportive of women's careers. Again, take Judith Briles' (1987) new book: *Woman to*

Woman: From Sabotage to Support. Fifty-three percent of women surveyed said that other women had treated them unethically in the workplace through such acts as vindictiveness, back-stabbing, lack of support, and betrayal of commitment. Briles found that women undermined each other again because of "resentment, fear and low self-esteem." Eighty-four percent of *Cosmopolitan* readers, it was reported in their "Sex and the working mother" (1986) issue, preferred not to work for a woman boss.[2]

Much of this is because women are pitted against women. We are either feminists or nonfeminists, mothers or career women, women who support women or women who want to get ahead of women in a "men's world." Interestingly Carolyn Heilbrun (1985), a leading feminist literary critic at Columbia University, perpetuated these myths by pitting all these classifications against each other in her presidential address to the MLA in 1984. She started out with what seemed to be an idealized exhortation to feminists:

For the very heart of feminism and, I suspect, of our theories of gender has to do with solidarity and identification with other women: how many of us are there, and do we greet one another as peers and comrades? For a woman to be a feminist, I would suggest, is to be where women are and to value the presence of women there. And to see to it, if one does not find oneself where women are, that women are soon where one is. (p. 282)

But soon she turned to Adrienne Rich who spoke of childbearing as "prescribed destiny" that pushes women into the Cro-Magnon cave. And so women with children are pitted against women without children in the academic workplace. Heilbrun was questioned about this by Dr. Vitz (1986) of NYU who felt she had enjoyed her "childbearing destiny" as a warm and sundrenched spot—and now had a successful career. But what of those of us who attempt both at the same time? Are we then to be labeled as somehow incapable or handicapped with our merit evaluation, noting "she is not on campus enough; she has a baby"? Who is to provide support for us or are we simply to be everyone's whipping boy?

One semester as I was working registration, I described the present study to a feminist colleague who said, "Why should I support women who are not feminist?" It is interesting that after years of "feminism," "liberation and enlightenment," women are unable to cut across the labels we have devised for each other and use these labels through the printed word to plague each other. Often all of this is chalked up to the nature of women—the old Miltonic idea that women can't be trusted—thus causing further divisiveness among women and further hampering the development of networks. Should we in our cynicism just say, "Women can't support women, they never have"? After all it was Eve who introduced "mutual accusation" to paradise and we just vindicate Milton who wrote,

Thus it shall befall
Him who to worth in Woman overtrusting
Lets her Will rule; ...

Paradise Lost, Book IX, Lines 1182–84

NOTES

1. My small town's newspaper.
2. *Cosmopolitan's* survey, "Working for a woman vs. working for a man": 60 percent say gender doesn't matter. The big surprise was that of the 43 percent who say gender does matter, one out of three would rather work for a man.

REFERENCES

Briles, J. A. (1987). *Woman to Woman: From Sabotage to Support.* New York: New Horizon Press.

Burke, O. (1987, February). Editorial. *Working Mother,* p. 8.

Burke, O. (1987, March). Editorial. *Working Mother,* p. 6.

Cesarian controversy. (1985, March). *Glamour.*

Grove, V. (1987, March 19). Spotlight. *London Times.*

Heilbrun, C. G. (1985, May). Presidential Address 1984. *Publications of the Modern Language Association of America,* pp. 281–285.

Hewlett, S. A. (1986). *A Lesser Life: The Myth of Women's Liberation in America.* New York: William Morrow.

Infographics. (1987). U.S. Department of Commerce. In *Las Cruces Sun–News,* November 20, 1987, p. 1C.

Jones, K. (1987, July 29). Christian parents are aided by faith. *Las Cruces Sun–News,* p. 2C.

Las Cruces Sun–News. (1987, November 20), p. 1C.

Nightline. (1988, January 21). ABC Television.

Quindlen, A. (1987, October 14). When a bored wife and mother feels like chucking it all. *Las Cruces Sun–News,* p. 2A.

Rao, R. (1984). *Kanthapura.* New York: New Directions.

Vitz, E. G. (1986, March). [Letter to the editor]. *Publications of the Modern Language Association of America,* pp. 247–248.

When mothers work. (1986, November). *Cosmopolitan,* pp. 297–362.

Working Mother. (March, 1987), p. 152.

Zeucey, E. (1987, April 1). *The Chronicle of Higher Education,* p. 104.

11

Communication Styles in Higher Education: Differences Between Academic Men and Women

Susan Schick Case

To an outsider, the academic world is fairly homogeneous in that its members are associated with books, libraries, laboratories, and teaching. As a group, academics are more like one another in background and interests than they are like, for example, construction workers. However, there are marked differences among groups of academics. A wide variety of careers are pursued within the academic world by a wide variety of people with a wide variety of interests and goals in a wide variety of institutions. Professors differ from administrators, and both differ among themselves. Scientists differ from philosophers, and even within the field of science, specialists in one area differ from those in another.

Academic women share in all of these differences, but they also differ in many ways from academic men. One such way is in their use of language. Because of their gender, women and men have had different life experiences and participated in different activities growing up. Thus, it would not be surprising that they would have different perceptions, beliefs, and categories for describing experiences (Alderfer, 1977; Alderfer & Smith, 1982; Miller, 1983). Much academic behavior occurs through linguistic activity, yet organizational analysis of behavior has paid almost no attention to how people actually speak (Mintzberg, 1973; Gronn, 1983; Levine, et al., 1984). Since the language people use and the association they make reveal how they see and interact with their world, the experiences of women, and their increasing presence in the higher education work force, mandate under-

standing their cultural perspective and respecting their differences where these exist.

In our research, we were interested in how men and women talked when they interacted with one another. We suspected that some gender differences would be revealed in the language used in problem-solving and decision-making settings that involved leadership and influence, partly as a function of differing equations of power held by men and women.

Unfortunately, when behavioral differences between the sexes are found or merely believed to exist, token women's behavior is often labeled "deficient" or "deviant," not "different." For instance, women's language is believed to reflect uncertainty and weakness, men's rationality (Rubin, 1976). There is little evidence to support this view. Yet the belief in women's speech "deficiency" has led to the proliferation of numerous "assertiveness" training programs in the past decade aimed at changing women's tone of voice, sentence structure, and other speech-style traits so that they are less feminine (Lakoff, 1975; Stone & Bachner, 1977; Eakins & Eakins, 1978; Kramarae, 1982; Thorne, Kramarae & Henley, 1983). Women take these courses believing that by changing their speech they will more likely be able to overcome organizational barriers to advancement.

Most of the information we have about the obstacles and barriers that women in upper-level positions in organizations face comes from research done in the private sector. But most of this information applies to higher education as well.

Many researchers have found that women have difficulty "fitting" into male-centered organizations (Bartol, 1978; Marshall, 1985). Traditionally, most profit-making companies have been established by men, and are often filled with male employees. As increasing numbers of women have been hired into these companies during the past decade, their path has not been an easy one.

One reason for the difficulty is that advancement in hierarchical organizations is fundamentally political in nature (Harragan, 1977). Women are generally rejected for promotion to upper-level positions because they do not fit the normative model of an ideal executive (Offe, 1976; Martin, Harrison & Dinitto, 1983). They are less likely to be viewed as qualified for the job (Epstein, 1975), particularly for positions entailing extensive authority over others (Wolfe & Fligsteen, 1979), or for decision making affecting substantial resources or capital (Silver, 1981). Yet access to and control of resources, and centrality in organizational interactions, make an individual important to the organization (Smith & Grenier, 1982). The formal system in organizations puts women at an overall disadvantage (Bartol, 1978).

A second reason for the difficulties women in upper-level positions face is that they are disproportionately few in number (Kanter, 1977). Because they are few, they receive more attention than their male peers. Not only does this increased visibility create performance pressures, but being

noticeable makes their mistakes more public and their differences seem more deviant.

Kanter (1977) reported that male managers exaggerate the differences between their own and women's cultures. For example, normal conversational flow gets interrupted by reminders of women's differences when a man apologizes for swearing in a woman's presence. Sexual innuendos and traditional "male" topics (such as sports) tend to increase when token women are present (Dyer & Devine, 1986). These perceptions of difference lead to the exclusion of women from informal groups.

Thus, for women, tokenism exacerbates the problems inherent in being in a male organization. Women may work there, but they do not really belong there, often feeling socially isolated (Devine, 1984; Marshall, 1984; Richbell, 1976). An individual's success is linked to the informal system of relationships in an organization. Informal social contacts are essential for information and guidance, especially for new organizational members (Schein, 1979). In fact, these informal processes may contradict these in the formal system. For example, decisions may be made during a golf game; information necessary to a task may be passed along in a men's locker room or at lunch. Furthermore, the closer one is to the top of an organization, the more commonly evaluations and rewards are determined by subjective criteria, and the more powerful the informal system is. Failure to belong to this informal system leads to both feelings of estrangement and a lower probability of quality performance and career success (Marshall, 1984; Devine, 1985).

It is not clear whether these conclusions are generalizable to other organizational contexts. But it is clear that women academics tend to be less satisfied with their colleagues than their male counterparts are, and more dissatisfied with promotion and merit-pay procedures (Fedler, et al., 1983). They also feel typecast into stereotyped roles, reporting more attention paid to their discrepant characteristics such as physical attributes (Dyer & Devine, 1986). These findings fit in with reports from token women in private corporations. Add to this the evidence from 217 academic employment discrimination grievances filed by individual women scholars in the United States (Farley, 1982), and it becomes reasonable to believe that the source of these problems lies in issues of male-oriented organizational structure and tokenism. Even though it is not clear whether these conclusions are generalizable to other organizational contexts, they serve as a useful guide to better understand the experience of academic women.

Our work is one piece in a larger body of studies about language use within which diversity of speech repertoires, ways of speaking, and choices among them find a natural place (Case, 1988). In it we analyzed the natural conversation of women and men as they worked together.

Research on men's and women's language styles primarily has been based on two types of studies. One approach has been to measure people's

"perceptions" of the kinds of language men and women use (Lakoff, 1973, 1975; Key, 1975; Thorne & Henley, 1975; Baird, 1976; Rubin, 1976; Kramer, 1977; Fisher, 1980; Kramarae, 1980, 1981, 1982; and Bonanno, 1982). Most of this research has been done through informants, anecdotes, and structured observation, all methods highly susceptible to influence by preconceptions.

For example, in work situations, women are often expected to be nurturant, emotional, and expressive, just as they are responsible for providing emotional support to family members, whereas men are expected to be rational and ignore feelings (Rubin, 1976). Perceptions of the language of the sexes seems shaped to be consistent with generalized sex-role images. Since women are thought to be emotional, indecisive, submissive, supportive, and interpersonally oriented, their speech is rated likewise; similarly, since men are seen as behaving aggressively, instrumentally, bluntly, and decisively, their speech is also rated consistent with that role image (Key, 1975; Baird, 1976).

Conclusions based on these studies contain all of the problems of subjectivity and selectivity inherent in any investigation of people's opinions of a topic. In some cases, empirical findings actually invert the stereotypes. For example, women are said to be more talkative than men, but when men and women talk together in groups, the finding has consistently been reversed: Men talk more than women (Strodtbeck, James, & Hawkins, 1957; Doherty, 1974; Aries, 1976).

A second class of studies addressing gender differences in language has involved empirical linguistic description of certain isolated speech elements in actual conversations (Shuy et al., 1967; Fasold, 1968; Barron, 1971; Labov, 1972; Mitchell-Kernan, 1972; Trudgill, 1972; Kramer, 1974; Bodine, 1975; Swacker, 1975; Aries, 1976; Gilbert, 1976a, b; Fishman, 1978; and Bonnano, 1982). Three generalizations about sex-based language are most consistently validated. These include:

1. When communicating, men more often assume task roles, women more often expressive socio-emotional roles.
2. The speech of women is more likely to be correct in terms of pronunciation.
3. In mixed-sex interaction, men talk more than women do.

But many results from studies contradict each other. For example, Lakoff (1975) conjectured that women use more tag questions ("Sally stayed in school, didn't she?"), making their language sound uncertain. Both McMillan, et al. (1977), studying mixed-sex discussion groups of college students, and Fishman (1980), studying heterosexual couples talking at home, found evidence for Lakoff's conjecture that women use more tags in their speech to elicit responses from uncommunicative male conversational

partners. Yet Baumann (1976) found no differences in tag use by gender in a classroom setting. In contrast, men have been found to use more tags in at least three situations: informal conversation (Lapadat & Seesahal, 1977), at a professional conference among participants (Dubois & Crouch, 1977), and when in a leadership role as a device to sustain interaction (Johnson, 1980). In these examples, the same feature appears to be used differently depending on the situation and the gender composition of the group, leading to questions about language function and use (McConnell-Ginet, 1980).

The results of empirical studies of the past few years encourage caution before making sweeping generalizations about extensive gender differences in speech. Basically, descriptions of linguistic gender differentiation are uneven and incomplete. Among the methodological problems are the facts that only small segments of conversation have been analyzed, that only a few traits have been examined, as well as that men and women have been compared on different scales, from which it is invalidly concluded that they are, in fact, different. Moreover, conversations usually have taken place in contrived situations rather than natural settings. In the latter, one can examine the give-and-take flow of actual conversation between men and women in formal or informal organizational groups and simultaneously think about the effects that the setting, topic, or roles might have as they interact with gender. Furthermore, the groups and contexts selected have varied from study to study.

The much-publicized data regarding the difference between male and female speech is overreported, polarizing gender stereotypes, and has yet to be demonstrated empirically in a systematic, comprehensive, and thorough way. There is a need for descriptive, exploratory studies of language differences within the context of the give-and-take of actual talk (Berryman & Eman, 1980; Fishman, 1983). Measuring many variables of speech with the same speakers, also would enable more general claims to be made about sex differences in talk, at least for that group (Thorne, 1986).

Our study improves on previous methodology by using a natural setting, lengthy conversational interactions, and comprehensive analysis of the language interaction in a natural work context. We asked the question, "What are the characteristics of typical male and female speech?" The natural conversation of women and men as they worked together in a group over time was empirically analyzed and quantified, and a speech profile for each gender was developed, enabling women and men to be compared on 34 speech traits. Based on the differing experiences of men and women in our culture, two predominant styles of speech were expected: a facilitative/personal style, used mostly by women, which would be more relational and integrative; and an assertive/authoritative style, used mostly by men, which would be more directive and commanding. Gender-related speech was also expected to correspond with influence in the group, with the more

influential masculine-style speech. What this study does is provide in-depth data on smaller numbers, drawing attention to similarities and differences in the speech of the women and men in this group.

METHOD

The study was conducted in a ten-person group (five women, five men) at a leading eastern management school. The group worked together in an unstructured setting, observing and attempting to understand their own leadership and influencing behavior as it occurred, coming face to face with issues of power, uncertainty, and normlessness. Group members were of comparable age (29–40), status (similar work roles and experience in higher education), social class (upper middle), and ethnicity (Caucasian), which should decrease linguistic variation. Since the group formed naturally, the fact that we were able to exclude many potential linguistic determinants due to race or social class was serendipitous. It meant there was little variation that would be expected in language except that due to gender differences.

Audiotaped, 45-minute sessions completed over 15 weeks were made from group formation until termination. All tapes were transcribed by the experimenter, who recorded as accurately as possible everything that was said without altering the grammar or verbal form of speech. A man and a woman from the group were used to help fill in sections of the transcripts because of a confidentiality contract among group members that allowed only group members to listen to the tapes. Reliabilities for the transcript process were a 96 percent agreement for words and 93 percent for utterance boundaries (where one speaker began and ended). Reliability is slightly lower for the latter because it is harder to establish when one speaker ends when more than one person speaks at the same time. Numbers were substituted for names so that analysis of data could be done without regard to the sex of participants.

Participant observation of group sessions occurred simultaneously, supplementing verbatim transcripts and empirical scoring schemas to record language interactions and comments on the social life of the group. Without the participant observation, the complexity, and dynamic nature of what occurs in conversational interactions is lost.

Analysis of Transcripts

From an initial 22 hours of taped conversation, four randomly selected one-hour tapes were analyzed for codification of each member's speech. Each was drawn from a different four-week calendar block to eliminate differences in speech that might have occurred as the result of group development over time (Bales, 1953; Bennis and Shepard, 1956; Schutz, 1958;

Bion, 1961; Alderfer, 1980). All tapes were used to illustrate the relationship between gender-related speech patterns and influence.

Phonological, morphological, semantic, and structural analyses of each member's speech were completed. Overall, 34 different language traits were examined. The phonological variables included differences in pronunciation, intensifiers (such as *so* or *such* used in an expressive way), and discourse length. Morphological variables included (a) the smallest meaningful units of language, and (b) syntactic usage (conjunctions, interjections, qualifications, and types of sentence construction). Semantic variables, related to the meaning of what was said, included pronoun choices, proof strategies (referring to outside experts or personal experiences), and conversational topics and themes. The structural variables included communication patterns of language organization and arrangement in interaction, such as turn taking, patterns of interruption, topic changes, who talked to whom about what, and messages of inclusion and exclusion.

A ranking and weighting schema for establishing influence behavior at each stage and for influence in the group as a whole was used (Case, 1985). Nine indicators of influence were employed, corresponding to five general measures: who talks, how much, to whom, about what, and in what way (Bales, 1950, 1968; Bales & Cohen, 1979; Hare, 1972; Borgatta & Bales, 1980) (see Table 11.1).

Table 11.1
Influence Measures

AREA	INDICATOR
Who talks	1. Frequency of initiation
How much	2. Mean utterance length 3. Percentage of total words spoken
To whom	4. Frequency of being talked to 5. Number of persons talked to per session 6. Frequency of talking to group as a whole
About what	7. Frequency of being talked about 8. Frequency of ideas being talked about
In what way	9. Proportion of fillers and qualifiers

Procedure for Establishing Speech Styles

Frequency of occurrence for each of the 34 traits was counted for each person, as well as the proportion of trait usage. Individual language profiles were then drawn. The extent to which an individual consistently employed certain linguistic features and patterns determined his or her predominant communication style. Reliability was obtained independently by a colleague who did not know the purpose of the study but who took the transcripts and did the same tasks with influence and scoring categories. Reliability on influence measures ranged from 93 to 100 percent and from 88 to 100 percent on each speech style scoring category for each individual.

Profile Categorization

A short experiment was developed to verify patterns in the profiles and to ascertain whether grouping of patterns corresponded to gender. Individuals sorted the profiles and put them in categories based on their perception of similarities or differences in the patterns. We expected that the more overlap the profile had, the more certain people would be of the similarities of the profiles.

Five men and five women sorted the profiles, with no gender-identifying characteristics on them. Two distinct groupings emerged from these examinations: a group made up of male profiles and a group made up of female profiles. Three profiles did not quite fit the pattern; yet, despite uncertainty, women were placed with women, and men with men. In all other cases, individuals were completely certain of their pairings.

RESULTS

Three speech styles were thus identified. In this chapter, we report on two of them: a predominantly feminine style (N=5) and a predominantly masculine style (N=5). We also found a wide verbal repertoire style used by two men and one woman, which still maintained gender-appropriate patterns. See Case (1985, 1987) for a description of this speech style.

Table 11.2 identifies two separate profiles, one for men's speech and one for women's speech. Within each variable (phonological, morphological, semantic, and structural) traits were ordered from high-to-low usage for men and low-to-high usage for women. The greater the contrast between percentage of occurrences of the variables for men and women, the more likely the importance of the variable as a distinguishing characteristic.

Table 11.2

Statistical Significance of Group Variance and Mean Difference on t-Test and Mann Whitney U

Variable	Mean Frequency Use		Group Difference		Variance Homogeneity
	Female	Male	t (one-tailed test)	U	F Value
Phonological:					
Informal pronunciation	1.4	13.6	-2.20**	2.0***	21.59****
Intensifiers	4.4	.8	1.90**	5.0*	9.59**
Varied discourse length	51.3	28.6	1.24	8.0	7.29**
Morphological:					
Conjunction topic shift	2.8	.8	3.24****	2.0****	1.71
Imperative construction	.4	4.4	-2.81***	1.0****	11.62**
Passive agreement	1.6	0.0	2.36***	2.5****	0.0
Tag questions	6.2	.2	1.95**	.5****	236.0****
Modal construction	32.6	16.4	1.71*	5.0*	4.25
Active agreement	3.0	8.8	-1.41*	6.0*	2.26
Interjections topic shifts	4.2	11.2	-1.39*	4.0**	1.59
Approximation/qualifiers	27.0	17.8	1.13	7.0	1.98
Exact words	8.4	16.8	-1.13	7.0	1.94
Compound sentences	8.2	6.4	.42	11.5	6.4**
Incomplete sentences	8.4	9.6	-.35	9.0	2.39
Compound-complex sentences	8.4	9.6	-.16	5.0*	11.57**
Semantic:					
Talks competition/aggression	8.4	30.6	-3.16****	2.0***	1.55
Slang	1.6	24.0	-2.49***	0.0****	63.25****
Third person/depersonalizes	48.2	111.2	-1.63*	4.0**	1.18
Jokes	.4	2.2	-1.52*	6.5*	7.75**
Swears	0.0	1.6	-1.43*	5.0**	0.0
Proof personal experience	15.0	1.8	1.25	3.5**	89.11****
Proof authority	.4	4.2	-1.17	5.5*	64.63****
Talks relations/responsibility	62.2	25.8	1.06	7.0	4.63
Hyperbole	1.4	3.4	-1.00	7.5	3.19
First person/personalizes	114.2	86.8	.42	9.0	15.96**
Structural:					
Changes topic	5.8	13.8	-1.80*	5.5*	1.92
Interruptions	1.2	3.2	-1.32	6.5*	1.43
Disallows interruptions	.4	1.2	-1.26	6.0*	1.5
Allows interruptions	2.2	.6	1.23	7.0	9.63*
Talks more	58.6	72.4	-.85	7.0	2.13
Builds on utterances	11.4	17.6	-.72	9.0	1.05
Confronts/attacks	5.4	9.4	-.61	9.0	2.14
Asks questions	14.8	17.6	-.49	10.5	1.71
Answers questions	6.4	6.0	.14	9.0	7.66**

*p <.10; ** p <.05; *** p<.025; **** p <.01

Note. U was obtained using a one-tail P corrected for ties.
In female and male group n = 5.

In spite of the fact that our group consisted of well educated men and women, who should be more similar in their speech (Maccoby, 1966), there were 23 traits that occurred more than two-thirds of the time in only one gender group, and of these all but five were statistically significant (p < .05). Of the five that were not, all were so close to significance (p < .1) that with the small population (n = 10) and gender samples (n = 5), each was suggestive of further examination. The results included below are of the traits that were significant.

The phonological and morphological areas both had some of the most extreme gender contrasts on traits. Phonologically, the group was not an exception to the usual predicted patterns. Women used more refined enunciation, sounding more polite in their speech than the men, whereas men sounded more challenging with their informal pronunciation. Women also varied the tone of their speech more through the use of intensifiers.

In the morphological area, the group also was not an exception to the usual predicted patterns. The women used tag questions (a shortened question added to a declarative sentence such as "the idea is good, don't you think?"), conjunctions rather than interjections to introduce topic shifts, and *mm hmm* as passive agreement, all adding to a sense of the women being more uncertain in their speech. Yet their manner of speaking seemed more socially facilitative. The men's speech included statistically significant differences in such traits as imperative construction (a form of commanding, implying obedience), interjections for topic shifts, and active agreement like *"right"* or *"yeah,"* all assertive, direct, authoritative forms of speaking.

A major contrast centered around semantic variables, with a different set of themes and styles of speaking utilized by each group. The data of this study demonstrate that the substance of male and female messages may be quite different. Five-sixths of the utterances counted as indicators of male traits were made by men, whereas only three-fourths of those labeled female were made by women (see the ratios in Table 11.3). Female themes included responsibility, affiliation, fairness, understanding, and commitment to the group, with use of words implying feeling, emotion, and personal references to their own experiences as they talked involving extensive self-disclosure. Women almost exclusively used personal experiences, rather than authority, as proof to convince others of their point of view. The responsibility/affiliation theme of female talk is illustrated by the following comment, "I think we pushed Linda outside. We're going to lose her." The themes used in our group by the women support Gilligan's (1982) notions of a different voice.

Semantically, there were significant differences in male use of swearing, slang, depersonalization and third-person usage, and competitive/aggressive talk about violence, victimization, one-upmanship, taking charge, control, superior status, and fear of self-disclosure. A man said,

Table 11.3
Gender-Speech Congruity Contrast by Linguistic Areas

Speech Traits Ascribed to Gender	Men	Women	Ratio*
	\% of Utterances		
	Phonological		
Masculine	90.7	9.3	9.8:1.0
Feminine	15.4	84.6	1.0:5.5
	Morphological		
Masculine	71.8	28.2	2.6:1.0
Feminine	27.9	72.0	1.0:2.6
	Semantic		
Masculine	84.3	15.7	5.4:1.0
Feminine	27.7	72.3	1.0:2.6
	Structural		
Masculine	65.1	34.9	1.9:1.0
Feminine	45.5	54.5	1.0:1.2

*Note: The ratio given for both men and women is their proportion of usage of more typical masculine to more typical feminine speech.

"I'm waiting for a leader to establish himself so I can go for his throat." Another male group member said, "I don't feel particularly like that much of a civilized adult, and I guess I don't trust anyone else in the group to be that much of a civilized adult. If I stick my neck out, someone will take out a razor blade and knock my head off." In contrast to women's use of personal experience as proof, men used proof from authoritative sources, appealing to objectivity.

A significant contrast was expected between gender groups in the structure of speech interactions, including patterns of language organization and arrangement, such as changing topics, interrupting, and disallowing interruptions. But the contrast did not occur. Although men were almost twice as assertive in the group as females, including interrupting women ($p < 0.1$), which was expected, females did *not* follow the expected conversational behavior of being significantly less talkative or more supportive in their language. Men also were different from what was predicted: answering questions, asking questions, and building on utterances. Women and men were the most similar in the structural area, as can be seen by the ratios in Table 11.2. Some of the women in the group had learned to hold

their own among the men, not allowing interruptions, changing the topic, and asking questions. Yet what they all chose to focus on thematically, and how they chose to express their ideas morphologically, were different.

In general, men were more mixed than women in their speech, using the traits that had been more frequently identified by previous research as male traits in a 3:1 ratio to those which had been more frequently thought to be female traits. In contrast, women had less variation in their speech with a more extreme 7:1 ratio of female-to-male traits (See Figure 11.1).

All confirmed female traits were expressive in function, contributing to a facilitative, personalized style. All confirmed male traits were authoritative in function, contributing to a take-charge, depersonalized, emphatic speech style.

In addressing the nature of the difference between masculine and feminine speech styles, it is clear that men attempted to assert status and establish dominance in interpersonal situations. They were more direct, informational, and action oriented. This included extensive use of the imperative form in making demands, commands, and requests. The masculine speech style was an assertively aggressive one that proposed, opposed, competed, and used proof from other sources. It was a style that pressed compliance on a listener, or led to an argument. It was also a style that withheld personal information, a strategy Sattel (1983) argues helps men exercise and maintain power over others. In general, the masculine style, with verbal gestures of dominance through use of words like *confront* and *attack*, and patterns of conversational assertiveness and control, was action oriented in its use of imperative construction, and exploitive in its themes of competition and aggression with little personal information revealed.

It is also clear that the feminine style was slightly more accommodative, with conversation heavily revolving around intimacy through self-revelation, and concern with internal states and behavior. Female talk seemed to attempt to manage relations with others. But it was not done by the expected use of supportive speech. Through their speech style, information was provided to the listener in forms of placating the listener or proof from personal experience about how the speaker thought and felt including emotional needs, hopes, wishes, likes, and dislikes. Even when the women were angry, they tended to talk about "manipulation" and "control" in terms of *feeling manipulated* or *feeling controlled.* By providing such information, the woman speaker seemed to hope the listener would respond with the desired behavior. Her concern was expressed more passively, yet it expressed the effects of conflict and feelings of victimization. As a style, feminine speech was more polite and indirect, employing many softening devices, such as tags and modal construction, to avoid imposing beliefs or agreement on others through strong statements or commands. In general, the feminine style was collaborative in its drawing out of other speakers,

Figure 11.1
Ratio of Gender-Speech Congruity of Individuals

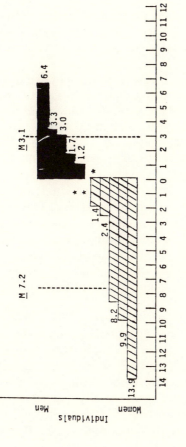

Notes:

1. Female ratios given are the proportion of typical feminine to typical masculine speech: male ratios are the proportion of typical masculine to typical feminine speech.

2. * Those individuals who were also called wide-verbal-repertoire

3. = women

   ▮ = men

sharing of emotions and personal knowledge, and respecting others' conversational space.

The research described above points to clear differences in men and women's speech styles. But my main claim is that these *differences* do not involve *deficiencies*. The two most influential members of the group were a man and woman. We had expected that masculine-style speech would correspond with influence in the group. Yet, in the case of these influential members, both used speech that combined masculine and feminine characteristics in differing frequencies and proportions. They had the lowest proportions of masculine to feminine speech traits ([Man 1.2:1, woman 1:1.4]. See Figure 11.1) Yet, the woman's speech was predominantly feminine (particularly in the semantic area) and the man's speech was predominantly masculine. The diversity of speech repertoires used by these individuals, which included action and ambition, as well as gentleness and sensitivity, was not in opposition to their leadership activities. Thus, neither the masculine style nor, in particular, the feminine style hindered their leadership activity. Both used both sets of speech traits. We turn to a more detailed discussion of differences without deficiencies in the next section.

IMPLICATIONS

The results we found were clear support of our hypothesis that conjectured a masculine speech style spoken predominantly by men and a feminine speech style spoken predominantly by women. It was clear that the different sexes used certain characteristics of speech more frequently and in sharply distinctive ways, although the speech of all women and all men was not homogeneous. A more accurate representation would be that there exist gender-based distributions with variably occurring differences and similarities in the frequency with which women and men use specific features of a shared language depending on the context of linguistic interactions. For example, we would expect some variation in individual speech used by men and women depending on their role in a group and the issues being discussed, when working in single-sex work groups, in mixed-sex work groups, and as they work in a group over time. Yet in general, there was a more feminine and a more masculine style.

It is a pitfall to believe that a given speech form is intrinsically strong or weak, and that for academic women to be effective, they must talk and act like men (Bennis, 1984; Case, 1985). In fact, there may be organizational and personal costs to attempts to shape all female academics into imitators of traditional organizational males, honing in on the rational, analytic, and competitive, at the expense of traditionally female, relation-oriented skills such as understanding, listening, awareness of others' feelings, and collaboration. Men and women have sufficiently different cultural histories that

may be responsible for their different modes of communication, different skills, and different ways of personal presentation.

The intergroup framework we use to understand the problem of gender contrasts in speech style usage suggests that groups automatically teach their members about their own and other groups. Even very educated, achievement-oriented women who indicated a desire for power and prestige spoke differently than similar male counterparts along a variety of dimensions. This polarization was sufficiently unexpected to suggest further research to understand persistence of the different voice. We suspect that both men and women learn to speak like others in their identity groups very early in life.

One cannot dispose of prejudice or discrimination by eliminating or ignoring such group differences. Intergroup theory recognizes the differences. Differences often lead to defining problems in different ways. How problems are defined frequently provides the solution. Therefore, if females view things in different ways and use a different voice (Gilligan, 1984), they may then define problems differently and generate different solutions. Intergroup theory attempts to find ways to negotiate among groups with minimal damage to either the group or to individual interests (Alderfer, 1986; Alderfer & Smith, 1982).

IMPLICATIONS FOR WOMEN

Many feminists believe that women's language reflects too much uncertainty and nonassertiveness (Lakoff, 1973, 1975; Eakins and Eakins, 1978; Kramarae, 1982; Miller, 1983). They argue that women in the professions should adopt "the stronger" forms of the male communication style and consciously work at eliminating their more female-like speech characteristics through assertiveness training, so that they will not be perceived as lacking confidence and be unable to take on leadership positions.

Some women did adopt the "stronger" masculine take-charge style, believing that if they spoke the language of power, they too would be powerful. But women who adopted this strategy were not treated equally. Self-confident, assertive, masculine speech, when used by women, was often perceived as overly aggressive or overbearing (Johnson and Goodchild, 1976; Fulmer, 1977). Men resented assertive, unemotional women for acting like men, but they also judged women who were passive and emotional as unsuited to management (Kanter, 1977). Researchers have also found numerous other cases of similar male/female speech being perceived and evaluated differently (Condry & Condry, 1976; Macke, et al., 1980; McConnell-Ginet, 1983; Bradley, in press). These role-conflict studies have done an excellent job in illuminating paradoxes that result from incongruencies between femininity and demands of work roles. If women exhibit the culturally defined traits of women, then they are

deemed unacceptable as managers. If they act according to male-defined traits of a leader, then they are criticized as too masculine.

Others disagree that the speech characteristics more frequently used by many men should be taken as the norm of desirable organizational speech. Bennis (1984:330) states:

There's a mythology of competence going around that says the way for a woman to succeed is to act like a man. . . . What we see today are all kinds of workshops and seminars where women undergo a metaphorical sex change, where they acquire a tough-talking, no-nonsense, sink-or-swim macho philosophy. They're told to take on traits just the opposite of those Harvard psychoanalyst Dr. Helen H. Tartakoff assigns to women: "endowments which include the capacity for mutuality as well as maternity . . . for creativity as well as receptivity." In short, she sums up, "women's feminine heritage, as caretaker and peacemaker, contains the potential for improving the human condition."

There does seem to be a need for empirically based solutions on communication strategies to redefine or transcend the paradox. Our research showing semantic differences in speech implies a permanence to intergroup differences along this dimension. Perhaps the literature on female friendship networks would be more useful in informing us about women and work and men and women as colleagues in organizations rather than the concepts gleaned from the traditional organizational theory literature of Weber, Fayol, Barnard, and Simon, "father figures" of organizational theory.

The women we studied in our research were not unassertive in the structural area that looked at speech interaction. They spoke up. Yet, they did not monopolize conversation or frequently interrupt others. Even though they spoke up, their speech was very different from the more "masculine" style. This type of difference typically has been interpreted as indicating that the way most women talk is intrinsically weak. The major difference in their speech was in the values expressed through their themes, which showed different perceptions, beliefs, and categories for how they saw and interacted with their world. Thus, even if these women tried to copy a more direct, combative style of speaking, it is likely that the substance of the messages would still differ. It was interesting to us that these women seemed to have resisted the pressure to adopt the more masculine style.

Changing language, if possible, assumes that issues of women in academe are at the individual level rather than focusing attention on transforming the organizational system. Making one group attempt to shift language styles (the "sex role" school of thought), is an attempt to retrain women to be like men. This wastes potentially valuable organizational resources. Also, work on the psychological structure of women, or sex-role stereotypes, makes no sense if the existing barriers to advancement are at the organizational and institutional levels.

Women's speech has strengths that men might benefit from sharing and that women might benefit from valuing (Aries, 1976; Kalcik, 1975; Goodwin, 1980; Thorne, Kramarae, & Henley, 1983). For example, in general, women in our study used language in a way that was more relative, more descriptive, more indirect, and more structured by the desire to include others in the solicitation of ideas rather than to assert their own ideas. Based on current organizational realities such as increasingly multicultural organizations, competition, goal variety, and the heavy legal context in which universities must operate, it is very plausible that features of women's speech (indirection, mitigation of criticism, solicitation of others' ideas) are useful organizational functions.

We certainly found in our results a personal, context-bound orientation in how our women talked, with abundant use of softening devices in speech, like tags and qualifiers, that allowed alternative ideas to be easily expressed. This could be especially helpful in the management of conflict or potential conflict within and among groups that influence the performance and goal attainment of the organization as a whole, as well as in developing complex and novel decisions that require pulling together perspectives and information from many different groups. This style was in contrast to the impersonal, authority-oriented speech style used by men, with its use of competitive and confrontative devices such as imperative construction, proof from authority, and interruptions to get a point heard.

Our position is that it is better for women to utilize their own style of speech rather than trying to copy the speech of others, realizing that what they possess is unique. It is especially important to women's careers that they recognize and value the diversity of speech repertoires used by people. And it is important for women whose speech may be different from the more typical organizational speech style to value precisely their own differences and what these differences can contribute to organizational effectiveness by seeing problems in different ways.

Since beliefs about differences in language use and its perceived impact are so important, how groups react to these differences becomes an important part of organizational life. However, it is true that if men retain real power, women's style may still not be valued and accepted as valid, since masculine speech embodies the stereotyped images of competence, intelligence, and leadership because of its association with those who have power (Miller, 1983). It might be that a *few* distinctions in speech of men and women cause those rendering perceptions to attribute more differences to a message than are actually present in the message. This explanation is consistent with stereotyping, which implies selective perception and attribution by categorization. Where some differences do exist, it is the negative perception of these differences that may lead to problems in power relationships and career development. Yet women most likely will be no worse off using their own speech style than those who copy men, and will

at least have preserved their integrity. Hopefully, ways will be found to enable those who make career advancement decisions to expand their images of competence. Intergroup theory helps focus our attention on the many factors that color our interpretation of the language used by women and men. An awareness of how our group memberships affect what we see, hear, and know can help us consider and incorporate alternative points of view.

IMPLICATIONS FOR HIGHER EDUCATION ADMINISTRATION

A major function of upper level administrators is to sense what is going on so that the administrator can detect and respond to potential problems before they become major problems. Good listening is an active process of making sense out of what is heard, although to many people it is an unrecognized process. The women we studied were better active listeners than their male counterparts.

They were the ones to rephrase ideas, ask for clarification, and use qualifiers and model constructions in idea generation. It is far more common in an interaction to let one's mind wander, to think about what to say next, and when to jump in with an idea, thus missing what is being said. Men in the group showed the latter characteristic by cutting off others to make their points and by changing the topic of conversation.

In our group, women's speech permitted the examination of differing value positions through supportive listening, sensitivity to others' needs, and mutual sharing of emotions and personal knowledge. It seemed to be a style driven by a vision of end values, rather than by a particular method and means to get there. It would appear to be an appropriate style when response to change is needed, when coping with ambiguous situations, when problems require a long-range perspective, and when a variety of values need to be understood. The speech used by women in our group helped consensus to be reached by competing groups, increased the interaction and the empowerment of others, and was generally a cooperative style, which fostered participation and communication rather than domination. The results of this study also suggest that such behavior is compatible with leadership activity.

This style is in contrast to the more impersonal, authority-oriented, dominating, and controlling style used by most of our male group members. Women's language is not being adopted by men, because it is not valued as a competent, articulate leadership style (Zimmerman and West, 1975; Jakubowski-Spector, 1973). Yet, ironically, at least in corporate management, men are being encouraged through sensitivity training programs to shed some of the same masculine characteristics that women are trying to imitate (Bennis, 1984).

Women currently in leadership positions, perhaps out of fear of softness or stereotypical labeling, may help perpetuate the stigma attached to the feminine style. Yet few women can develop enough of the qualities valued by the dominant male culture in a way that eliminates the effect of their gender. For example, assertiveness training may help a woman learn to hold the floor, disallow interruptions, and actively agree in decision-making groups. But it does not focus on the substantive semantic content of feminine speech, which is the area that most reflects the different voice and that most reflects the type of value orientations that women have learned in our culture.

We are not suggesting that the women's different voice is a "better voice." But it is much better to have both represented than any omitted. If both voices are included in organizational decision making, conversation is transformed and problems can be seen in different ways.

IMPLICATIONS FOR MANAGEMENT OF CULTURAL DIFFERENCES

Multicultural organizations are a major feature in modern society, raising new issues about what constitutes effective management of human beings in organizations. In a study of a multinational organization with offices in over 40 countries, Hofstede (1984) confirmed that generally masculine norms pervade American management techniques: individualism, tolerance of uncertainty, and achievement striving. Such norms also pervade academe. Hofstede pointed out that these norms do not work well in cultures such as those of Israel, Mexico, and Taiwan that value the collective over the individual, or ones like Thailand or the Scandinavian countries that emphasize feminine values such as nurturance and support. Management practices not only need to be adjusted to cross-cultural management in other nations, but also need to be adjusted for day-to-day work relations with those people who identify with different subcultures with the United States, whether these are based on sex, race, age, religion, or education.

The experiences and knowledge of both women and minorities, and their increasing presence in universities, mandate understanding their cultural perspective, respecting their differences, refining one's notion of it as more than merely exceptional, and addressing the blind spot in all areas of knowledge that segregate or avoid what has been defined as irrelevant. Organizations are too complicated to have only one set of rules, behaviors, and skills that apply to women or men in their attempts to succeed.

Futurologists have predicted that the values of our urbanized society will center on cooperation, de-emphasize competitiveness, and foster an increased need for alternative styles of speaking and for pluralistic management in which many voices can be heard (Rosener & Schwartz, 1980; Toffler, 1980; Naisbitt, 1984). The new leader will need to be a facilitator,

not an order giver (Naisbitt, 1984). The growth of information in our society involves increased interaction and communication. Having both the feminine and masculine style represented in administrative roles could help increase organizational effectiveness. By including both voices in organizational decision making, problems will be seen in new ways. The differences, then, would be assets, not deficiencies.

This research is important in making clear the powerful masking effects of style. Individual language styles themselves each have unique and positive attributes that can contribute to organizational effectiveness. By understanding the differences in speech style, and not focusing on perceptions of deficiency, we may be able to transcend them so that individuals can be judged on their organizational contributions rather than through the "veil of style" that they use. Further research is needed to help generalize the results.

REFERENCES

Alderfer, C. P. (1977). Improving organizational communication through long-term intergroup intervention. *Journal of Applied Behavioral Science, 3,* 193–210.

———. (1980). Consulting to underbounded systems. In C. P. Alderfer & C. L. Cooper (Eds.) *Advances in Experiential Social Processes: Vol. 2.* London: Wiley, 267–95.

———. (1986). An intergroup perspective on group dynamics. In J. W. Lorsch (Ed.) *Handbook of Organizational Behavior.* Englewood Cliffs, NJ: Prentice-Hall, 190–222.

———, and Smith, K. (1982). Studying intergroup relations in organizations. *Administrative Science Quarterly, 27,* 35–65.

Aries, E. (1976). Interaction patterns and themes of male, female, and mixed groups. *Small Group Behavior, 7(1),* 7–18.

Baird, J. E., Jr. (1976). Sex differences in group communication: A review of relevant research. *The Quarterly Journal of Speech, 62,* 179–92.

Bales, R. F. (1950). *Interaction Process Analysis: A Method for the Study of Small Groups.* Reading, MA: Addison-Wesley.

———. (1953). The equilibrium problem in small groups. In T. Parsons, R. F. Bales, & E. A. Shils (Eds.). *Working Papers in the Theory of Action* (pp. 111–61). New York: Free Press.

———. (1968). Interaction process analysis. In D. L. Sills (Ed.), *International Encyclopedia of the Social Sciences: Vol. 7.* New York: Macmillan & Free Press, 465–71.

———, and Cohen, S. T. (1979). *SYMLOG: A System for the Multiple Level Observation of Groups.* London: Free Press.

Barron, N. (1971). Sex-typing language: The production of grammatical cases. *Acta Sociologica, 14(1–2),* 24–72.

Bartol, K. (1978). The sex structuring of organizations: A search for possible causes, *Academy of Management Review,* October, 805–15.

Baumann, M. (1976). Two features of "women's speech." In B. L. Dubois & I. Crouch (Eds.), *The Sociology of the Languages of American Women.* San Antonio, TX: Trinity University, 33–40.

Bennis, W. G. (1984). False grit. In D. Kolb, I. Rubin, & J. McIntyre (Eds.), *Organizational Psychology: Readings on Human Behavior in Organizations.* Englewood Cliffs, NJ: Prentice-Hall, 330–34. (Reprinted from *Savvy Magazine,* June 1980).

————, and Shepard, H. (1956). A theory of group development. *Human Relations, 9,* 415–37.

Berryman, C. L., and Eman, V. (1980). *Communication, Language, and Sex: Proceedings of the First Annual Conference.* Rowley, MA: Newbury House Publications.

Bion, W. R. (1961). *Experiences in Groups.* New York: Basic Books.

Bodine, A. (1975). Sex differentiation in language. In B. Thorne & N. Henley (Eds.). *Language and Sex: Difference and Dominance.* Rowley, MA: Newbury House Publications, 130–51.

Bonanno, M. (1982). Women's language in the medical interview. In di Pietro (Ed.), *Linguistics and the Professions.* Norwood, NJ: Ablex Publishing Co., 27–38.

Borgatta, E. F. & Bales, R. F. (1980). Interaction of individuals in reconstituted groups. *Sociometry, 16,* 302–20.

Bradley, P. (In press). The folklinguistics of women's speech: An empirical examination. *Communication Monographs.*

Case, S. S. (1985). *A sociolinguistic analysis of the language of gender relations, deviance and influence in managerial groups.* Unpublished doctoral dissertation, State University of New York at Buffalo.

————. (1987). Communication Styles in Management: Recognition of wide-verbal-repertoire speech. In Chapter 3, The Saliency of Cultural Boundaries, *Information and Organizations: Internal and External Perspectives, Proceedings of First Texas Conference on Organizations,* Austin, TX: UT Press, 1987, 9–12.

————. (1988). Cultural Differences, Not Deficiencies: An Analysis of Managerial Women's Language, in Larwood, L. and Rose, S. (eds.), *Women's Careers: Pathways and Pitfalls.* NY: Praeger Publishing, forthcoming.

Condry, J. and Condry, S. (1976). Sex differences: A study of the eye of the beholder. *Child Development, 47,* 812–19.

Devine, I. (1984). The social isolation of professional women in organizations, Paper presented at *CRIAW Annual Conference,* Saskatchewan, November.

Doherty, E. G. (1974). Therapeutic community meetings: A study of communication patterns, sex, status, and staff attendance. *Small Group Behavior, 5,* 244–56.

Dubois, B. L., and Crouch, I. (1977). The question of tag questions in women's speech: They don't really use more of them, do they? *Language in Society, 4,* 289–94.

Dyer, L. and Devine, I. (1986). Tokenism and academic culture: Women in Canadian business schools, *International Conference on Women and Organizations,* Chicago, 1986 (unpublished paper).

Eakins, B., and Eakins, G. (1976). Verbal turn-taking and exchanges in faculty dialogue. In B. L. DuBois & I. Crouch (Eds.), *Papers in Southwest English IV: Pro-*

ceedings of the Conference on the Sociology of the Languages of American
Women (pp. 53–62). San Antonio, TX: Trinity University.

———. (1978). *Sex Differences in Human Communication.* Boston: Houghton Mifflin.

Epstein, C. (1975). Institutional barriers: What keeps women out of the executive suite? In F. E. Gordon and M. H. Strober (eds.) *Bringing Women into Management.* New York: McGraw-Hill, 7–21.

Farley, J. (1982). *Academic Women and Employment Discrimination.* New York State School of Industrial and Labor Relations. Ithaca, NY: Cornell University.

Fasold, R. W. (1968). *A sociological study of the pronunciation of three vowels in Detroit speech.* Washington, DC: Center for Applied Linguistics. Unpublished manuscript.

Fedler, F., Counts, T., and Smith, R. (1983). A survey of job satisfaction of women professors in Mass Communication, Paper presented to the Mass Communication and Society Division, Annual Convention of Association for Education in Journalism and Mass Communication, Oregon State University, August.

Fisher, A. B. (1980). *Group Decision Making: Communication and the Group Process, 2nd ed.* New York: McGraw-Hill.

Fishman, P. M. (1978). Interaction: The work women do. *Social Problems, 25,* 397–406.

———. (1980). Conversational insecurity. In H. Giles, W. P. Robinson & P. M. Smith (Eds.), *Language: Social Psychological Perspectives.* New York: Pergamon Press, 127–32.

———. (1983). Interaction: The work women do. In B. Thorne, C. Kramarae, & N. Henley (Eds.), *Language, Gender, & Society.* Rowley, MA: Newbury House, 89–102.

Fulmer, R. M. (1977). *Practical Human Relations.* Homewood, IL: Richard D. Irwin.

Gilbert, S. J. (1976a). Anxiety, likability, and avoidance as response to self-disclosing communication. *Small Group Behavior, 7,* 423–32.

———. (1976b). Empirical and theoretical extensions of self-disclosure. In G. R. Miller (Ed.), *Exploration in Interpersonal Communication* (pp. 197–216). Beverly Hills, CA: Sage.

Gilligan, C. (1982). *In a Different Voice.* Cambridge, MA: Harvard University Press.

———. (1984, October). Invited panelist, Forum on feminist discourse and the law. State University of New York at Buffalo Law School.

Goodwin, M. H. (1980). Directive-response speech sequences in girls' and boys' task activities. In S. McConnell-Ginet, R. Borker, and N. Furman (Eds.), *Women and Language in Literature and Society.* New York: Praeger, 157–73.

Gronn, P. C. (1983). Talk as the work: The accomplishment of school administration. *Administrative Science Quarterly, 28,* 1–21.

Hare, A. P. (1972). Four dimensions of interpersonal behavior. *Psychological Reports, 30*(2), 499–512.

Harragan, B. L. (1977). *Games Mother Never Taught You: Corporate Gamesmanship for Women.* New York: Warner Books.

Hofstede, G. (1984). Motivation, leadership, and organization: Do American theories apply abroad? In D. Kolb, I. Rubin, & J. McIntyre (Eds.), *Organizational*

Psychology: Readings on Human Behavior in Organizations. Englewood Cliffs, NJ: Prentice-Hall, 309–30.

Jakubowski-Spector, P. (1973). Facilitating the growth of women through assertive training. *The Counseling Psychologist, 4*(1), 75–86.

Johnson, P. B., and Goodchild, J. D. (1976). How women get their way. *Psychology Today, 10*(5), pp. 69–70.

Johnson, J. L. (1980). Questions and role responsibility in four professional meetings. *Anthropological Linguistics, 22,* 66–76.

Kalcik, S. (1975). " . . . like Ann's gynecologist or the time I was almost raped": Personal narratives in women's rap groups. *Journal of American Folklore, 88,* 3–11.

Kanter, R. M. (1977). *Men and Women of the Corporation.* New York: Basic Books.

Key, M. R. (1975). *Male/Female Language.* Metuchen, NJ: Scarecrow Press.

Kramarae, C. (1980). The voices and words of women and men [Special issue]. *Women's Study International Quarterly, 3*(2–3). (Reprinted as C. Kramarae [Ed.], *The Voices and Words of Women and Men.* Oxford, England: Pergamon Press, 1981).

———. (1981). *Women and Men Speaking.* Rowley, MA: Newbury House Publications.

———. (1982). How she speaks. In Ellen Bouchard Ryan and Howard Giles, eds. *Attitudes toward Language Variation: Social Applied Contexts.* London, England: Edward Arnold, 84–98.

Kramer, C. (1974). Women's speech: separate but unequal? *Quarterly Journal of Speech, 60,* 14–24. (Reprinted in B. Thorne & N. Henley [Eds.], *Language and Sex: Difference and Dominance.* Rowley, MA: Newbury House Publications, 43–56.

———. (1977). Perceptions of female and male speech. *Language and Speech, 20,* 151–61.

Labov, W. (1972). *Sociolinguistic patterns.* Philadelphia, University of Pennsylvania Press.

Lakoff, R. (1973). Language and woman's place. *Language in Society, 2,* 45–79.

———. (1975). *Language and Women's Place.* New York: Harper & Row.

Lapadat, J. & Seesahal, M. (1977). Male versus female codes in informal contexts. *Sociolinguistics Newsletter, 8*(3), 7–81.

Levine, V., Donnelson, A., Giora, D., & Sims, K. P., Jr. (1984). Scripts and speech acts in administrative behavior: The interplay of necessity, chance, and free will. *Educational Administration Quarterly, 19,* 93–110.

Maccoby, E. E. (1966). Sex differences in intellectual functioning. In E. E. Maccoby (Ed.), *The Development of Sex Differences.* Stanford, CA: Stanford University Press, 25–55.

Macke, A. S., and Richardson, L. W., with J. Cook. (1980). *Sex-typed Teaching Styles of University Professors and Study Reactions.* Columbus, OH: The Ohio State Univ. Research Foundation.

Marshall, J. (1985). *Women Managers: Travellers in a Male World.* New York: Wiley.

Martin, P. Y., Harrison, D., and Dinitto, D. (1983). Advancement for women in hierarchical organizations, *Journal of Applied Behavioral Science, 19,* 19–33.

McConnell-Ginet, S. (1980). Linguistics and the feminist challenge. In S.

McConnell-Ginet, R. Borker, & N. Furman (Eds.), *Women and Language in Literature and Society.* New York: Praeger, 3–25.

————. (1983). Intonation in a man's world. In B. Thorne, C. Kramarae, & N. Henley (Eds.), *Language, Gender, & Society.* Rowley, MA: Newbury House Publishers, 69–88.

McMillan, J. R., Clifton, A. K., McGrath, D., and Gale, W. S. (1977). Women's language: Uncertainty or interpersonal sensitivity and emotionality? *Sex Roles, 3*, 545–59.

Miller, M. G. (1983). *Enter the stranger: Unanticipated effects of communication on the success of an organizational newcomer.* Unpublished manuscript, Yale University.

Mintzberg, H. (1973). *The Nature of Managerial Work.* New York: Harper & Row.

Mitchell-Kernan, C. (1972). Signifying and marking: Two Afro-American speech acts. In J. Gumperz & D. Hymes (Eds.), *Directions in Sociolinguistics.* NY: Holt, Rinehart, & Winston, 161–79.

Naisbitt, J. (1984). *Megatrends.* New York: Warner Books.

Offe, C. (1976). *Industry and Inequality.* London, England: Edward Arnold.

Richbell, S. (1976). De facto discrimination and how to kick the habit, *Personnel Management, 8.*

Rosener, L., and Schwartz, P. (1980, October). Women, leadership and the 1980's: What kind of leaders do we need? In *The Report: Roundtable on New Leadership in the Public Interest.* New York: NOW Legal Defense and Education Fund, 25–36.

Rubin, L. B. (1976). *Worlds of Pain: Life in the Working-class Family.* New York: Basic Books.

Sattel, J. W. (1983). Men, inexpressiveness, and power. In B. Thorne, C. Kramarae, & N. Henley (Eds.), *Language, Gender, & Society.* Rowley, MA: Newbury House Publishers, 119–24.

Schein, E. H. (1979). Organizational socialization and the profession of management. In D. A. Kolb, I. M. Rubin, and J. M. McIntyre (eds.), *Organizational Psychology.* Englewood Cliffs, NJ: Prentice-Hall.

Schutz, W. C. (1958). *FIRO: A Three-dimensional Theory of Interpersonal Behavior.* New York: Holt & Rinehart.

Shuy, R., Wolfram, W., and Riley, W. (1967). *Linguistic Correlates of Social Stratification in Detroit Speech, Final report* (Project 16–1347). Washington, DC: US Office of Education.

Silver, C. (1981). Public bureaucracy and private enterprise in the U.S.A. and France: Contexts for the attainment of executive positions by women. In C. F. Epstein and R. L. Coser (eds.) *Access to Power: Cross-national Studies of Women and Elites.* London, England: George Allen and Unwin, 219–36.

Smith, H. L., and Grenier, M. (1982). Sources of organizational power for women: Overcoming structural obstacles, *Sex Roles, 8*, 733–46.

Stone, J., and Bachner, J. (1977). *Speaking up: A Book for Every Woman Who Wants to Speak Effectively.* New York: McGraw-Hill.

Strodtbeck, F. L., James, R. M., and Hawkins, C. (1957). Social status in jury deliberations. *American Sociological Review, 22*, 713–19.

Swacker, M. (1975). The sex of the speaker as a sociolinguistic variable. In B.

Thorne & N. Henley (Eds.), *Language and Sex: Difference and Dominance.* Rowley, MA: Newbury House Publications, 76–87.

Thorne, B. (1986). Personal correspondence.

———, and Henley, N. (1975). Difference and dominance: An overview of language, gender, and society. In B. Thorne & N. Henley (Eds.), *Language and Sex: Difference and Dominance.* Rowley, MA: Newbury House Publications, 5–42.

———, Kramarae, C., and Henley, N. (1983). *Language, Gender, and Society.* Rowley, MA: Newbury House Publications.

Toffler, A. (1980). *The Third Wave.* New York: Morrow.

Trudgill, P. (1972). Sex, covert prestige, and linguistic change in the urban British English of Norwich. *Language and Society, 1,* 179–195. (Reprinted in B. Thorne and N. Henley (Eds.), *Language and Sex: Difference and Dominance.* Rowley, MA: Newbury House Publications, 1975, 88–104).

Wolfe, W., and Fligstein, N. (1979). Sex and authority in the workplace. *American Sociological Review, 44,* 235–52.

Zimmerman, D. H., and West, C. (1975). Sex roles, interruptions, and silences in conversation. In B. Thorne & N. Henley (Eds.), *Language and Sex: Difference and Dominance.* Rowley, MA: Newbury House Publications, 105–29.

12

The "Female-Determined Relationship": Personal and Professional Needs of Academic Women in Commuter Marriages

Sharon Hileman

Some sociologists believe that the most influential occurrence of this century is the proliferation of dual-career marriages (Winfield, 1985). Clearly this phenomenon can have wide-reaching effects not only in personal and professional spheres but also in ideological ramifications. One of the newest aspects of dual-career marriage to interest researchers is its frequent evolution into a commuter marriage. The last three years have seen the publication of books such as *Commuter Marriage: Living Together, Apart* (Winfield, 1985) and *Commuter Marriage: A Study of Work and Family* (Gerstel & Gross, 1984), as well as the articles "Weaving the Threads: Equalizing Professional and Personal Demands Faced by Commuting Career Couples" (Johnson, 1987) and "'Commuter Marriages' a Growing Necessity for Many Couples in Academe" (Heller, 1986). This last article, which appeared two years ago in the *Chronicle of Higher Education*, emphasizes what many of us already realize: More than 50 percent of commuter marriages involve academics, and the percentage is probably continuing to grow. Because men and women are affected somewhat differently by their involvement in such a marriage, it is important that the personal and professional needs of such women be identified.

Most studies of commuter marriage estimate that there are at least 700,000 couples participating in this relatively new and necessary lifestyle. This figure was used in an article in *Time* magazine in 1982, so it has probably increased since then. Even with this figure, though, we can as-

sume that more than 350,000 such couples are academics. Theoretically, the nature of work in academia—independent and unsupervised—as well as the possibility of flexible scheduling and lengthy vacations allows for fairly satisfactory commuting arrangements. Couples can have professional lives apart and still spend a considerable amount of time together.

The distances, frequencies, and methods of commute may differ significantly for those involved. Some couples commute several hundred miles while others commute cross-country. Not surprisingly, the shorter commutes, where couples are usually reunited every weekend (or extended weekend), are the least stressful. Longer commutes, which may be quite expensive, due to air fare costs, can result in fewer reunion periods. Some of these couples may see each other only once a month. One couple, he in San Diego and she in Minneapolis, commuted every two weeks and were the subject of an article in *Money* magazine entitled "Marriage as a Fortnightly Affair" (Seixas, 1981). Couples who are just beginning careers in academia certainly find it difficult to finance numerous cross-country airtrips. More established couples may have more money, making it more likely that they will reunite more often. Whether or not there are children at home with one of the spouses can also be a major factor in determining how the commute is structured. For most of the commuting couples involved in studies that have been done, there were no children or children were grown.

Despite such variations, what remains constant in all cases, whether in academia or industry, is that the commute is decided upon so that both partners can pursue professional opportunities and goals. In academia, nepotism laws may make it impossible for a couple to find mutual employment at one institution, or the simple scarcity of positions may prevent the couple from both working at the same place. Consequently, commuting may offer one of the spouses the *only* means of being employed in his or her chosen field. Occasionally, though, the commute may be undertaken because of an offer of a more prestigious and/or more highly paid position.

If sociologists are correct, it is not surprising to find increasing numbers of commuter marriages. The nuclear family, sociologists point out, replaced the extended family because of postindustrial society's need for units possessing geographical mobility (Gerstel and Gross, 1984). Now with dual-career marriages, the continued need for such mobility may separate couples. Because of this recurring physical separation, the term *marriage* may need to be redefined.

Today most people assume that married people will live together. The U.S. Census Bureau defines a married couple as "same household," which, incidentally, makes it impossible to determine how many dual-residence marriages there actually are. As of 1983, commuter marriage was legal in only five states since there are only five states that say a married person can establish his or her own domicile (Winfield, 1985).

Certainly most commuter couples who have participated in research

studies stress that their commuting arrangement is a temporary one. Such couples realize they are perceived as deviant in their practice of marriage, and, while they may not like the physical separations in their lives, they may also be trying to neutralize such negative judgments.

Social stigma is one of the numerous problems faced by commuting couples. Colleagues and friends usually assume that commuting spouses are in the first stages of a divorce. Often these colleagues don't feel comfortable including a "married single" in social plans. The outside world looks at commuter couples critically, but the target of most criticism is the woman (Winfield, 1985). Instead of fulfilling a more traditional role as "trailing" spouse or un- or underemployed helpmate, a woman in a commuter marriage values her career as much as her personal relationships. Although husbands share these values, the commuting life-style usually benefits women most directly, which is why the relationship is said to be "female-determined." From the perspective of traditional values, such a relationship is by definition "deviant."

While the major drawback of commuter marriage is probably the physical separation itself, an additional and significant problem is the cost of such a life-style. Two households must be maintained, and whether the couple owns one primary residence and rents a secondary residence, rents in both places, or owns the two residences, major costs usually result. In addition, there are the commuting expenses, which may run into thousands of dollars in airfare or large investments in automobiles and their maintenance. One couple who commutes weekly within the state of California estimates that their costs are more than $1000 a month, as does another couple commuting every six weeks between Boston and New Orleans (Heller, 1986). Since daily face-to-face interaction is impossible, many couples rely on daily telephone calls to replace the physical intimacy of their relationship. The results can be astronomically expensive. (One woman reported that any monthly telephone bill under $300 was a gift.) For some couples there are no tax benefits from commuter marriage, either. Instead, they pay taxes in two states, not just one. The couple in the *Money* magazine article (Seixas, 1981) estimated that their commuting costs over a seven-year period had been approximately $40,000. This included $28,000 for airfare, $10,000 to furnish a second house, and $1600 for long-distance phone calls. During this time their combined income ranged from $27,500 in 1973 to $57,000 in 1981. One tax adviser consulted by the magazine recommended that the couple consider divorcing since they would thereby save $1800 in federal taxes!

Emotional costs may take several forms. The physical separation is difficult for both spouses, but then there is also a difficult "re-entry" period when the commuting spouse returns to the primary residence. This is especially evident in women, who frequently report experiencing a "stranger" phenomenon in response to their husbands. Such an unsettling, recurring

experience needs to be researched further and then written about instead of being ignored by psychologists and psychiatrists.

Time is needed to readjust to being together, and time is the one thing that most commuter couples lack. For this reason, couples usually try to spend the time they have together doing things together, with a resulting exclusion of friends and relatives. Unrealistic expectations for time spent together, whether planned activities include domestic chores, sex, or entertainment, can contribute stress to the relationship.

Finally, there is bound to be some physical cost to the commuting spouse, who may experience major fatigue or exacerbated stress as a result of the commute.

Why, then, do couples continue such an arrangement? Don't the stresses contribute to a higher divorce rate for people in commuter marriages? The answers to these questions are interrelated, primarily because such a marriage tends to be a "female-determined" one. The couple has undertaken the venture of commuter marriage because both are committed to the belief that the wife's career is as important as the husband's. Sharing such an assumption makes it easier for both to accept the hardships that characterize the arrangement. Nor is sexual infidelity the problem that so many onlookers expect it to be. In fact, one study showed infidelity decreasing rather than increasing after couples began commuting. Eight percent of couples in this study had had no affairs before commuting but did have them while commuting, whereas 11 percent, who had had affairs before commuting, discontinued the practice while commuting. The study verified that those who had been faithful in their marriages before beginning to commute (60 percent) remained faithful during the commute period (Gerstel and Gross, 1984). The divorce rate is no higher for commuting couples than for single-residence couples.

In terms of sexual behavior, then, commuting did not introduce significant changes into the lives of the commuters. Changes did occur in other areas, however. The most important of these changes for women was that commuting led to a decrease in their domestic duties and a concomitant increase in their work-related productivity. In fact, women were almost twice as likely as men to increase their professional work involvement (76 percent vs. 43 percent in Gerstel and Gross's study). Other studies have already shown that married professional women (specifically women with doctorates), with or without children, spend three or four hours less per week on employment and professional activities than a married male professional, with or without children. The female professional is usually trying to be a superwoman, so that while she may spend several fewer hours professionally than her male counterpart, she then spends 18 to 19 hours a week managing the household, with an additional 10 hours devoted to child care (Centra, 1974, cited in Arfken, 1985).

Most men in commuter marriages experience no change in their profes-

sional activity, although they find themselves undertaking more domestic tasks. Perhaps for this reason, it is not surprising to find that more husbands than wives in Gerstel and Gross's study disliked the commuter marriage. According to this survey, 62 percent of husbands disliked the commuter marriage more than their wives; only 16 percent of the wives disliked such an arrangement more than their husbands. The study concluded that since men are the prime beneficiaries of most single-residence marriages, they therefore lose more than women from commuter marriage.

Questions about exactly what women gain need to be asked, however. It is true that women may become more productive professionally, but this effect results from the compartmentalizing of personal and professional selves. That is, a week is divided according to where one spends one's time: while separated from a spouse, a woman is likely to immerse herself in professional activities, and 14-to-16-hour workdays are not uncommonly reported among survey respondents. The corollary of such an intense work schedule is to seek complete respite from it during reunion time with spouses. Of course, such total compartmentalizing is not always possible, but its desirability is usually unquestioned. However, one respondent in a survey conducted by Sharon Ervin Johnson (1987), stated: "My life becomes dichotomized. It's all business during the week and all family on the week-end. There is no time for myself."

In other words, a dual identity may simply add new stresses to the stresses already imposed by the physical and emotional burdens, not to mention the social stigmas and ostracizings, that the commuter experiences. It does seem that the phenomenon of dual identity would help explain women's experiencing their husbands as "strangers" when they reunite. However, it is not the husband who has become a different person; it is the wife.

The change in location also involves a change in self-concept: A woman is no longer fully independent when she adds the role of wife (and perhaps mother) to the role of professional. Studies have shown that simply sharing living space with a man makes most women feel they must assume a more domestic role than they would when living alone. A countertransformation must also occur when the workweek commences. It is probably because time is needed to effect these changes that so many commuting wives express their appreciation of the hours spent driving or flying to their workplaces. One respondent in a survey used the term "mental flip" to describe what happens halfway between the two homes as the commuter switches to the second role (Johnson, 1987).

Some women may wish to retain the increased number of hours invested professionally as a result of their commuter marriages, but for others it may be important to realize that they can have social lives away from their husbands. Gerstel and Gross's study showed that women were more likely than men to establish friendships while separated from their spouses. Such

friendships were usually with other professional, single women. Most commuting wives were afraid to make gestures of friendship or issue invitations to men for fear of having such actions misinterpreted as sexual advances. Perhaps more noncommuter couples need to define themselves as "married singles" so they will be able to pursue friendships as individuals and bring singles, "married" or otherwise, into couple-dominated activities.

Another possibility for commuters is participation in some sort of network or support group. Local and national groups could provide immediate contacts, invaluable information, coping strategies, and the means of effecting some long-reaching professional changes. (Only one such network, in Arizona, seems to be operating currently.)

Change is needed so that those things that discriminate against the dual-career couple in the academic world are challenged. Nepotism restrictions, for instance, prevent many spouses from even being considered for employment at the same institution. Clearly, the removal of such restrictions could make it less likely that a couple might have to commute.

But for those couples who do need or choose to commute, the stigma attached to such a life-style has to be removed. Several candidates for academic positions have been the victims of hostile questioning on this issue during interviews. The attitude of department chairs and personnel committees tends to be that a commuter would not be committed to his or her work or institution. One administrator at Clark University, quoted in the *Chronicle*'s articles, stated, "I think that any department that told you it wasn't concerned about the amount of time an individual puts into a program would be devious . . . ," although he added that a commuter would still be considered for a position (Heller, 1986). Of course, academic institutions, like corporate institutions, need to become more active in helping spouses find employment when the other spouse is offered a position. Universities definitely trail industry in making such attempts.

Some commuting academics are even afraid to ask for three-or four-day teaching schedules that maximize their time at the primary residence. They fear that their "commitment" will be questioned. In one situation a colleague resented a commuter's not having to teach Fridays and demanded a four-day schedule for himself as well. But flexible schedules are supposedly one of the hidden benefits of academic employment. Certainly the lure of flexible schedules is used to entice those working in industry to accept an academic appointment. It would seem that a maximum four-day schedule could be arranged for commuting faculty.

There are corporations that make their relatively inexpensive telephone lines available for commuting employees' personal long-distance telephone calls. There is even one corporation (Xerox) that pays the airfare between Texas and California for one of its commuting employees (Winfield, 1985). Perhaps, as Fairlee Winfield, professor of business at Northern Arizona University, author of a book on commuter marriage, and herself a per-

son who commutes 400 miles each week, suggests, it would not be outrageous for academic institutions to help commuting employees in some ways with travel expenses. Finally, since tax deductions for a second business residence and its expenses are available only for "temporary" employment, nine-month contracts could probably be worded to permit such tax benefits. Eventually tax laws themselves could even be changed.

Such long-term possibilities are not as unlikely as they may sound. With more and more women receiving doctorates and seeking positions in academia, it is quite probable that many of them will eventually be involved in a commuter relationship, if not marriage. These couples are going to make demands for improved schedules, greater compensation, and additional benefits. As today's commuters are discovering, commuting is a temporary arrangement only in their dreams. Unless more academic positions become available in more places, commuters will continue to find that the road does indeed go on forever.

REFERENCES

Arfken, D. (1985). *Running at Double Pace: Women in Dual-Profession Marriages.* Milwaukee, WI: National Association for Women Deans, Administrators, and Counselors.

Gerstel, N., and Gross, H. (1984). *Commuter Marriage: A Study of Work and Family.* New York: The Guilford Press.

Heller, S. (1986). Commuter marriages' a growing necessity for many couples in academe. *Chronicle of Higher Education, 31,* 1.

Johnson, S. E. (1987). Weaving the threads: Equalizing professional and personal demands faced by commuting career couples. *Journal of the National Association for Women Deans, Administrators, and Counselors, 50,* 3–10.

Seixas, S. (1981). Marriage as a fortnightly affair. *Money, 10,* 78–83.

Winfield, F. (1985). *Commuter Marriage: Living Together, Apart.* New York: Columbia University Press.

13

Attitudes Toward Women as Managers: The Hispanic Influence

Deborah Diane Payne
Wilma Hoffman

The difficult struggle within the last two-and-a-half decades to increase the number of women in the workplace and to address the inequalities that exist has provided both relevant and interesting information concerning working women. Lawyers, economists, management researchers, educators, psychologists, sociologists, and historians have provided information that has simultaneously created, changed, and resolved the focus of many of the controversial topics within the subject area.

One of the interesting points that has been documented is that the presence of women in the workplace is not a phenomenon that is unique to the last two decades, nor is it entirely a result of the women's movement. Women have worked outside the home for many decades, although in the past economics was the primary reason for their employment. Those jobs, however, have been in areas traditionally thought of as being suitable for women: teachers in the elementary grades through high school, secretaries, administrative assistants, waitresses, clerks in retail establishments, and nurses. What has changed in the last two-and-a-half decades is the type of work women are doing: They still teach, but now it is not uncommon for women to be professors in colleges and universities; women in top executive positions are still rare, but women in managerial jobs are not; women as attorneys, doctors and professionals in other fields are not much more common than they were 20 years ago, although, in general, women are

seeing more opportunities than before in fields where only a few years ago there was almost no opportunity.

The question addressed by this chapter is: Where does the bias against women in managerial positions begin to manifest itself? The El Paso area and the University of Texas at El Paso (UTEP) are unique in several respects. First, the majority of the people residing in El Paso and the majority of the student body are of Hispanic origin. Second, those students graduating from UTEP usually continue to reside and pursue their careers in the El Paso area. The students in the College of Business at UTEP are usually employed while also attending the university, hence they have an insight into the work they desire to pursue. Yet, if one considers the work force of the cities of El Paso and Ciudad Juarez one notices that the majority of the management personnel are male. Two questions of importance are: (1) Is the bias towards male managers present before the students begin their careers or is it manifested after graduation? and (2) Does ethnicity play a role in generating the negative bias towards women as managers?

REVIEW OF LITERATURE

Although few people argue that the opportunities for women in the workplace have increased, few would claim that their acceptance in the workplace is complete or that no obstacles remain. One of the areas where the literature offers some of its most interesting data is in the area of the acceptance of women in the workplace, particularly in the acceptance of women in managerial and executive positions, and in the study of attitudes toward women as managers. The study of this aspect of women in the workplace touches on many topics. Three of these topics that have received attention are:

1. the current attitudes of male managers toward women workers and a study of the comparative differences between male and female managers,
2. the problems typically encountered by women managers separate and apart from the typical management concerns and dilemmas resulting primarily from the fact that they are women, and
3. the difficulty in addressing the problems encountered by women managers and executives, particularly in the areas of recruiting, training, and development.

This literature will present the current findings of researchers on these topics. The major emphasis will be on studies that address the problem of attitudes that are to a large extent preformed by and stereotypical of women managers. In discussions of women in managerial positions, there are usually two major areas of interest. First, the attitudes toward women as managers and the initial perceptions of women as managers. Second, how do

those attitudes and perceptions manifest themselves in producing problems and difficulties for women managers.

When considering the existing attitudes toward women as managers, interest centers on determining and/or explaining gender differences in managerial situations and in trying to locate, if possible, the origination of these attitudes toward women and women managers. In their study of lower-, middle-, and upper-level male managers and staff positions in the Rochester area, Bass, Krusell, and Alexander (1971) provide interesting results based on a 56-item questionnaire. Age (grouped by under-30 and over-30 categories), marital status, level within the organization, and the subject's current assignment involving working with women were used to analyze the participant's responses. Identifying seven factors that affected the male managers' attitudes and acceptance of women, Bass et al. found deference was the strongest factor, that is, "the rules of etiquette and politeness between the sexes in public." The study found strong implications of a well-defined societal role for men and women, the deference factor together with the responses that women and men would both "prefer" male supervisors, and a negative perception of a woman's dependability were the three strongest negative factors in the manager's attitude toward women workers. The study addresses the finding that men who did not work with women had more positive responses than men who did. Bass et al. state that the solution for integrating women into the work force requires more than just the hiring of more women (which may, in fact, contribute to reinforcing old stereotypes about women in the workplace). The study suggests that managers should examine their attitudes toward working women; reexamine the data on women—their skills, their dependability, and their orientation toward work; and, finally, put men and women in work situations where they have to interact "as equals." Placed in a situation where they can see how the goals and values of working men and women are both similar and different, perhaps the stereotypical and unjustified attitudes of male managers will be changed.

Davidson and Cooper (1987) examined the similarities and differences between male and female managers in Britain. Using recent studies of women in British industry, the authors found far more similarities than differences in the ways men and women manage in the areas of efficiency and performance. The authors found less similarity, but not significant differences existed in the demographic profiles of male and female managers, in job status and employment factors, in their career development, and in occupational stress levels. The authors did, however, address the problems stemming from the attitudes that female managers are not as capable as male managers. Davidson and Cooper found women managers were more likely than men to be married; there were no significant age differences; and that women managers had more formal qualifications than men. The authors found basic similarities in attitudes toward careers and career de-

velopment, with the exception of the area of career breaks where the discussion centers, not surprisingly, on pregnancy and the raising of the children. Davidson and Cooper report the majority of barriers to women managers stem from preconceived attitudes that in most cases cannot be substantiated. The study addresses the prejudicial attitudes associated with leadership and leadership style—particularly that managerial qualities are more likely to be found in men than in women, and differences in the attitudes of men and women managers. The major differences between male and female managers do not stem from gender difference in relation to leadership, qualifications, mobility, efficiency, or performance factors. Rather, the authors found that demographic profiles, job status, employment factors (where women managers are typically in types of work still thought of as suitable to women), career development, and attitudes are the areas where the most significant differences exist. The authors recommend that one way to lessen the attitude differences between male and female managers can be achieved by accommodating dual-career couples and families. Specific recommendations include flexible working arrangements, reasonable parental leave policies (maternity and paternity), career-break and retraining schemes for women who take time away from employment for child bearing and raising, adequate day-care facilities, and changes in relocation policy.

In determining those factors that influence the attitudes toward women as managers and the perception that women managers differ so strongly from male managers, the examination of both the personal and the managerial viewpoints are important. Powell, Posner, and Schmidt (1984) surveyed 6000 members of the American Management Association (10% of whom are women) to study the similarities and differences between personal value systems (PVS) of men and women and the effect of PVS on managerial value systems. Powell et al. concluded that the similarities between men and women in managerial value systems outweighed the differences and, in fact, did not substantiate typical beliefs or stereotypes concerning men and women managers. Particularly striking was the fact that women were more likely than men to emphasize success in the job, even to the extent of requiring sacrifices in their family life. Women derived more satisfaction in their lives from their careers, when contrasted with home life or other interests. Powell et al. identified 11 organization goals. Women identified high productivity, good organization, leadership, and organizational stability as more important more often than men did. There were no significant differences in the evaluation of the remaining goals. In fact, the study found that the stereotypes of women's views of business issues were not upheld by the data, and that men and women managers could not be distinguished appreciably, at least in the area of their attitudes and perceptions toward business and managing.

A study by Pearson (1984) identifies the prevalent perceptions about

women as managers, identifies the actual sources of the problems, and discusses the prospect for change in the perceptions toward women as managers. The perceptions about women managers focus on three points: (1) a woman can't make "hard" decisions because they are too delicate; (2) the woman's place is in the home; and (3) the notion that a woman manager deprives a man of a job, a corollary to the second perception. An interesting perception made by Pearson is that those women who do make the "hard" decisions and do display a toughness or aggressiveness are often labeled as hard-nosed or unfeeling. In conclusion, women managers cannot be successful since the majority do not have the ability to make difficult decisions, or if they do have the ability to make difficult decisions, that strength makes them unsuitable for a managerial role. The actual problem facing women managers is that they usually take a break in their career to bear and raise children. Closely tied with this fact is the tendency for women managers, in all but the top level, to place primary importance on the husband's career. The result is that companies hiring a woman as a manager fear that when the husband relocates, the wife will also relocate. Pearson identifies two factors that may, over time, help to dispel these misperceptions about women managers. The current generation is the only one to see the majority of women working. The ideas of women working, of women growing within an organization, and of women rising to managerial positions will seem perfectly natural to the children of today's generation. A second misperception is that women managers and, in particular, those women who reach senior executive posts, will be in a position to provide moral support for other women in their roles as managers and executives.

The existing attitudes toward women as managers are, as researchers have found, often severe obstacles to women in managerial posts. The problems women managers face can largely be traced to the prevailing attitudes about working women and about their ability to exercise a managerial role. Those attitudes can create difficulties for women managers, who, in effect, cannot fail in a managerial role without having someone trace the reason to the "fact" that women can't manage.

Norgaard (1980) provides information gathered from 124 women managers concerning their perceptions of the problems and the progress made in their careers. The study found that the problems identified by the managers, with the exception of employer discrimination, were not these problems that are commonly cited. Norgaard concludes that the evaluation of women managers is more complex now, primarily because each woman reacts based on her specific situation. Since more women managers are being hired, it is likely that there will be a variety of reactions to the different managerial situations. The problems identified by women managers include discrimination (though not so much with hiring and getting a job, but with acceptance and reactions once they have been hired), child care factors (almost half, 43%, saw children as a neutral factor), and difficulties

with spouses (although cited infrequently). In the area of career attitudes, Norgaard found women working for the same reasons as men and, in general, taking satisfaction from the same things: financial rewards, career development (career commitment on the part of the women was strong), and promotion and advancement opportunities. Norgaard concludes that although the general consensus is that women will advance in both managerial and executive positions in businesses, it is going to be increasingly difficult to assess their progress. The difficulty results from the varied and complex factors involved in measuring and assessing a person's progress. Two of the major factors involved in this assessment are the business in which the woman is employed and the type of work that the manager does.

A study by Lirtzman and Wahba (1972) revealed that "in a clearly competitive situation in which outcomes are subject to risk," women adopt the same coalition strategy as men. The study was based on data gathered on 48 female undergraduate students. Lirtzman and Wahba argue that the major determinants of coalitional behavior are the demands of the situation, rather than the sex role. The implications to organizational situations are obvious, since a woman's decisions and actions are predicted by men to be based on reasons different than a man's. Specifically, the ideas that Lirtzman and Wahba refute (that sex roles are a determinant of behavior in organizations) are exactly those ideas that many women have cited as being perhaps the significant problem for their advancement in an organization. The authors' findings "raise questions about the traditions of business that bar the accession of women to high organizational positions precisely because it is expected that women will act naturally according to sex-related roles; that is, noncompetitively." Furthermore, the authors conclude that "If women are told the rules and rewarded for appropriate behavior, their coalition formation decisions should be undistinguishable from those of men."

Norgaard's study rejects the ideas of many women managers that getting hired is not the primary factor any longer, the primary factors are their acceptance and progression in an organization. Supporting Norgaard's research are two studies that conclude that women act not on sex role determinants or along predictable lines, but according to other situational factors. Hjelle and Butterfield (1974) compared two groups of college-aged females, 20 liberal and 20 conservative, to examine the differences in the degree of self-actualization in relation to the attitudes toward women's rights and women's roles in society. This study examined the question of women's attitudes concerning their role in society and made determinations concerning largely political and attitudinal questions not necessarily having a direct impact on managerial concerns. The study concluded that women react in different ways to different situations, and that stereotyping the type of behavior of women is not valid. In that sense, Hjelle and Butterfield illustrate the breakdown of the stereotypes concerning wom-

en's attitudes and behavior, and by extension their actions in a workplace setting.

A second study conducted by Feather and Raphelson (1973) analyzed stories written by Australian and American college students that were based on the verbal cues from a prior study. The study revealed that both Australian and American males wrote more fear-of-success stories based on the "Anne" (female) cue than on the "John" (male) cue. Australian female students also wrote more fear-of-success stories to the "Anne" cue than to the "John" cue. Feather and Raphelson were interested in determining why, though, the American women students wrote fewer fear-of-success stories based on the "Anne" cue than to the "John" cue. One conclusion is that American women are redefining their conceptions about what are appropriate achievements for women in society. Feather and Raphelson suggest further research to determine more precisely the role of motive and sex role stereotypes in these reactions. For the subject of this chapter, it is important that the interpretations include the possibility of sex role stereotypes, in both the male and the female populations.

A final study dealing with the basis for performance evaluation of females was conducted by Karabenick and Marshal (1973). The study used a substitution test for females with male opponents, female opponents, and no opponents. The substitution tasks were performed under achievement-oriented conditions. The intention was to determine whether fear of success, fear of failure, and opponent could be determined to have any basis on the outcome, and whether the outcome was related to sex role orientation. The research found that the women subjects had a higher fear of failure when presented with the same test tasks as men. Again, the implication for determining the nature of responses by women managers and executives seems clear, and the evidence provided by research of this type will be important in discussions about the motivations and actions of women managers as well as the attitudes toward women managers.

The final section of this review addresses the problems of women managers in the workplace. The issues involved in this discussion include recruiting, training, and development.

Mottaz (1986) investigated satisfaction in the type of work, work rewards, and the determinants of work satisfaction. The interest in this area is a direct result of the increase in the number of women in the workplace and an interest in determining the existence of gender differences and job attitudes. As Mottaz reports, no significant differences exist between men and women, and the cause of this conclusion needs to be determined. Possible causes include different expectation levels (women expect less and men more) or men and women may be using different criteria to determine satisfaction. Mottaz's study supports the conclusion that gender and overall work satisfaction are unrelated. However, the causes, though centering on the expectancy and value explanations, are not clear. Neither the expec-

tancy nor the value approach is able to explain the similarity in work satisfaction between men and women in upper-level occupations. In upper-
level occupations, both sexes perceive their jobs as fulfilling important
work values. In lower-level occupations, men and women do differ in work
satisfaction. Women assign more importance to intrinsic rewards, and they
place more emphasis on the social aspects of their work. A possible explanation for the difference at this level is that basic differences exist between
the sexes in regard to sex role socialization; however, Mottaz argues that if
the sex role differences were so important, they should also appear in the
upper-level occupations. Again, further research could help more precisely
to determine the extent to which gender differences exert in the work
setting.

Knowing what motivates employees of either sex is important to any organization's personnel recruitment and development practices. Lathan,
Ostrowski, Pavlock, and Scott (1987) focus on the accounting profession's
recruitment of women and attempt to determine the differences between
men and women in their reactions to the interview process. The authors
surveyed 676 graduating seniors (348 male, 328 female) at 23 universities
about the interviewing and the general recruiting practices of accounting
firms that visited their campus. The authors did find differences between
men and women respondents, particularly in the areas of salary expectations, the long-term prospects with the firm, and the perceptions with respect to interview topics that are both important and appropriate. The
authors found a 6 percent difference in the number of persons who expected to leave accounting within six years (61% women, 55% men) and
over twice as high a percentage difference, 13 percent, in the number of respondents who expected to be partners (38% of the women, 51% of the
men). The authors speculated that the differences resulted from the wom-
en's perceived lack of success in the accounting field, based perhaps on beliefs that their success and progress will be based on biases and sexual
stereotyping rather than on actual merit. There were significant differences
in salary expectations, perhaps stemming from the fact that women foresee
less success in the accounting field and do not expect to attain the higher
salaries. The second-year men expected a salary approximately $1000
higher than that expected by women. The difference in the sixth year salary expectations was on the average almost $6000 more, and in the fif-
teenth working year the difference was over $13,000. More women than
men (41% to 31%) preferred to work for a non–"Big 8" firm. Finally, men
placed more importance during the interview process on promotions and
future earnings, while women indicated that the important issues for them
are the training and continuing education programs, a youthful and dynamic personnel, an interesting client mix, fringe benefits, and little or no
travel or overtime. The authors concluded that both male and female respondents found the overall interviewing and recruiting process was

poorly done and recommended changes to improve every firm's standing in the view of the future personnel. Both male and female students felt the interviewers asked questions that were inappropriate and nonessential. The authors' most salient point in the area of recruiting and gender-based differences was that only a few women recruiters were used by firms recruiting on college campuses. It was concluded that women applicants could not get useful answers to many of their questions from men and that an increase in women recruiters would help firms both recruit women and perhaps retain them.

Buzenberg (1975) identified five areas where women managers need additional information. He advocated the use of university classes, in-house training, and development programs by businesses to provide information in the specified areas. The five areas identified by Buzenberg: (1) consciousness-raising and confidence building; (2) the impact of working women on society and the economy; (3) how to be professional; (4) effective management—feminine style; and (5) marriage and career. Though published in 1975, many of these same points are currently being addressed and retain their relevance to the question of women in the workplace. Buzenberg's model of training and development is based on the premise that women have not been prominent in either executive positions or training programs in the specified areas. In the area of consciousness-raising and confidence building, the ability of women to manage and make decisions is addressed because the complaint has been made that women lack those skills. Enormous changes in social and economic spheres have occurred and will continue as a result of the increasing number of women in business. The question of sexism and how to combat it is also addressed. Buzenberg's inclusion of how to be professional is based on an absence of professional role models for women. This topic has not been included in management classes simply because male students have always had professional role models; however, women have not. Effective management—feminine style is included in the training and development curriculum, because, neither talent nor intelligence recognizes gender differences, and there is no need to minimize feminine qualities in a management or executive setting. Finally, because the question of marriage and career is important to every woman manager, this topic is also included in Buzenberg's training and development curriculum.

Women managers are a relatively recent phenomenon, and much of the data on attitudes toward women managers, the success of women managers, and their training and development are not nearly as abundant as the data on male managers. The continued influx of women managers and the retention of women managers depends on the training of women managers, the opportunities provided for women to step into managerial positions, and the strategies used to retain the women who are selected and trained for management positions. Stereotyping, lack of opportunity, and

inexperience in management positions—each of these problems remains significant in a woman's climb to the top managerial and executive posts in business and industry. Because many studies will be conducted and additional data will be collected on women managers and women in the workplace, some of the issues presented here may be more precisely defined and even resolved in the near future. The nature of some of the problems indicates that women managers and executives are not likely to be widely and completely accepted in the near future, and many of the stereotypes and unjustified attitudes toward women managers will continue to exist. However, as more women are given the opportunity to enter management more insight into the problems of women managers will develop, and resolutions to the problems will emerge.

THE STUDY

When does the negative bias toward women as managers develop and does the Hispanic influence have an effect? The purpose of the study is to provide some insights into these two questions. To address these questions a survey consisting of two sections was used. The first section was a questionnaire developed during the past decade by Herbert and Yost (1984). This questionnaire is titled "Attitudes Toward Women as Managers" (ATWAM). The tool consists of 12 questions. In each question the respondent is forced to make a decision concerning his or her personal opinions. These closed-end questions are then scored using a scale developed by Herbert and Yost; the scale gives a ranking of 1, 3, 5, or 7 to each possible response. The higher the score the more negative was the respondent's attitude toward women as managers. The scores for ten of these questions are added together and the resulting total then represents the composite attitude. (Two of the questions are specified by the developers as being neutral.) A total score greater than 50 represents a strong negative attitude, whereas a total score less than 40 represents a strong positive attitude. The second section of the survey gathered demographic information. The demographic information included work history, ethnicity, sex, religion, age, and educational background.

The resulting two-part survey was administered to students enrolled in the College of Business Administration at the University of Texas at El Paso during the 1987 fall semester. Of the 136 questionnaires administered, 97 were able to be used in the resulting analysis.

The respondents to usable questionnaires were surprisingly uniform in their demographic characteristics. The respondents were almost equally split in the characteristics of sex (male-female), ethnicity (Hispanic–non-Hispanic), and employment (currently employed–not currently employed).

To draw conclusions, the total of the ten ATWAM question scores were compared to a nationwide ranking composed by Herbert and Yost. The

study concluded that overall the respondents (13%) were not as negatively biased as the nationwide results (25%). This finding tends to imply that the negative bias appears to manifest itself after a person enters the workplace. When comparing the responses for Hispanic (14%) and non-Hispanic (12%) respondents, the Hispanic influence that was expected to be present failed to appear. Finally, when comparing the responses of the male participants to those of the female participants, there was a marked difference. While only 5 percent of the females exhibited a negative bias, 20 percent of the males exhibited a negative bias. This final finding may eventually provide insights concerning the development of the negative attitude toward women in management, for the vast majority of managerial positions in business are currently being held by men.

CONCLUSION

When then does the bias against women as managers manifest itself? This question must be answered if women are to be considered the equals of men in their professional careers and the negative bias prevented. Equality in the workplace could be defined as providing the same opportunities for advancement and placement to both men and women having the same capabilities. The study, conducted using the instrument developed by Yost and Herbert, concluded that the bias against women as managers is already present among the male participants before they finish their formal education. Yet the women participants were found to still be confident that they would have the same opportunities as their male counterparts in the workplace, that is, the bias was not yet present. Ethnicity did not play as big a role in this bias as had been hypothesized. While there was a definite bias among the respondents of Hispanic origin to have a negative attitude towards a woman manager, quantitatively it was not as extreme as had been expected.

REFERENCES

Bass, B., et al. (1971). Male managers' attitudes toward working women. *American Behavioral Scientist, 15,* 221–236.

Buzenberg, M. (1975, Fall). Training and development of women executives: A model. *Collegiate News and Views,* 19–21.

Davidson, M., and Cooper, C. (1987). Female managers in Britain—A comparative perspective. *Human Resource Management, 26* (2), 217–242.

Feather, N., and Raphelson, A. (1973). Fear of success in Australian and American student groups. *Journal of Personality, 42,* 191–201.

Herbert, T., and Yost, E. (1984). Development of the attitudes toward women as managers scale. Unpublished paper.

Hjelle, L., and Butterfield, R. (1974). Self-actualization and women's attitudes to-

ward their roles in contemporary society. *The Journal of Psychology,* 87, 225–230.

Karabenick, S., and Marshal, J. (1973). Performance of females as a function of fear of success, fear of failure, type of opponent, and performance-contingent feedback. *Journal of Personality,* 42, 220–237.

Lathan, M., et al. (1987). Recruiting entry level staff: Gender differences. *CPA Journal,* 57 (1), 30–42.

Lirtzman, S., and Wahba, M. (1972). Determinants of coalitional behavior of men and women: Sex roles or situational requirements? *Journal of Applied Psychology,* 56 (5), 406–411.

Mottaz, C. (1986). Gender Differences in work satisfaction, work related rewards and values, and the determinants of work satisfaction. *Human Relations,* 39 (4), 359–378.

Norgaard, C. (1980, Winter). *MSU Business Topics,* 23–28.

Pearson, D. (1984, October). Inaccurate perceptions about women as managers. *Supervisory Management,* 29–34.

Powell, G., et al. (1984). Sex effects on managerial value systems. *Human Relations,* 37 (11), 909–921.

SECTION FOUR

WOMEN IN ADMINISTRATION

The focus of this section is women in their administrative roles—their challenges and their difficulties. Several authors discuss the strategies that women use to get the job done.

The use of team skills is the subject of study by Merrion and Thompson. Twenty-three team play skills are studied and their importance to the administrative role of women is identified.

Durnovo, in a study of women administrators in community colleges in Texas, found that women are gaining greater access to higher administrative positions. Significant in this access to the higher positions was the possession of a doctoral degree.

The unique position of being a female manager of a university physical plant is discussed by Patton. She discusses the challenges that she faced and how she solved problems as administrator.

In discussing the relative benefits and costs to and for women administrators, Simmons and Jarchow indicate that women administrators make significant personal sacrifices throughout their careers. Benefits such as personal growth, autonomy, and "perks" are explored.

14

Administrative Team Play

Margaret Merrion
Donna Thompson

Administrators in higher education must both cooperate and compete with one another in a myriad of ways. They give and take much like team players involved in a competitive sport. Specialized team play skills, however, are highly valued far beyond the athletic sense. Today, the corporate, political, and educational sectors of society recognize the importance of executives, managers, and leaders having skills as team players.

Differences in team play skills have been noted, particularly within the business sector (Loden, 1985). In a recent *Wall Street Journal* survey, a large percentage of women (60%) reported a sense of not fitting in as "one of the boys" (Rogan, 1984). The female applicants for flight attendant positions in a major airline are required to pass a psychological screening "to determine their sense of cooperation and sense of team work" (Peters & Waterman, 1982, p. 253.) It seems that certain skills and behaviors allow entry into the "men's hut" which appears to be the rite of passage for both men and women in the business world (Ritti & Funkhouser, 1977).

And perhaps the most familiar arena in which team play skills are openly discussed as criteria for candidacy is in political appointments, where a candidate's strength might be his or her ability to be more of a team player (*Time*, 1985).

Though the nature of higher education is somewhat different from corporate and political administrative structures, administrators in higher edu-

This chapter is reprinted from copyrighted "Leadership in Education," Journal of the National Council of Administrative Women in Education, Geraldine Chapey, Ed.D., Editor.

cation engage in team play function much like chief executive officers in corporate and political structures. Perhaps some of the difficulties are parallel within administrative teams in higher education.

Team building within organizations appears in the literature with some frequency (Patten, 1981). There is a paucity of literature, however, relating to team play skills as such. Since team play skills have not been researched in a formal sense, 23 specialized specific examples of team play were brainstormed by a team of women at the University of Northern Iowa* using Nominal Group Techniques (Delbecq, et al., 1975). These skills were:

1. playing several roles
2. practicing public relations skills
3. identifying appropriate tasks for team accomplishment
4. delegating tasks to team members
5. being willing to spend time that is necessary to work with a team
6. losing gracefully
7. giving and taking
8. facilitating the brain power of team members
9. listening to team members' input
10. practicing decision making models
11. sacrificing individual goals for group goals
12. computerizing planning strategies
13. attending to the process as well as content of team work
14. recognizing what one does well and doing it within team operations
15. practicing conflict-resolution skills
16. competing
17. communicating without conflict
18. completing the job
19. trusting team members' expertise/judgment
20. practicing problem solving approaches
21. cooperating
22. sharing/rotating leadership roles
23. maximizing the use of group resources

A rating scale of 1 to 5 was employed to indicate the "use" and "importance" of these 23 skills. Regarding the skill's use, the scale ranged from never use (1) to most used (5). Similarly, in rating a skill's importance, the scale ranged from unimportant (1) to most important (5). Administrators

---

*Pat Bassett, Mary Engen, Mary Franken, Elaine Kalmar, Margaret Merrion, Bev Taylor, and Donna Thompson.

were asked to indicate to what extent they used the particular team play skill and to what extent they thought the skill was important.

Of the 23 skills, all were rated from moderate (lowest average response: 2.19) to high (highest average response: 5.00) range in use and importance. When these responses were examined for differences, a number were found. The responses were first examined for significant differences (a) among respondents in different administrative positions, (b) between administrators in independent and public institutions, and (c) between male and female administrators.

When comparing the average responses of presidents, vice-presidents, and deans, the use of one skill was found statistically significant in tests of Analysis of Variance at the .03 level. That particular skill was "cooperating." Presidents indicated a very high mean score (4.7) reflecting an extensive use of cooperation in their administrative team roles. Vice-presidents reported a high average score of 4.3 while deans reported a moderately high score of 4.0. Among the Iowa administrators it appears that presidents of institutions of higher learning use the skill of cooperating significantly more often than vice-presidents and deans.

With respect to differences among the skills' importance ratings, one skill was found statistically significant: "Sharing and rotating leadership roles." The average responses were different in that the vice-presidents reported the highest mean (3.6), followed by the deans (3.3), and the presidents (2.6). These differences were noted at the .01 level. It appears that the skill of sharing and rotating a leadership role within team operations is more important to the vice-presidents in this study than it is among the deans and presidents.

When the data were analyzed for significance with respect to affiliation, two differences were found. Two skills used by the independent and public college administrators were markedly different. "Being willing to spend time that is necessary to work with a team" was reported as used to a greater extent by public university administrators. Their average response was 4.8 indicating a very extensive use. Independent college administrators reported a moderately high average response of 3.8.

The team play skill, "sacrificing individual goals for group goals" was similar in response pattern. Administrators of public universities reported a significantly higher usage of this skill (average response: 4.4) than their colleagues in independent colleges (average response: 3.5). This difference was noted at the .03 level. It appears, then, that administrators within public universities are more willing to spend time that is necessary to work in team situations and that they tend to sacrifice their individual goals for group goals more so than administrators in the independent colleges in the study.

Analyses of variance in the administrators' responses according to position uncovered no significant differences in importance ratings among any

of the 23 team play skills. There appears to be some commonality in the values assigned to the skills between independent and public college administrators.

Examining the responses according to differences in gender yielded additional significance. In each instance, the average responses were higher among female than male administrators. The use of "giving and taking" among women was collectively high (average response: 4.7). Male administrators reported a high usage (average response: 4.1) but significantly different at the .03 level. The importance of this same skill was a source of further significant difference. The female respondents indicated that "giving and taking" was close to most important. Their average score was 4.9 and the male respondents reported an average score of 4.2—somewhat less in importance. This difference was noted at the .02 level. "Giving and taking" as a team play skill was the only skill in which both use and importance differed significantly.

Male and female administrators assigned significantly different degrees of importance to "playing several roles." Males' average rating was 3.5; females' average rating was 4.4. Again, this difference was at the .02 level of significance. Women in administration appear to place more importance on playing several roles in their team interaction than men do.

Although both male and female administrators assigned high values of importance to the skill of "cooperating," it is interesting to note that the average score among the female respondents was 5.00—each administrator had rated cooperating as most important. It was also of interest to note that only six of the skills were given higher "use" ratings by men. These six included: "identifying appropriate tasks," "attending to process as well as content of team work," "recognizing what one does well and doing it within team operations," "practicing conflict-resolution skills," "competing" and "maximizing use of group resources." The single skill which men found more important than women was "competing."

This research was limited to a descriptive nature—measuring the use and importance of specific skills administrators use in teamwork. It would be conjecture to offer explanations which provide a rationale for what emerged in this study. It is appropriate and possible, however, to identify other research and literature which corroborates findings. Certainly these theories and theses can interpolate understandings on the topic.

Piaget (1932), for instance, observed differences in male and female children's attitudes toward game rules, rule breaking, and innovation. Lever (1976, 1978) studied children's play and game behaviors extensively and concluded that strikingly different sets of social skills were cultivated through the diverse play experience of the sexes. Boys, for instance, engaged in team sports; girls did not. Boys learned how to compete; girls tended to cooperate. Boys took on different roles and "used" team members' expertise; girls did not appear to have parallel play experiences. Boys

played in large groups; girls played in small groups. Boys participated in more complex games attending to the process of the game; girls played games with fewer rules. In fact, if disputes arose, girls terminated play; boys worked out their differences. Boys also played to win; girls played for the fun of it.

Educational psychologist Gilligen (1982), in analyzing adult moral behaviors, agreed with Lever, noting that women tend to make different sense of their experience and base this sense on their knowledge of human relationships. She poses the hypothesis that women do not have the same moral ethics as males. Their behavior and moral decisions, then, are based on a different sense of morality.

Are the play behaviors Lever observed coming back to haunt us in the team behaviors of adults? Are the differences Piaget noticed in young boys' and girls' attitudes toward game rules, attitudes that are carried into adult team play? If women bring different experience and sense to their adult roles as Gilligen suggests, should these differences be valued and cultivated in adulthood?

To be sure, from these philosophical, sociological, and psychological studies one can see sometimes subtle, yet distinct sets of team play skills practiced. Whether these diverse team play skills complement one another to enhance the likely success of administrative teams is a subject for further investigation. Meanwhile, the nature of administration in higher education will continue to involve teams of people in competitive and cooperative situations. Administration will also entail complex rules, conflict, extensive communication, innovation, and moral judgments—much like the game behaviors learned in childhood. It behooves administrators to look seriously at team play skills.

This study has illuminated the use and importance of 23 team play skills among administrators in Iowa's institutions of higher education. The study identified differences in the responses of administrators depending on their position in the institution, the type of institution, and the administrator's gender. It is recommended that this study be replicated in other states and regions to determine if the results can be generalized to a wider population of administrators. Although these findings are limited to the responses of administrators in one state, as administrators assume or change positions in higher education, they may wish to consider the differences this study uncovered.

REFERENCES

Delbecq, A. L., et al. (1975). *Group Techniques for Program Planning*. Glenview, IL: Scott, Foresman and Co.
Gilligen, C. (1982). *In a Different Voice*. Cambridge, MA: Harvard University Press.

Lever, J. (1976). Sex differences in the complexity of children's play and games. *American Sociological Review*, 43, 471–83.

————. (1978). Sex differences in games children play. *Social Problems*, 23, 478–87.

Loden, M. (1985). *Feminine Leadership or How to Succeed in Business without Being One of the Boys*. New York: Times Books.

Patten, T. (1981). *Organizational Development through Teambuilding*. New York: Wiley–Interscience Publications.

Peters, T., and Waterman, R. (1982). *In Search of Excellence*. New York: Harper & Row.

Piaget, J. (1932). *Moral Judgment of the Child*. New York: The Free Press, p. 75.

Ritti, R., and Funkhouser, G. (1977). *The Ropes to Skip and the Ropes to Know*, 2d Ed. New York: John Wiley and Sons, Inc.

Rogan, H. (October 29, 1984). Women executives feel that men both aid and hinder their careers. *The Wall Street Journal*.

Time. (November 18, 1985). p. 51.

PARTICIPATING INSTITUTIONS

Briar Cliff College	Maharishi University
Buena Vista College	Marycrest College
Central University of Iowa	Morningside College
Clarke College	Mount Mercy College
Coe College	Mount Saint Clare College
Cornell College	Northwestern College
Divine Word College	St. Ambrose College
Dordt College	Simpson College
Drake University	University of Dubuque
Graceland College	University of Iowa
Grand View College	University of Northern Iowa
Grinnell College	Upper Iowa University
Iowa Wesleyan College	Wartburg College
Iowa State University	Westmar College
Loras College	William Penn College
Luther College	

15

Emerging Characteristics of Women Administrators in Texas Public Community and Junior Colleges

Maya Durnovo

Only in the last two decades have women joined men as college leaders. Today, the proportional representation of women in top-level administrative positions is substantially greater than it was ten years ago (K. Moore, Twombly, S., & Mortorana, S., 1985). Yet, relatively little is known about women who occupy administrative positions below the level of president. The sparse number of studies are a reflection of the small percentage of women in administrative posts in higher education.

The literature suggests that women administrators tend to build careers in some areas or tracks more easily than in others (Etaugh, 1985; Green, 1984; K. Moore, 1984). Most women administrators work in community colleges, in lower level positions (Etaugh, 1985; Kistler, 1979). On the whole, women are not mobile (Green & Kellogg, 1982; Moore & Sagaria, 1981; Stokes, 1984). According to most studies, mentoring has been found to be important for career advancement (Evans, 1985; Green & Kellogg, 1982; Ironside, 1983; K. Moore, 1982).

The research on women who have attained high-ranking positions indicates that these women not only expanded traditional roles, but developed qualities such as self-reliance, ambition, and assertiveness. The common personality characteristics that have emerged in most studies have been a high need for achievement, a strong desire for recognition, a deeply embedded work ethic, a need for challenge, and a willingness to accept responsibilities (Eaton, 1984; Kistler, 1979; Ironside, 1983; Nieber, 1975).

This study was the first to examine the characteristics of women administrators in Texas public community and junior colleges. Specifically, the study examined (a) what positions women administrators occupied, and where they were located in Texas public community and junior colleges; (b) their educational, professional, and personal background; (c) career mobility issues; (d) the significance of mentoring; (e) factors that shape careers: the differences among qualifications, mobility, mentoring, age, and marital status on administrative rank; and (f) factors that contributed to success.

METHOD

All Texas public community/junior college women administrators from the level of coordinator to chancellor were surveyed in 1987. Adapted from the *Today's Academic Leaders* (Moore, K., et al., 1985) the *Women Administrators in Texas Community/Junior Colleges* questionnaire was sent to 294 women. An 80 percent response was achieved with 212 or 72 percent usable surveys. Descriptive statistics (e.g., percentages, means, and standard deviations), analysis of variance, and the chi-square test were used to analyze the data. A chi-square test found a significant difference among the three administrative levels, indicating that there were more women in mid-level positions than in upper or lower levels, and significantly more in upper than lower levels. A 10 percent sample of the respondents were interviewed by phone to obtain data on factors leading to success.

RESULTS

Results of the study revealed that women administrators in Texas community colleges function at every level, except chancellor. Fifty percent were directors, 30 percent were above director level, and 20 percent were below director level. The majority function in midmanagement positions. This is an encouraging increase when compared to Kistler (1979), who found California community college women administrators clustered in lower-level positions. Table 15.1 reports the frequencies and percentages of respondents' administrative positions.

EMPLOYMENT BY TEXAS COMMUNITY/JUNIOR COLLEGE

The majority of the 49 Texas community colleges employ, on the average, between one and five women administrators. Table 15.2 lists the frequencies and percentages of women administrators per community college in Texas.

Table 15.1
Respondents' Administrative Positions

Position	Frequency	Percentage
Vice-Chancellor	1	.5
President	4	1.9
Assistant to Chancellor	1	.5
V.P. for Instruction	1	.5
V.P. for Student Services	5	2.4
Executive Dean	1	.5
Dean of Instruction	5	2.4
Dean of Student Services	10	4.7
Dean of Vocational/Tech.	2	.9
Dean of Continuing Education	3	1.4
Dean (other)	5	2.4
Associate Dean	7	3.3
Campus Director	3	1.4
Chair	15	7.1
Directors	107	50.5
Officer	11	5.2
Registrar	5	2.4
Business Office	5	2.4
Coordinator/Manager	15	7.1
Head Librarian	3	1.4
Other	2	.9
Total	212	100.

EDUCATION

The highest degree earned by most of respondents, 53.8 percent, was a master's degree. Table 15.3 displays the highest degrees earned.

FIRST PERSON TO HOLD ADMINISTRATIVE POSITION

Over one-half of the respondents, 53.4 percent, were "founding" administrators for at least one of their positions. This suggests that women are gaining access to new positions and to the creation of new departments. Ninety-seven of these positions were created in community colleges and 13 outside of higher education. Twenty-three of the respondents were "first person" in two and/or three new jobs. The most frequent new position was director.

TRACKS

The study was designed to determine if women administrators clustered in particular tracks and/or if they moved from those tracks. Tracks were

Table 15.2

Employment by Texas Community/Junior Colleges

College	Frequency	Percentage
Alamo Community College	3	1.4
Alvin Community College	3	1.4
Amarillo College	1	.5
Angelina College	1	.5
Austin Community College	4	1.9
Bee County College	1	.5
Blinn College	3	1.4
Brazosport	2	.9
Central Texas College	3	1.4
Cisco Junior College	2	.9
Claredon College	1	.5
College of the Mainland	2	.9
Collin Community College	6	2.8
Cooke County College	1	.5
Dallas Community College District	35	16.5
Del Mar College	7	3.3
El Paso	10	4.7
Frank Phillips	5	2.4
Galveston College	3	1.4
Grayson County College	1	.5
Hill Junior College	-	-
Houston Community College System	22	10.5
Howard County Junior College	4	1.9
Kilgore College	-	-
Laredo Junior College	3	1.4
Lee College	4	1.9
McLennan Community College	5	2.4
Midland	6	2.8
Navarro College	3	1.4
North Harris County Junior College	6	2.8
Northeast Texas Community College	3	1.4
North Lake College	4	1.9
Odessa College	2	.9
Panola Junior College	2	.9
Paris Junior College	5	2.4
Ranger Junior College	-	-
San Jacinto Junior College	2	.9
South Plains College	3	1.4
Southwest Texas Junior College	1	.5
Tarrant County Junior College	19	9.0
Temple Junior College	5	2.4
Texarkana Community College	1	.5
Texas Southmost College	2	.9
Trinity Valley Community College	4	1.9
Tyler Junior College	-	-
Vernon Regional Junior College	4	1.9
Victoria College	2	.9
Weatherford College	6	2.8
Western Texas College	-	-
Wharton County Junior College	-	-

Table 15.3
Educational Background

Highest Degree Earned	Frequency	Percentage
Associate	3	1.4
Bachelor's	39	18.4
Master's	114	53.8
Doctorate	46	21.7
Doctorate in Progress	5	2.4
Degree Earned in Texas	166	78.3
Degree Earned outside Texas	46	21.7

defined as student services, academic affairs (instruction), administration, continuing education, and business/accounting. The student services track held 47 percent, the largest number of respondents. Of these, only 8 percent have advanced into other areas, suggesting that women tended to remain in one administrative track. Table 15.4 reports the numbers and frequencies in each track.

PROFESSIONAL WORK EXPERIENCE

The average number of positions held was 3.5 in an average number of 16.2 years. Experience specifically related to community college employment indicated an average number of 2.2 positions in an average of 9.6 years. The current position was held for 5.1 years and the preceding position for 4.9 years.

MOBILITY

Of the 212 respondents, only 16 have worked in more than one Texas community college. The majority of the respondents have built their careers in one community college. This suggests that women tend not to be mobile within the state.

Are Women Mobile within Their Institution?

On the average, women administrators have held two positions during their community college work experience. A comparison was made between the current position and the preceding position. Administrative positions were divided into three levels:

Table 15.4

Respondents in Student Services Positions

Student Services	Number	Percentage
V.P. Student Services	5	2.4%
Dean Student Services	10	4.7
Director Student Services	61	28.9
Coordinator	15	7.0
Registrar/Admissions	5	2.4
Financial Aid	3	1.4
Total number	**9 9**	**47.1%**

Respondents in Academic Affairs Positions		
Vice President for Instruction	1	.5%
Dean of Instruction	5	2.4
Dean of Vocational/Technical	3	1.4
Chair	14	6.6
Director	13	6.2
Coordinator of Health Services	2	.9
Total	**3 8**	**18.1%**

Respondents in Administration		
President/CEO	4	1.9%
Vice-Chancellor	1	.5
Director Public Information	14	6.6
Director of Personnel	7	3.3
Campus Director	3	1.4
Director (other)	1	.5
Coordinator/Manager	7	3.3
Total	**3 7**	**17.5%**

Respondents in Continuing Education		
Dean of Continuing Education	3	1.4%
Director of Continuing Education	8	3.8
Total	**1 1**	**5.2%**

Respondents in Business Affairs		
Dean of Business	5	2.4%
Director of Business Affairs	5	2.4
Officer of Business Affairs	6	2.8
Total	**2 7**	**7.6%**

1. upper level—which included vice-chancellor, president, assistant to the chancellor, vice-president, executive dean, dean, chair and campus director (total = 62).
2. middle level—which included all directors (except campus director) (total = 107).
3. lower levels—which included assistant director, lead instruction, coordinator, registrar, librarian, business office related and manager (total = 44).

One-hundred and nineteen women administrators moved upward from a lower- or mid-level position to an upper- or mid-level position during their most recent job change, while 72 stayed in the same position. A significant difference ($p < .05$) was found between these two groups. This suggests that women are advancing from lower- or mid-level to mid- and upper-level positions.

MENTORING

Fifty-seven percent of the respondents indicated that they had a mentor in their career in higher education administration. Women who have had mentors were in significantly ($p < .05$) higher administrative positions than women who had not experienced mentoring, leading to the assumption that a mentor is an important factor in the career development and advancement of respondents.

The mentor was helpful with career advancement: providing opportunity, visibility, sharing information, providing encouragement and confidence, being a role model, encouraging the protégé to continue her education, and teaching how to be politically astute. Repeatedly, respondents, including those who have not had a mentor, recommend a mentor relationship.

Of those mentored, 62.9 percent had a male mentor, and the majority (87.9%) were Caucasian. Mentor relationships ranged from one year to 21 years. The most frequently cited time span was three years.

All the respondents indicated that the mentor relationship was important and valuable in their career development and career advancement.

HOW WERE CURRENT POSITIONS OBTAINED?

The best source for learning about the position currently held (see Tables 5.5 and 5.6) has been through personal contact, leading to the assumption that being well integrated in the collegial system and "knowing people" are the best ways to learn about new positions.

Table 15.5
Method for Becoming a Candidate to Current Position

Method	Frequency	Percentage
Applied directly	73	36.0%
Appointed by senior administrator	37	18.2
Mentor recommended	26	12.8
Nominated (other than mentor)	26	12.8
Assumed acting appointment	15	7.4
Other	15	7.4
Invitation from search committee	9	4.4
Created position and got it funded	2	1.0

Table 15.6
Best Source for Identifying Current Position

Source	Frequency	Percentage
Personal Contacts	86	43.2%
My mentor	36	18.1
Other	35	17.6
Institutions job announcement	25	12.6
Ad in newspaper, journal, etc.	16	8.0
Employment agency	1	.5

ARE WOMEN SEEKING A JOB CHANGE?

Only 14.6 percent of the respondents indicated they were actively seeking a job change, and 25.3 percent were not sure. This finding is similar to Moore et al. (1985), who found that women administrators were either not seeking a job change or were not sure.

Thirty-eight percent of those who did want to change (a frequency of 33 respondents), were seeking positions at a higher level in preferably another two-year public community college. They indicated that they were actively developing new contacts in order to find a new job.

PERSONAL BACKGROUND

Personal background revealed that the average woman administrator was 42.7 years of age. The Texas community college woman administrator was slightly younger than the national mean age, 46.4 years, found by Moore et al. (1985). Sixty-one percent were married and 37 percent were single. The majority of the women administrators, 84.4 percent, were Caucasian, 8.5 percent were Black, and 7.1 percent were Hispanic.

Close to one-half of the respondents, 48 percent, were firstborn in the family. The majority of firstborn administrators have held upper-level or mid-level positions, suggesting that firstborns tend to be in higher ranking jobs. In this study, administrators who were "only children" did not fall in upper-level positions, but rather in mid-level directorships.

The majority of respondents earned higher degrees than either parent. One-fourth of the fathers had only a high school education and slightly less than one-third of the mothers had earned a high school diploma.

WOULD YOU BE AN ADMINISTRATOR AGAIN?

In answer to the question, Would you be an administrator again, 71.4 percent indicated they would, 8.1 percent would not select administration, and 20.5 percent were not sure. Of the remarks that accompanied a "yes," the following representative opinions were made: (a) I enjoy my job; (b) Seek a doctorate early in your career; (c) I enjoy the responsibility and the rewards; and (d) I would have started earlier.

WHAT FACTORS SHAPE ADMINISTRATIVE CAREERS?

1. Were there significant differences among the administrative ranks that women administrators attain? A chi-square test found a significant difference among the three levels at the $p < .01$ level of probability. There were significantly more women in mid-level administrative positions than in upper or lower levels, and significantly more in upper levels than in lower.

2. Were there significant differences among qualifications, mobility, mentoring, marital status and age on administrative rank? A five-way analysis of variance revealed a significant, $p < .05$, main effect for mobility, degree earned, and mentoring on administrative level. Women who changed positions moved upward into a significantly higher level. Likewise, those who earned a doctorate and had a mentor relationship were also at a significantly higher administrative level. The interaction between mobility and degree was found to be significant. Women who changed positions and had a doctorate were more likely to advance to top-level administrative posts.

WHAT FACTORS LEAD TO SUCCESS?

A follow-up telephone interview was conducted with 10 percent of the sample, or 21 respondents. The telephone interview sought to probe more deeply into factors that led to success. Administrators were selected by region for a statewide representative sample.

1. *Did family background influence career?* The majority of the women interviewed had families who expected their daughter to achieve, to do her best, and to succeed. Family milieu facilitated, encouraged, and nurtured accomplishment. Six of the 21 women were firstborn or only children, and six were the first female. Eleven identified their fathers as being the influential figure, seven specified mothers, and three indicated that both parents were equally influential. In most cases, the respondent was the successful child.

2. *Did school years influence career?* All the women were outstanding students in high school, college, or graduate school. Most were remarkable scholars at every level of their education. Unanimously, they conceded that their motivation and drive to succeed, fostered from early childhood or tapped later in life, was the determining factor in their academic accomplishments.

3. *What other factors/people influenced career?* The majority (19) had mentors. Of those with a mentor, all highly recommended the relationship because it provided a valuable emotional and intellectual support system, as well as access to crucial information. In several cases the mentor was responsible for an important new job or promotion. Many urged other women administrators to become mentors.

4. *What characteristics were needed to be a successful administrator?* Success was dependent on having the right credentials, being able to get along with people, competence, leadership skills, tenacity and stamina, creativity, being political, conscientiousness, a "tough skin," practicality and the ability to actualize ideas, a sense of fairness, and patience. Mentioned repeatedly by most of the women was the willingness to work hard and the love of one's work. The theme of working ardently was reiterated again and again.

5. *What kind of experiences did women have in higher education?* Most respondents were very optimistic and observed progress with positive changes for women in administration over the past few years. Approximately one-third had a negative perspective; they felt discriminated against and not taken seriously. The topic of discrimination was volunteered by half of the respondents; others indicated that women were not treated seriously and that they must work extra hard to prove themselves. "It's still a man's world" surfaced three times. Overall, women experienced the need to work extra hard and accomplish beyond average expectations. The common explanation was that women were noticed more because they were infrequent in numbers.

6. *What were the rewards of working?* The rewards of working were very positive for the majority. Fulfillment and the opportunity to contribute something valuable was mentioned repeatedly. Without exception, all the women administrators loved the community college environment. Many were motivated by the challenge, others by serving students, and some by the prestige of being affiliated with an institution of higher education. The feeling of successful accomplishment was also a source of reward.

7. *What suggestions could be made for future women administrators?* Advice for women seeking careers in administration focused on being committed, acquiring the terminal degree, networking, always being a professional, and never giving up. Specific suggestions were: Dedicate yourself to excellence, do not be too pushy or aggressive, be a mentor for other women, become politically aware, and build solid underpinnings. Overall, respon-

dents felt that it was possible for women to succeed in community college administration.

CONCLUSIONS

1. Women administrators are found throughout Texas community colleges and they are gaining access to higher-level administrative positions. According to this study, a significant number of women have moved into upper-level positions during their last job change. While the majority of the respondents are directors, the number of administrators above director level is significantly greater than the number below director, which implies that it is possible to reach high-ranking positions. The path is marked by an education, a mentor relationship, an opportunity to advance, a commitment to excellence, and a personal approach that is positive and confident.

2. Each administrator who was interviewed for this study had indicated that she was also an outstanding student in high school, undergraduate, or graduate school, suggesting that scholastic achievement may be related to future success in higher education. Perhaps the early pattern of success and leadership fosters a positive relationship with education that develops into a successful future career.

Furthermore, there is a significant relationship between upper-level administrators and those with a doctorate, which leads to the conclusion that a terminal degree is necessary for women seeking advancement.

3. Mentoring is another significant factor in the career development and promotion of women administrators in Texas. There is a significant relationship between women who are mentored and administrative rank. This suggests that a mentor relationship is important, not only for learning the tools of the trade, but also for advancement. All respondents have described mentoring as a positive experience that increases career satisfaction, personal growth, and advancement. Therefore, it may be implied that a mentor may make the critical difference.

4. Over one-half of the respondents to this survey have been the first person to hold a newly created position. This result is encouraging in that it affirms the conclusion that women are gaining access to administrative posts. These positions are important because they provide the groundwork for the creation of the scope and quality of the position.

5. The best way to learn about a new job is through personal contact, according to the respondents of this survey. This suggests that it is important to network, to become well integrated with one's colleagues, both within the college setting and outside. Only 18.1 percent consider their mentor to be the best source for identifying their current position. This may be explained by the fact that most women have built their administrative careers in one community college and most mentor relationships have tran-

spired between two administrators. In other words, most relationships begin when the respondent is already employed in her college.

6. Women administrators are not geographically mobile and they are not interested in seeking employment elsewhere. Only 14.6 percent of the respondents are actively pursuing a job change. The majority have built their careers at primarily one community college, implying that women have chosen not to be geographically mobile.

7. According to this study, women rarely move from one administrative track to another. This supports the literature that indicates that once launched in a given track, individuals do not move easily to another track (K. Moore, 1984). Women in this study are pocketed in the student services areas.

8. The majority of Texas women administrators are Caucasian. Although Black and Hispanic administrators are found at every administrative level, their representation is noticeably small.

9. Three salient themes emerge from the interview data on factors leading to success: (1) Career opportunities for women administrators are improving. (2) The path to upper level administrative posts is difficult because women administrators perceive some discriminatory practices. (3) Success is achieved through a commitment to excellence, a willingness to work hard, and a positive attitude that reaches beyond barriers or discrimination and embraces only a challenge.

10. The experiences reported by respondents of this study ranged from highly laudatory to extremely critical. The reason for this diversity points in only one direction, the woman herself. The personal histories of each woman who has been interviewed reflect not only her opinions, but also her personal makeup, her personal bias and perspective, and her personal attitude. And it is in the personal approach to her present experience and her future opportunities that the answer to success lies. A positive resolve to succeed is what gives birth to a champion. This resolve is not found within the college setting, or in policy and procedure manuals, or in legislation. It is found within the woman herself.

RECOMMENDATIONS

From the findings and implications of this study, several recommendations can be proposed. The first recommendation is that women administrators should strive to develop a mentor relationship. In turn, they should become mentors for other women seeking a similar career path. The findings of this study indicate that women who have mentors are more likely to reach upper level posts. The value and importance of a mentor has also been verified through telephone interviews and previous research.

The second recommendation is that women should pursue a terminal degree if they seek advanced positions in higher education. The significant

relationship between administrative rank and women with doctorates strongly suggests that the terminal degree is a necessary qualification. This finding was affirmed repeatedly through the interviews. Learn to network is the third recommendation emerging from this study. The process of networking not only assists in learning about new positions, but also fosters a support system among women administrators.

The women in this study are success stories. Their success is built not only on skills and qualifications, but also on their positive approach, their personal commitment, their dedication to excellence, and their love of the community college, leading to the fourth recommendation: One must strive toward excellence and work because of a personal commitment. Through this type of involvement, women administrators not only achieve success, but also become powerful role models for both male and female colleagues, as well as influence the aspirations of young students.

REFERENCES

Eaton, J. (1984). Tapping neglected leadership sources. In Eaton, J. (Ed.), *Emerging Roles for Community College Administrators: New Directions for Community Colleges*, (Ser. 46, Vol. VII, 94). San Francisco, CA: Jossey-Bass.

Etaugh, C. (1985, April). Changes in the status of women faculty and administrator in higher education since 1972. Paper presented at the annual meeting of the American Educational Research Association, Chicago, IL.

Evans, N. J. (1985, March). Career development issues facing women in student affairs administration. Paper presented at the annual meeting of the American College Personnel Association, Boston, MA.

Green, M. F. (1984). Women and minority ACE Fellows in the ascent toward administrative posts. *Educational Record*, 65, 46–49.

Green, M. F., and Kellogg, T. (1982). Careers in academe: Confirming the conventional wisdom? *Educational Record*, 63, 40–43.

Ironside, E. (1983, March). Women administrators in higher education: Qualitative data for values questions. Paper presented at the annual meeting of the Association of the Study of Higher Education, Washington, DC.

Kistler, K. M. (1979). Equal opportunity: Women in administration in the California community college. U.S. Department of Education (Eric Document Reproduction Service No. 217 896).

Moore, K. M. (1984). Careers in college and university administration: How are women affected? In Tinsley, A., Secor, C. & Kaplan, S. (Eds.), *New Directions for Higher Education: Women in Higher Education Administration*, 45, 5–15. San Francisco, CA: Jossey-Bass.

Moore, K. (1982). The role of mentors in developing leaders for academe. *Educational Record*, 63, 22–28.

Moore, K., and Sagaria, M. A. (1981). Women administrators and mobility: The second struggle. *Journal of the National Association for Women Deans, Administrators and Counselors*, 44, 21–28.

Moore, K., Twombly, S., and Mortorana, S. (1985). *Today's academic leaders*. Uni-

versity Park, PA: The Pennsylvania State University, Center for the Study of Higher Education.

Nieber, N. A. (1975). There is a certain kind of woman. *Journal of the National Association for Women Deans, Administrators and Counselors, 38,* 99–103.

Stokes, J. M. (1984). Organizational barriers and their impact on women in higher education. Washington, DC: National Association of Women Deans, Administrators and Counselors. (Eric Document Reproduction Service No. ED 264 747).

16

Women Managers in Higher Education

Karen L. Patton

This chapter was written to raise the awareness of the public to the concerns of the often forgotten position of women managers in higher education. This is the woman manager at universities and colleges who works behind the scenes and who is very rarely in the public eye.

INTRODUCTION AND PERSONAL BACKGROUND

I have Bachelor's and Master's degrees from Ball State University. My major was Business Education with minors in French, Russian, and Vocational Education—all of this completed with the intention of teaching after graduation. I did teach one year in the Indianapolis public schools and then decided to spend the next six years as a full-time homemaker, wife, and mother.

When it came time for me to return to the work force, we had just moved, because my husband had taken a new teaching and coaching position. I hit the street looking for employment. For the next school year I taught as a temporary instructor at Ball State University within the Business Education Department. Following that, I worked as a secretary for a department head within the university. It was at this time I received a call from the local General Motors Plant where I had submitted an application and was offered a position as a receptionist—no prestige, but twice the money, and I took it!

After a year answering phones and greeting salespeople, I was offered

the opportunity to go out on the manufacturing floor and become a production supervisor. (I was told by management that I had the education,
now all I needed was about six months' experience and I could really climb
the corporate ladder!) When I made this decision, I had absolutely no experience supervising people, had never seen a factory in action, and certainly
knew nothing about machines and their workings. But my first thoughts
were, 'Well six months can't be too bad and look at all the experience. Boy!
Will I have an advantage.'

My responsibilities in this position were the direct supervision of 20–50
men and control of 75–100 machines. Along with the usual clerical duties
of recording absences, sick time, overtime scheduling, daily and monthly
reports on efficiency and quality control, I had to handle the grievance procedures with the union and EEO responsibilities, in addition to maintaining
acceptable efficiency with a low scrap count. I must admit it was during this
time that I learned more about people, life, and work than any book I had
read or class I participated in could teach me. This was a world *not* like any
other, but after all, anyone could endure six months! The fact that I was the
first and only woman to go from the office to the manufacturing floor
didn't bother me as much as the men!

Four years later I received the news that due to a slump in the economy
and because I was a production supervisor I was to be laid off. Totally im-
material were the facts of where I had started, what I had been told, my education, or the experience I had gained during the past four years.

Following this, I started my own bookkeeping business. This gave me yet
another opportunity to expand my awareness of the business world and
the people who exist in it. While I was working at establishing my business
I also kept my application current at many of the businesses in town. After
two years, I received an interview and an offer for employment as the Superintendent of Building Service, Moving, and Storage at Ball State University. My destiny seemed to be calling me to continue within the university
setting but now I had a chance to use the skills I had acquired in the business world. I have been in this position now four years.

I am responsible for six supervisors on two shifts, 130 service staff, 80
buildings, maintenance of 3,000,000 sq. feet, and a $2,000,000 budget. I
interact and maintain good public relations with 18,000 students and 2500
faculty and staff. It is my responsibility to interview, hire, terminate, develop, and administer policies and procedures, and train my employees
along with following OSHA and EEO guidelines. I must maintain quality
control and standards for the custodial staff, moving and storage laborers,
their products and equipment. I entered this position as the only woman
superintendent and the only person under 50 years of age, following a man
with 25 years' experience.

I would like to say that I like my position—it is by far the best job I have

ever had. It is with this perspective in mind that I would like to consider the woman manager in higher education.

The real-life woman manager in higher education works within an area in higher education where little or no research is done and where there is very little documentation to draw from. Therefore, beyond quoting from the various sources that do exist, I will share some knowledge I have gleaned from personal experience.

First, the background of this woman manager: Who is she? How did she get there? and What is the area in which she must work?

THE WOMAN MANAGER, WHO IS SHE?

Even though little research has been done and little information can be gathered from written works, a comparative parallel can be drawn between the woman who is in middle management in a large corporation and the woman manager in higher education. Even though she is in higher education—whether considered staff, management, or professional—she is a true manager in every sense of the word. Her scope of responsibilities and communication skills run the gamut from service staff (who may not be able to read or write) to the educated professor with a doctorate and distinguished publishing record. She must supervise and communicate with the goal-oriented professional as well as the employee who is satisfied with his present position and has no desire for any advancement in any area of his life. She manages the young and old, women and men, wealthy and poor.

Even though we think of the educational institution as a progressive thinking organization, most positions of upper management in higher education are filled by men. Barbara K. Dopp and Charles A. Sloan in *Clearing House* (1986) recently commented

Since 1950, the number of women in educational administration has declined as administrative positions have been redefined as management rather than teaching positions. (p. 120)

And as stated in a recent article entitled, "Men Still Dominate Higher Ed Despite Women's Gains," in the August, 1987 issue of *Higher Education and National Affairs,*

Despite the significant gains women in higher education have made in the last 15 years, women are still rarely viewed as leaders in what remains a male-dominated field, according to the Women's Research and Education Institute. (p. 3)

THE WOMAN MANAGER, HOW DID SHE GET THERE?

The typical woman manager has progressed into the lower levels of management that exist in higher education. She has often started as a custodian or dining service employee, and from there she may have moved to group leader, then to supervisor, and then superintendent. In each instance she had to spend the appropriate time in each position before advancing. This is an area not quite unlike business which has been dominated by men, who are well entrenched through the "good old boy" system. In her article entitled, "Women Administrators: Profiles of Success" (1985), Lillian C. Woo's first statement is: "Women are distinctly under-represented at the higher levels of the education profession" (p. 285). She goes on to mention a characteristic of a woman who has made it to the top as having the ability to continue within the mixed messages of society. As the woman manager progresses from one position upward to another she has had to correctly interpret the messages given by each level of management.

The woman manager in higher education is often seen as the Affirmative Action Director, an Associate Dean, or the Director of some special program. This is an area that is very visible to the public and can be counted easily. On rare occasion you will see her as the Dean, or perhaps Vice-President. This is not to minimize the attainment of these middle management positions, but this is to recognize that there should be many other higher levels of responsibility awarded to the woman manager in higher education. What about the hundreds, even thousands, of positions that are behind the scenes? How many can you count within your organization? It has been too easy to keep men in the high profile position areas with an occasional token female.

Most recently, women managers in higher education are found in minority specialties, traditionally women-oriented fields, with a few exceptions thrown in for good measure. The women managers who are actually subjected to public scrutiny in higher education often have had a background common to the men who have occupied these positions in times past. In many cases, these women managers' education and experience will far exceed those of the males who are chosen for these positions.

I would like to call your attention to the woman in higher education who has great possibilities to attain positions of professional importance but who is not in the public eye or who has not been able to break the male-dominated barrier, yet who has the qualifications equal to or greater than the men who are the leaders of this domain. Old boy networks yield reluctantly to the new girl networks; eventually these gender networks will give way to become competency-based networks. According to Dopp and Sloan (1986), accepting the idea of women business managers requires new attitudes about women and leadership.

THE WOMAN MANAGER, WHAT IS THE AREA IN WHICH SHE MUST WORK?

The women managers within the physical plant of the university, and the women managers within the student areas such as housing, dining, or the student center, are often the managers "behind the scenes." These behind-the-scenes managers are typically women—supervisors of custodial department (who does toilet bowls better than a woman?); dining services (who knows a kitchen best but a woman?) and housing directors (who knows how to make a bed better or watch after children than a woman?).

Rarely, does one find a woman as the physical plant director, superintendent of skilled trades, director of the heating plant, or vice-president of student relations (remember she does an excellent job on the ground level taking care of the student) or the head of the student center operations. Perhaps a woman is good as the hotel manager or manager of housekeeping, but not as the sole person in charge of finance, budgets, labor relations, or "skilled trades." However, in the same frame, who manages most of the financial matters of today's family and who works continually within the confines of the family budget to see that everyone gets what they need. Who is the labor relations arbitrator of the many people and personalities that make up the "family sphere." I bring all of this to your attention to emphasize the obvious—it is a man's world, and it will be a man's world for a long time to come.

I met a friend of mine who works at a local bank and whose name I had read many times in the paper as she moved up the banking ladder. When I congratulated her on her successes she was quick to point out that she now has a new boss. He is a much younger man than his predecessor and really reads the things she puts out and actually communicates with her on a common ground, not father to daughter as had been the case before. She remarked that the difference in age and outlook on life and career that this symbolized was the remarkable difference and one of the keys to her successes.

Age and tradition are barriers that are perpetually working against women as they try to make strides to promote themselves in this predominately male-oriented world. Perseverance and grace could be the bywords for this campaign (Insel, 1987). As brought out in the article "The Making of A Top Manager" (Insel & Jelinek, 1987) if a woman can produce solid evidence on how her performance exceeds that of her male counterpart, then her colleagues will be less gender conscious and it has been found that in younger industries one is more likely to find men who are tolerant of having young women around them in positions of power.

A woman manager in higher education is in the minority. Equality within the ranks may also be in the minority. As Charol Shakeshaft (1986) stated in "A Gender At Risk,"

Funding and support for equity-related issues have nearly disappeared at the federal and state levels. Equity is not merely out of fashion in the Department of Education—it has been declared an enemy. The reality is that excellence cannot be achieved without equity. Although an equitable system might not be an excellent one, true excellence in education cannot exist without equity. The two are not at odds; rather, they are dependent on each other. (p. 499)

An additional note comes from "Preparing Women School Administrators," (Shakeshaft, Gilligan & Pierce, 1984) that during 1970, 50 percent of the total enrollment in school administration programs were women and this was considered normal. Now, in the 1980s, there has been no noticeable increase of women in major administrative positions (Allison & Allison, 1985). Until I hired in at the university there were no women superintendents.

The woman manager in higher education has some additional post–high school training and is goal oriented. She has worked often with men and is usually comfortable working in a male-oriented organizational structure. She is not stagnant in her thinking, her ideas, or methods of management. She has come to her position through the ranks, by taking the ladder one step at a time, by serving her time and paying her dues to each level and completing the requirements for the next progressive step. In most cases, she is a concerned, well-read, sincere, and compassionate person and most definitely could be classified as a "people" person. Experience and education play an integral part of the qualifications for the position, but it would be unrealistic to say that affirmative action has not been an influential factor.

Why does a woman manager in higher education really want to manage? If asked this question, most women managers would say they wanted to develop new skills and have an impact on the organization. In addition, greater responsibility, more money, and security are important but secondary. Power holds the least amount of draw for a woman who wants to move to a higher career level (Woo, 1985).

On paper and in theory the possibilities for promotion are endless. In practicality the odds and barriers are formidable as they are ingrained with tradition and culture, the very values that have run our world since time began.

THE WOMAN MANAGER: THE PROBLEMS SHE FACES

The second area to be discussed in this chapter are the problems actually facing the woman manager in higher education. By comparing the university environment with that of a large corporation, the following parallels can be drawn:

Both are male dominated

Both offer service to a customer

Both have many layers of hierarchy

Few females are CEOs

Middle management is often caught between the layers of union/service staff and professional/management.

Beyond coping with the obvious problems that any manager would have with his/her subordinates, the woman manager in higher education in support areas of the university or college has some concerns unique to the area. Very often her subordinates come from a varied socioeconomic background. There will be some who are working as a hobby while others are struggling to pay for each month's rent. Within this same group of people there is a large number who cannot read or write. Communication which is a vital link to accomplish the mission of the organization is often strained and difficult. Differences in culture, education, family experience, and lifestyle present challenges in communication and shared values.

On the other end of the scale, this manager also has very close dealings with the faculty and staff. The people are usually highly educated persons, goal oriented and with often very different life-styles and cultures than the service staff. Both groups are sincere, dedicated, hard working, and committed employees but each demands its own method of communication and level of understanding.

The custodial staff and moving crew are part of the service organization, understanding that they are employed to maintain the quality of the life of the student, staff, and faculty at an optimum. Most are eager to please and more than willing to be of service. I often stand between these people and the faculty who expect and demand more and better service at their convenience. An example of this is when we try to maintain the conditions of the floors by buffing them with automatic machines. There is some noise involved as when any machinery is working, however, numerous times the custodian has been asked not to buff the floors, run the sweeper or do any job while class is being held in a nearby classroom. This sounds reasonable and acceptable to all except there are only so many hours allotted in the day for the cleaning of these specific areas. If this demand is repeated across the campus, there is no way that the custodian can get all of his/her work done in only a few hours time. Here again, diplomacy and finesse must become the manager's bywords. This is just one small example of the vital communication necessary between and among the levels of personnel at the university. Regardless of the area in which a woman manager has responsibility, to be outstanding she must be able to cope and function well within the system.

Whether it be corporate life or educational life, some problems experienced by a woman manager may have been brought on by herself. These

problems may be caused by her attitude and inexperience in working with men and women of all skill levels, educational backgrounds and cultural differences.

Her idea of what the ideal appearance and dress for a woman in management is may create problems that she is totally unprepared for and is unable to see. Just because a man wears a pin-striped, three-piece suit does not mean that it is the proper attire for the woman manager. A woman does not have to imitate a man in order to accomplish her goals. A woman is a woman and the dress will not change that. Why not build on it. A woman can still accomplish her mission in a smart-looking shirtwaist dress or tailored skirt and sweater combination. The idea of the woman in the double-breasted suit has gone the way of many stereotypes in management.

Another area of concern for the woman manager in higher education is her ability to function and work within the system. It's a system full of "good-old boys" and a long tradition of men and the male culture. She must be able to work within this system to achieve her goals. In addition, her lack of extensive education may work against her, or limited hands-on experience and training in the field she supervises or has cross dealings with.

Some other external barriers that the woman manager will have to overcome in order to obtain the leadership position she wants are sex role stereotyping, discrimination in the university and society, lack of adequate professional preparation, too few role models, along with the demands of her family and home life. Internal barriers may consist of low career aspirations, self-limiting beliefs and attitudes, lack of motivation, and poor self-image (Shakeshaft et al., 1984).

Another area that often presents itself as a problem for the woman manager is the pay scale and how the organization rewards its people monetarily. Often the custodial or skilled trades service staff will make more money than the secretarial and lower professional staff as well as being highly competitive with the managerial staff. As in any hierarchy where the competition for advancement is keen, jealousies will be of prime concern. This jealousy comes not only from the men who are used to dealing with the traditional male culture which must adjust to working with the female culture, but also from other women below, on the same level, and those above who are afraid of the upcoming competition.

Working within the system of higher education, the structure, culture, and tradition of the university or college will present some unique problems as well as opportunities for the woman manager. In most universities or colleges, as in most large corporations, there are many levels between the top level of administration—president, chancellor, and so on—and the woman manager. As suggested by Dr. John Urice in his address to the Association of Colleges and Universities Building Services Supervisors at their 1987 Fall Conference, the university setting as a work environment presents the following special problems for the manager:

- unclear job description
- difficulty in gauging success
- irrational power structure
- atrocious salary structure
- inadequate or inappropriate use of staff and money
- the individual has very little control over his environment, yet much responsibility
- labor intensive with short amount of space
- work cycle is cyclical and episodic
- changes are frequent and irrational to explain
- very rank conscious with subtle but conscious way of demonstrating credentials

The woman manager must know exactly in what order of personnel her ideas or proposals must be presented. She must be constantly aware of these status feelings and the weight they hold not only within her department but as they ripple across the campus through various departments, deans, vice-presidents and her entire area of influence.

The woman manager may present problems for herself in that she is just that—a woman. Even though the workplace does not call for strong emotions, and sensitive involvement, it is a typical characteristic of a woman. At this point she can be her own worst enemy and must fight strongly against being overly emotional while still trying to be sensitive to the needs of her employees—to remain strong mentally and physically with her male counterparts watching—but also be humanistic and sympathetic to those who are responsible to her. The woman manager must be able to break away from the popular public image of the mothering, nurturing woman who's duty is to stay home and tend the family unless she be ridden with guilt for all times. The working woman must learn to rein in the traits that are stereotypically labeled "female," since this behavior is what men have learned to devalue and to deride (Gould, 1985).

Those who are her peers often feel threatened by the new woman, the educated woman, the woman with ideas or whatever attributes assigned to her. The attributes that may have helped her obtain the job are now the very things that her peers may find offensive and unable to work with. The jealousies and experiences of her coworkers along with their service time with the organization all seem to be valid concerns that the woman manager must anticipate and be able to work with.

The woman manager must also make some personal choices. Is it really possible to give all that is necessary to a career and to a husband and family at the same time? I believe this is close to impossible. Something must give. Most CEOs and women in top administrative positions have attained their

goal with the sacrifice of husband and family. There is just rarely enough of a woman to cover all areas.

THE WOMAN MANAGER: SUGGESTIONS FOR SUCCESS

The third area to be addressed is what it takes to be a top female manager, whether in education or the corporate structure, and some suggestions for obtaining the goals that women managers have. First, it must be realized that if these problems are not resolved, she will find herself isolated from her peers and the wheels that keep the organization in motion. A woman does not have to be like the stereotypical male manager to succeed. The best features for success for any woman manager are:

- Competence—she must be intelligent, educated and have a variety of experience
- Persuasive—she must be able to accomplish her mission within the organizational structure
- Controlling—she must be able to draw her valuable resources of people and material together and cause them to work harmoniously
- Quick—she must be able to deal quickly and competently in many situations
- Compulsive—she must have drive and dedication
- Image—she must represent success in her entire presence, while being flexible to each situation (Insel & Jelinek, 1987).

The woman manager in higher education must work to change the cultural expectations for women (Dopp & Sloan, 1986). She must see herself as successful and as a professional who has the experience, motivation, and skill to be a success regardless of the setting. Other attributes that successful women in higher education exhibit are sensitivity, good interpersonal relationships, visibility, positivism and optimism, good conflict resolution skills, hard work, high energy level, and honesty.

By the mere virtue of being a woman in a traditionally male oriented field calls for some extra work on the part of the woman manager in higher education. This calls for a balancing act between the traditionally female staff position and the predominately male supervisor. In order to maintain the integrity and character of the service staff and to enhance their positions and morale along with meeting the demands of the men who will ultimately decide her fate causes a great deal of juggling of personalities, needs, and priorities, and so on. Women must raise men's awareness of their abilities and worth by winning their acceptance in the workplace (Gould, 1985).

Some specific suggestions for success in management in higher education are:

- set very high goals, be precise and enthused about them
- remember your past successes and keep a record of them
- promote someone else who is also successful as soon as possible
- stick up for your people, know their concerns
- make clear decisions and let them be known
- if you don't know the answer, say so
- laugh, enjoy yourself, your people, and your work
- don't promote the father/daughter syndrome with your colleagues
- be outgoing, but not flirtatious; be aware of your public relations at all times
- be professional in the way you present yourself, your office, and your area of concern
- be warm, concerned, and remember the compassion you need is also a need of those above and below you (Allison & Allison, 1985).

To summarize, the woman manager in higher education is a rare figure with problems in common with corporate management but to which are added the uniqueness of the university or college setting. Obviously through hard work, sacrifice, and dedication, she is now making a place within the traditionally male-dominated world. It will take all of her skills, education, and hands-on experience for this progress to continue. She can do it, of course, but the woman manager in higher education must remember where she is and what the culture of the workplace is. She must be able to adapt, change, and cope with the special problems and concerns of the university and college. It must be brought to the attention of the influential powers, the mentors, those seeking equality, and those in the public eye that there is a creature known as the woman manager in higher education, what she is, where she is, what problems she encounters, and that her potential is infinite. The woman manager in higher education is a success, an asset not to be wasted, but an asset of great value within the total structure whose time has come—if she is given the opportunity!

REFERENCES

Allison, M. A., and Allison, E. W. (1985, October). Managing men. *Working Woman*, 37.

Dopp, B. K., and Sloan, C. A. (1986, November). A career development and succession of women to the superintendency. *Clearing House*, 120.

Gould, R. E. (1985, April). Why can't a (working) woman be more like a man? *Working Woman*, 104.

Insel, B., and Jelinek, R. (1987, May). The making of a top manager. *Working Woman*, 105.

Jelinek, R. (1987, May). What makes top managers different? *Working Woman*, 109.

Shakeshaft, C. (1986, March). A gender at risk. *Phi Delta Kappan*, 499.

Shakeshaft, C., Gilligan, A., and Pierce, D. (1984, March). Preparing women school administrators. *Phi Delta Kappan*, 67.

Urice, J. (1987, September). *Stress management*. Address given at 1987 Fall Conference Association of Colleges and Universities Building Services Supervisors.

Woo, L. C. (1985, December). Women administrators: Profile of success. *Phi Delta Kappan*, 285.

17

Women Administrators: Benefits and Costs

Barbara Simmons
Elaine Jarchow

Women administrators must balance their personal and professional lives carefully. In order to better understand their dilemmas, this chapter analyzes professional benefits/costs and personal benefits/costs.

PROFESSIONAL BENEFITS

When one examines the careers of women who have successful careers as administrators in higher education, several career benefits become apparent.

Recognition

Shakeshaft and Nowell (1984) report that women find satisfaction in administrative roles and that this feeling can be related to Maslow's ideas about self-esteem. The female socialization process places tremendous emphasis on love and the need to belong. In advanced countries women also can attain self-actualization and have the best of both worlds. Quoting from Maslow's *Motivation and Personality,* Shakeshaft and Nowell (1984) state:

It is possible for a woman to have all the specifically female fulfillments (being loved, having the home, having the baby) and then without giving up any of these

satisfactions already achieved, go beyond femaleness to the full humanness that she shares with males, for example, the full development of her intelligence, of any talents that she may have, and of her own particular idiosyncratic genius, of her own individual fulfillment.

Women administrators certainly gain status, recognition, respect, and intellectual fulfillment because of their positions.

Global Perspective

Through travel, networking, and utilization of professional growth opportunities, top-level women managers are able to attain a more global perspective. These contacts can be quite important when career decisions are made or when advice is needed. Morrison, White, and Van Velsor (1987) find that women take greater risks during career advancement. Their performance must be outstanding, whatever the degree of difficulty; however, little compensation is received for extra effort. When problems arise, consulting with a variety of capable colleagues nationwide and internationally is indeed advantageous.

Perks

Obvious benefits of advancement are financial security, longer vacations, insurance benefits, provision of an automobile, and payment for attending professional conferences. Because of higher salaries, many women are able to buy larger homes, take nicer vacations, drive more expensive automobiles, send their children to better universities, and retire comfortably. Material possessions are strong reinforcers but need to be supplemented with continuing development in other areas.

Intellectual Growth

One reward of advancement that is receiving considerable attention today is the mental stimulation that occurs as a result of experience. Brandehoff (1985) noticed the challenge of administrative tasks after interviewing several successful female administrators. The women handled diverse tasks by being strong communicators, creative problem solvers, good managers, attentive to details, and observant of the nuances of both verbal and nonverbal indicators. Such characteristics thrive when ongoing relevant training occurs, mentors are available, and personal support systems are developed.

PROFESSIONAL COSTS

In addition to receiving benefits, female administrators also make many investments in their careers and those of others. These investments also may be viewed as costs.

Expanded Responsibilities

A female administrator, according to Stiegemeier (1980), must be prepared, be informed, dress professionally, act professionally, have a good sense of humor, treat others with respect, accept support, plan to be successful, recognize her own accomplishments, become involved, be assertive, and believe in herself. Furthermore, many writers believe a woman must be more competent and work harder than a man in order to obtain the same career advancement.

Smith (1978) suggests that women can help each other by sharing information about new jobs, organizing groups to promote women as administrators, and serving as mentors. Unfortunately, in her book *Woman to Woman: From Sabotage to Support*, Brile (1987) found that women were more likely than men to sabotage women colleagues in the workplace. Acts of vindictiveness, back-stabbing, and betrayal were reported by 53 percent of the women in her study. Women must support other women or opportunities for female administrators will decrease rapidly.

Stereotypic Expectations

According to Loden (1985) women are beginning to find their own leadership styles—styles that may be different from males but equally effective. Contrary to the notion that acting like a man will signify authority, Shakeshaft (1987) observed that effective women administrators often strive to look less authoritative and less threatening and that they are more influential when using a consideration style as opposed to a dominant one. Loden (1985) also noted that women are beginning to challenge the dress for success, management without emotion stereotype that was used to characterize the successful managerial woman of the 1970s.

Shakeshaft (1987) found that many women leave their administrative roles because of the attitudes others have toward women. For example, a woman using a collaborative approach may be considered weak and ineffective even though research overwhelmingly indicates that such a style is quite effective. Professional behavior such as being directive and assertive (often considered appropriate for males) may be seen as "inappropriate" for women. Unfortunately, women also are more likely to be judged on their attractiveness rather than for their achievements (Sandler, 1986).

Morrison, White, and Van Velsor (1987) describe the conflict that can occur because of stereotyping:

The women described to us as successful were put through a number of hoops as they progressed up the corporate ladder. They had to show their toughness and independence and at the same time depend on others. It was essential that they contradict the stereotypes that their male bosses and coworkers had about women. They had to be seen as different, "better than women" as a group. But they couldn't go too far and forfeit all traces of femininity because that would make them too alien to their superiors and colleagues. In essence, their mission was to do what wasn't expected of them, while doing enough of what was expected of them as women to gain acceptance.

Narrow Options

Although advancement is usually an advantage, specific training and experience may limit the number of available jobs and make moving a necessity. In some cases, additional training may be required before a career change can be made, then the right job may not be open. Opportunity and timing become critical. A change in position may require seeking out new colleagues and professional associations or abandoning past contacts.

Time Limitations

A dedicated professional is likely to have less leisure time, more required after-work functions, and limited time with family members. The integration of personal and professional lives is considered by many to be female administrators' greatest challenge.

PERSONAL BENEFITS

Several personal benefits have been identified by female administrators.

Enhanced Self-Esteem

Because women administrators are placed in positions where they can "make a difference," both status and a sense of accomplishment are gained. This increased self-confidence is an important asset because women work in a sex-structured society that generates the belief that females lack ability (Shakeshaft, 1987). One woman observed (Brandehoff, 1985) that as a beginning professional she had a job but as an administrator she had a career.

Female administrators also feel a unique sense of pride when they are able to help other young professionals. Williams and Willower (1983) found that women superintendents recognize that the futures of other

women often depend on how well they performed; they are succeeding not only for themselves, but also for the sake of their gender.

Autonomy

Advancement increases the likelihood that women will have more control over their destinies. Important decisions are made independently on a regular basis; however, women are more likely than men to gather information from many individuals before taking action. Shakeshaft (1987) noted that power means different things to men and women. Men are less likely to give their power to others; whereas, women use power to empower others based on the belief that power is not finite but expands as it is shared.

Variety

Administrative jobs do have a certain amount of routine, but opportunities for innovation abound. A single phone call requiring rapid problem solving can change what might have been a routine day and promote a sense of accomplishment. Being open to creative ideas and contacting colleagues who have exciting plans are ways to increase options and make each day more rewarding.

PERSONAL COSTS

The sacrifices that are made by professional women must be examined in light of the personal benefits that can accrue.

Time Restraints

Increased responsibilities require spending more time on job-related tasks. Because the number of hours in a day is limited, juggling obligations is often a problem. Arranging adequate child care, commuting, entertaining, attending conferences, housecleaning, and shopping are just a few of the tasks that make it difficult for women to spend the desired amount of time with family and friends.

Stress

Women administrators in higher education need to be aware of the role that stress plays in their lives. McMillen (1987) describes universities as "stress factories" because there are too many tasks to be done within a limited time period. The myriad duties of academic life and unreasonably high expectations make stress management difficult. Although stress is not a problem unique to women, their responsibilities are often compounded be-

cause of family obligations. When symptoms such as weight gain and loss, illness, feelings of isolation, and lowered self-esteem appear, help should be sought. Talking with concerned colleagues, participation in a planned exercise program, learning to say no, managing time carefully, and hiring workers to do some household tasks make it easier to schedule personally rewarding experiences.

Marital Instability

Two-career families often have difficulty integrating their personal and professional goals. Marriages of women administrators often fail as their careers advance. While 96 percent of male superintendents are married, only 41 percent of the female superintendents are married (Rist, 1984). Heller (1986) reported that 700,000 couples have commuter marriages with academics making up a large percentage of the total. Separations are difficult for both spouses and children. When marital conflict occurs, everyone suffers. The combination of many factors including experiential background causes many women to have feelings of guilt when they are confronted with decisions that may have a negative impact on their family. Decisions about relocation and international assignments are particularly difficult.

Interpersonal Relationships

Numerous social functions increase the number of superficial contacts while decreasing time needed to nurture long-term friendships. Sandler (1986) reports that undue attention is paid to women's personal lives including marital status, sexual orientation, and dress. This lack of privacy results rapidly because of the many acquaintances an administrator acquires. In the office, administrative time is often spent dealing with petty situations created by individuals who are thinking only of their own personal needs.

Role Conflicts

Multiple roles create conflict in the minds of many female administrators. For example, decisions are most difficult when job advancement makes it necessary for a spouse to leave a good job, when children must change schools or when a conference interferes with an important piano recital. Often the ability to resolve such conflict depends on supportive family and friends.

CONCLUSION

Although female administrators make significant personal sacrifices throughout their careers, most women will confirm that the rewards they have experienced have made their investment worthwhile. Such women administrators hope that their success and commitment will make the path smoother for younger women who are striving for career advancement.

REFERENCES

Brandehoff, S. (1985, January). Spotlight on women managers. *American Libraries,* 20–26.

Brile, J. (1987). *Woman to Woman: From Sabotage to Support.* New York: Horizon Press.

Heller, S. (1986, January 22). 'Commuter marriage' a growing necessity for many couples in academia. *The Chronicle,* 21(19) 1, 22–23.

Loden, M. (1985). *How to Succeed in Business without Being One of the Boys.* New York: Time Books.

McMillen, L. (1987, February 4). Job related tension and anxiety: Taking a toll among employees in academia's "stress factories." *The Chronicle,* 33 1, (21), 10–12.

Morrison, A., White, R., and Van Velsor, E. (1987, August). Executive women: Substance plus style. *Psychology Today,* 18–26.

Rist, M. C. (1984). Superintendents: Here's how you work, live, play, and think. *The Executive Educator,* 6(9), 26–30.

Rist, M. C. (1984). Women school executives get serious about success. *The Executive Educator,* 6(3), 24–28.

Sandler, B. R. (1986). *The Campus Climate Revisited: Chilly for Women Faculty, Administrators, and Graduate Students.* Washington, DC: Project on the Status and Education of Women Association of American Colleges.

Shakeshaft, C. (1987). *Women in Educational Administration.* Newbury Park, CA: Sage.

Shakeshaft, C., and Nowell, I. (1984, Winter). Research on theories, concepts, and models of organizational behavior: The influence of gender. *Issues in Education,* 2(3), 186–203.

Smith, J. (1978, May). Encouraging women to enter administration. *NASSP Bulletin,* 62(418), 114–119.

Stiegemeier, L. (1980). Confidence: A necessity for women administrators. *NASSP Bulletin,* 64(440), 34–39.

Williams, R. H., and Willower, D. J. (1983, April). Female school superintendents' perception of their work. Tape presented at the annual meeting of the American Educational Research Association, Montreal, Canada.

SECTION FIVE

MENTORING AND WOMEN IN HIGHER EDUCATION

Mentoring is a subject of considerable interest to women in higher education today. The authors in this section look at all aspects of mentoring and the implications of mentor relationships for women.

Anderson and Ramey discuss the five distinct roles that mentors play: educator, sponsor, coach, counselor, and confronter. The use of these roles in administrative mentoring is explored.

The negative side to mentoring is often neglected in presentations and discussions about mentoring. Braun reminds us that there are negative consequences to the mentor/protégé relationship, particularly for women.

Alexander studied the attributes of a mentor/protégé relationship of administrators (deans) of nursing programs. She found that specific elements contributed to and supported the development of the mentor/protégé relationship such as the availability of frequent informal meetings and being well educated.

Mentoring is a regular part of the practice of social work. Farr explores this premise and its documentation in social work literature. She believes that "most of us function as part of a mentor dyad."

Thompson discusses mentoring among nursing faculty. She found in her study of the literature that mentoring was not used as a way to help neophytes learn their roles and responsibilities.

18

Women in Higher Education: Development Through Administrative Mentoring

Roberta T. Anderson
Pauline Ramey

It is likely that in some stage of career development, you have encountered someone who has had a significant impact on your professional achievements. Perhaps it was a teacher—a major professor, a supervisor, a dean, or a research adviser. This impact was indicative of the formative influence of others.

There are two general kinds of formative influence on professional achievements. First is the role model. A role model's influence is basically a passive influence. A person identifies a role model who possesses the skills or qualities that she or he lacks and yet admires and wishes to emulate. By observing the role model's performance and its consequences, the person develops an image and then mimics the behavior that evokes desired outcomes or accomplishments. Due to the individuality of the observer, the imitation is likely to be only an approximation of the skill or quality. The observer's appraisal of the outcome or accomplishment is based on comparison of personal performance through interpretation of role model standards. The process of observing can take place without direct interaction between the observer and the role model. It is possible that the role model may not be aware of her or his influence on another person.

The second formative influence in professional achievement is that of the mentor. In contrast to the role model, the mentor has an active influence on a protégé.

A mentor is a person who leads, guides, and advises someone more jun-

ior in experience toward career accomplishments. A mentor can be viewed by a protégé in an almost mystical sense by such encompassing descriptions as: wise adviser, powerful sponsor, gracious host, careful guide, exemplar, kind counselor, smart teacher, and surrogate family member. A mentor can be a key figure in a protégé's life for a brief and defined period of time or for a number of years.

Mentoring is the process by which the protégé is guided, taught, and influenced. There are mentoring events, self-mentoring strategies, and mentoring people. Mentoring events are those which stand out away from the regular or expected flow of life and are indeed significant formative active influences. Events which impact life, which result in growth or change in behavior can be referred to as mentoring events. These are often extrinsic events which have intrinsic, strong emotional impact. Early responsibilities, early experiences, early independence, and early leadership roles can be considered mentoring events.

There are also self-mentoring strategies. Questioning and listening is a primary approach to self-mentoring strategies. This requires good interpersonal skills through framing the right questions and sensing the timing. Also, there is the reading and researching approach to self-mentoring. A third approach using self-mentoring strategies is enrolling in educational programs. This approach combines reading and researching with questioning and listening, and often includes learning psychomotor skills. Last is the self-tutoring approach. This approach includes "figuring out," "mulling over," and "following dreams." This approach is reflective of many theorists, innovators, and entrepreneurs. Each of these four self-mentoring strategies are examples of "tapping your own resources."

DISCUSSION

For the purpose of this chapter "people" mentors and mentoring people will be the central focus.

Mentors seem to come in all shapes, forms, and guises. However, Darling (1985), identified four basic mentor types: (a) The Traditional Mentor; (b) The Step-ahead Mentor; (c) The Co-Mentor; (d) The Spouse Mentor.

The Traditional Mentor is one who is sufficiently able to give wise counsel to the protégé. The paradigm is the parent or the elder of a group. This mentor is usually ten or more years older than the protégé.

The Step-ahead Mentor is one who is able to pave the way, protect, or give valuable guidance to the protégé. The paradigm is the older sibling or more experienced colleague. This mentor is usually ten or fewer years older than the protégé.

The Co-Mentor is one who is engaged in reciprocal or mutual relationships. The two take turns providing guidance and assistance. They provide

help to each other in specific areas. The paradigm is the friend or classmate. The Co-Mentors are usually peers in both age and experience.

The Spouse Mentor is a special form of Co-Mentor. Spouse Mentoring can be either unilateral, with one person giving to another, or it can be reciprocal with each providing guidance and assistance to the other in specific areas.

Mentors perform five distinctly different roles: educator, sponsor, coach, counselor, and confronter. Each role is used to facilitate learning and elicit creative contribution (Peters & Austin, 1985).

The mentor as an educator shares knowledge about the organization that can take years to acquire. This can include unwritten practices, idiosyncrasies, rules that can be loosely observed and policies that must be obeyed to the letter. The hallmarks of the educator are identifying goals, roles, or conditions for the protégé, introducing protégés when they are new to a group and teaching new skills as needed. The tone of the educator is positive and supportive with an emphasis on the protégé learning and applying specific new knowledge. The key skills of the educator are the ability to articulate performance expectations clearly and a willingness to reinforce learning. The consequences for the protégé of an educator mentor are acquisition of new skills, an increase in confidence, and a broadened perspective on the institution.

The mentor as a sponsor widens the exposure of the protégé and reflects direct responsibility for guiding and developing the strong skills of the protégé through the mentoring process. From the women's movement, a nation of networking has emerged as a positive way to achieve outcomes. Protégés are not just introduced to the right people, they are made visible by serving on committees or working on projects that can display their talents. The hallmarks of the sponsor are informing significant others when the protégé can make a special contribution that could let an outstanding skill speak for itself. The tone of the sponsor is positive and enthusiastic with an emphasis on long-term development of the protégé and therefore contribution to the institution. The focus of the sponsor is the polishing, and fine-tuning of the protégé's talents. The key skills of the sponsor are the ability to debureaucratize, dismantle barriers to performance and develop collegial relationships, with a willingness to let go of controls and a willingness to provide access to information and people. The consequences for the protégé of a sponsor mentor are showcasing outstanding skills, contributions to the institution, greater experience, and potential promotion.

The mentor as a coach is face-to-face leadership that observes the protégé for cogitative, affective, and psychomotor skill development. This mentor observation provides data for constructive criticism in each realm of protégé development. Often the coach will play the roll of the devil's advocate by confronting and challenging the protégé. The protégé recognizes the mentor's role as such and trusts the mentor, which results in receptive-

ness to this form of mentoring. The hallmarks of the coach are encouragement before or after a "first" and to make simple but brief corrections. The tone of the coach mentor is encouraging, enthusiastic, preparatory, and explanatory. The key skills of the coach mentor are the ability to express genuine appreciation and to listen effectively. The consequences for the protégé of a coach mentor are enhanced confidence, skills, and improved performance.

The mentor as a counselor advises, listens actively, provides empathic support, and encourages problem solving. The counselor provides a milieu conducive to the introduction of innovative ideas by the protégé and renders clear feedback to the protégé. The hallmarks of the counselor are providing positive, caring support when problems alter the protégé's performance and after potentially traumatic education experiences or needed coaching. The counselor mentor can deter setbacks and disappointments and speed recovery of a protégé. The tone of the counselor mentor puts emphasis on problem solving, positive feedback, supportive comments, encouraging remarks, and structuring dialogue with the protégé. The key skills of the counselor mentor are the willingness to listen and the ability to give clear, useful feedback. The consequences for the protégé of a counselor mentor are an enhanced sense of self and an ability to solve problems. There is often an increased sense of accountability and a renewed commitment from the protégé.

The mentor as a confronter clearly identifies alternatives and consequences to the protégé. When chronic low performance prevails, the confronter provides constructive, caring responses and presents the consequences of unacceptable performance which may include termination of the relationship or reassignment. The confronter and the protégé must recognize that behavioral change is imperative. The hallmarks of the confronter are resolution of aberrant performance behaviors, when the protégé seems unable to meet expectations despite educating and counseling, or when the protégé is persistently failing in the current role. The tone of the confronter mentor is positive, calm, supportive, firm, with a clear focus on the need to make a decision and the time at which decision will be made. The key skills of the confronter mentor are listening and the ability to give direct, useful feedback with an ability to discuss sensitive issues without over-emotionalizing. The consequences for the protégé of a confronter mentor are reassignment with a chance to succeed in another position or have the current position restructured.

The ideal mentor can assess the protégé's needs for the specific mentoring role necessary to advance the protégé. The best mentors inspire continued learning and help a protégé to develop tolerance and coping mechanisms suitable for both the struggles and the applause in the unfolding of their skills and contributions.

Mentoring is not a simple rubric. Rather, it is a complex process which,

when done positively, is the best a mentor can give and when done negatively can be traumatic to both protégé and the mentor.

Positive mentors are best described by characteristics identified by protégés. Among these are: challenges me, is objective, follows through, celebrates my successes, inspires loyalty, reassures me, is optimistic, is courageous, is perceptive, and empowers me.

The positive mentor is an empowering mentor who creates a networking environment for the protégé. The empowering mentor educates, sponsors, coaches, counsels, or confronts the protégé, according to an assessment of what is needed to maximize performance. Recall that without full assessment there is a decrease in the likelihood of correct planning and implementation of the protégé's expectations, hence an invalid evaluation of performance will ensue. Further, the empowering mentor delegates authority with responsibility, includes protégé participation in decision making, and consults the protégé before making decision changes directly related to an area of responsibility delegated to the protégé. An empowered protégé is motivated with praise, challenging tasks, visibility, recognition, and trust in his or her ability. The underlying message of the empowering mentor is "You are a valuable resource," and "I respect, encourage, and promote your growth."

Mentor and protégé relationship inhibitors are described by Darling (1985) as characteristic of Avoiders, Dumpers, Blockers, and Criticizers. The Avoider underinstructs and is neither available nor accessible and ignores or does not respond. Dumpers will provide a large single set of instructions and then introduce new roles or situations. The Blocker demonstrates as the Refuser, the Withholder, and the Hoverer. The Refuser actively avoids meeting needs by outright refusal of requests. The Withholder controls by withholding either vital data or potentially growth-producing opportunities. The Hoverer is guilty of too close supervision and smothering behaviors which decrease self-confidence, self-esteem, and underdevelopment of potential skills. The Criticizer demonstrates as the Destroyer, the Belittler, and the Nagger. The Destroyer projects a negative image to others. The undermining techniques of the Destroyer are often subtle and it may take time to realize exactly what is being experienced. The Belittler is much more overt in behavior. Public reprimands and volatile temperament characterize the Belittler. The Nagger is always seeking an answer to the ever-illusive "why." "Why do you always. . . ." "Why can't you ever. . . ."

Mentors must be seen by the protégé as trustworthy and people to be counted on. Inattentiveness, erratic behaviors, and inconsistency in a mentor will not build trust in the relationship and these behaviors will lead to nonbonding between the protégé and the mentor. Excessive control on the part of a mentor leads to resistance by a protégé. Behaviors that suggest

control or manipulation deter bonding. Judgmental attitudes and task orientation of the mentor can lead to mentor resistance by the protégé.

There is also a danger of some women protégés transferring their own
dependency needs into the mentoring/protégé relationship. The conscious
or unconscious wish to be taken care of by others impacts both the protégé
and the mentor by endangering the effectiveness of each. This behavior
has been described as the "Cinderella complex" and is defined as personal
and psychological dependency, a network of largely repressed attitudes
and fears that keep women retreating from the full use of their minds and
creativity (Dowling, 1981). The chronic energy-sapping ambivalence of dependence versus independence by a protégé creates reluctance in the mentor to educate, sponsor, coach, counsel, or confront.

However, educating and sponsoring are two forms of mentoring which
can often be successful with a "Cinderella" protégé since the keys are
reinforcement of learning and access to information. On the contrary,
coaching, counseling, and confronting "Cinderella" tends to enhance the
personal and psychological dependence of the complex. Recall that these
three forms of mentoring are not totally positive. To coach a protégé can
mean that there are errors to be corrected. To counsel a protégé can note
deficits in performance and the need to solve problems. To confront a
protégé can entail admission of failure.

Protégés dependent on mentors deny their own capacity for learning,
doubt their own ability to cope, and fear being set apart. A protégé who ev-
idences dependency is likely to continue in a subordinate, different role
even when it no longer fits. A "Cinderella" protégé with an exceptionally
intuitive mentor can have a positive learning experience with professional
growth. The Pygmalion effect described by Rosenthal (1973) states that
people sometimes become what we prophesy of them. The power of expectation alone can influence the behavior of "Cinderella" from dependence
toward independence. Through the mentoring process and with time as the
needed catalyst, dependency behaviors are no longer viable and achievement results.

In reality, dissolution of mentor-protégé relationships does occur. Sometimes it is by growth of the protégé, geographic relocation, or it may come
as a result of trauma or neglect. The mentor who is unable or unwilling to
shift from the Traditional Mentor or Step-ahead mentor to Co-Mentor runs
the risk of dissolving the relationship as the protégé grows beyond the ap-
prentice or novice role and the mentor maintains control. In this incidence
a negative ending is eminent. The mentor may demonstrate the "after all
I've done for you" syndrome. This traumatic dissolution of relationship is
evidenced by mentor self-pity, jealousy, contempt, intimidation, or entrap-
ment of the protégé. The mentor becomes a controller rather than a sponsor privilege-giver and a punisher rather than a coaching supporter.

Neglect can bring an end to a mentor-protégé relationship. Disinterest or

inertia on the part of either the mentor or protégé initiates dissolution through neglect. Mentors may choose to drift away from the relationship in which there are not enough rewards to make mentoring worthwhile or there is protégé insensitivity to the mentor's needs.

SUMMARY

At its very roots, mentoring is a personal transaction and interaction between the mentor and protégé. A mentor, empowering or depowering, negative or positive, will impact on the professional achievements of a protégé. A protégé, whether she is demonstrating Cinderella behaviors or is an undiscovered Wonder Woman will impact on the mentor. Rogers (1986) contends that every paper published, every speech delivered, every honor received testifies to the mentors competence and leadership to the protégé. Mentoring in academe provides the vehicle for putting into context a professional value system; the teaching, research, and service missions of higher education; and personal career aspirations.

A valid way to acquire committed professionals, scholarly practitioners, and esteemed academicians is to create them through planned mentoring. In order to elicit professional achievements from a protégé, the mentor must be firmly committed to the components of the positive mentoring. The mentor must exercise the skills of assessment, planning, implementation, and evaluation of situations impacting a protégé. Further, mentors must determine their own distinct roles which facilitate learning and elicit creative contributions from protégés. Fostering and perpetuating positive mentoring is the responsibility of every prospective mentor, every prospective protégé, and everyone who is in a position to facilitate the association of the mentor and the protégé. Achievement requires taking risks.

> "Come to the edge," she said.
> They said, "We are afraid."
> "Come to the edge," she said.
> They came.
> She pushed them . . . and they flew.
>
> Guillaume Apollinaire (paraphrased)

EPILOGUE

The Morehead State University Academic Affairs Associate Program was recognized in the publication, *More Good Ideas,* in the fall of 1987 by the American Association of State Colleges and Universities. It stated that,

A university can bring benefits to both institution and professors by mobilizing existing administrative talents within the faculty. The vice president for academic af-

fairs identified six specific areas within the university which warranted either prompt attention or direct coordinating efforts. With the concurrence of the president, an Academic Affairs Associate Program was instituted at Morehead State University. The thrusts of the formal mentor/protégé program are to provide faculty members with an opportunity to exercise their administrative skills in their choice of specific areas, afford the university a structured method to utilize the administrative expertise of faculty, and provide faculty members experiences to expand their understanding of administrative processes. (p. 20)

REFERENCES

Darling, L. (1984). So you've never had a mentor . . . don't worry. *Journal of Nursing Administration*, 12, 38–39.

———. (1985). Mentors and mentoring. *Journal of Nursing Administration*, 3, 42–43.

———. (1985). What to do about toxic mentors. *Journal of Nursing Administration*, 5, 43–44.

———. (1985). The case for mentor moderation. *Journal of Nursing Administration*, 15(7 & 8), 42–43.

———. (1985). Cultivating minor mentors. *Journal of Nursing Administration*, 15(9), 41–42.

———. (1985). Endings in mentor relationships. *Journal of Nursing Administration*, 15(11), 40–41.

———. (1986). Self-mentoring strategies. *Nurse Educator*, 15(11), 24–25.

Dowling, C. (1981). *The Cinderella Complex.* New York: Summit.

Peters, T., and Austin, N. (1985). *A Passion for Excellence.* New York: Random House.

Ramey, P., and Anderson, R. (1987, June). *Academic Affairs Associate Program.* Morehead, KY: Pauline Ramey, Morehead State University.

———. (1987). *More Good Ideas.* Washington, D.C.: American Association of State Colleges and Universities.

Rogers, J. (1986). Mentoring for career achievement and advancement. *American Journal of Occupational Health*, 40(2), 79–82.

Rosenthal, R. (1973, September). The Pygmalion effect still lives. *Psychology Today*, pp. 56–63.

Umiker, W. (1986). Mentoring: A tool for career development. *Medical Laboratory Observer*, 18(8), 71–72.

19

The Downside of Mentoring

Ronnie Braun

Articles proclaim, "Everyone Who Makes It Has a Mentor," "Mentoring: A Legacy of Success." It has generally been assumed in much of the theoretical and general literature (Phillips, 1977; Roche, 1979; Hennig and Jardim, 1977a & b; Shapiro et al., 1978) that mentoring is a virtually totally positive experience. Rarely has the issue been addressed in anything but glowing terms.

Unfortunately, that is not always the case. By day, while writing my doctoral dissertation, I was struck by the poignant renditions of subjects whose mentoring experiences either did not work out or developed in a hurtful manner. At night, people would come up to me at parties and describe their relationships and then say—brightly and with determination—"That's a bona fide mentoring relationship, isn't it?" because in our culture it is generally assumed that mentoring is a good thing. I would respond with a smile and then say that one of the most common misconceptions about mentoring is that it is always a good thing.

If pressed, I would tell them about one of my subjects who was completing his doctorate at a major university. His dissertation adviser and mentor was a Nobel Laureate. The protégé—my subject—felt that his mentor was a combination of God, Christ, and Einstein, and that he, the protégé, would always only be a B+ student by comparison. That was not the consensus of the faculty, but it was my respondent's perception of reality, and he turned it into a self-fulfilling prophecy.

The purpose of this chapter is to examine some aspects of the downside of mentoring—what happens when mentoring does not work out—in order to present a more balanced perspective of the phenomenon.

Daniel J. Levinson (1978, p. 251) has observed that the "presence or absence of mentors is . . . an important component of the life course during the 20's and 30's." Not every individual has a mentor, but Levinson suggests that a mentor relationship usually has a major (and primarily beneficial) impact on a young adult's development. A *mentor* may be defined as an older adult who takes under his wing a younger adult who is still in the early stages of an occupational career, marriage, family career, or other adult relationship. The mentor acts as a guide, teacher, critic, and sponsor. At best, the mentor "bestows his blessing" on the younger person, and the relationship enables the younger person to relate as an adult with an older person "who regards him as an adult and who welcomes him into the adult world on a relatively (but not completely) mutual and equal basis" (Levinson, 1978, p. 252).

While one of the most important functions of the mentor is to "bestow one's blessing" upon the protégé, what happens when the mentor negates his or her blessing? What happens when the dream is shattered? When the mentor leaves the protégé behind? When the mentor is not a good mentor? When the mentor has his or her own problems? Or perhaps, the relationship—full of hope and promise—never blossoms. There is also, of course, the very real possibility of gender difficulties.

Only a very few studies have even noted any negative aspects of the mentoring relationship (Missirian, 1982, Halcomb, 1980, Bowers 1985). Researchers are just beginning to investigate the downside of mentoring (Auster, 1984).

Donald Auster (1984, p. 142), as one who has dealt with some of the negative consequences, suggests a conceptualization of the mentor-protégé relationship "as a power-dependent, dyadic role set with a strong potential for role strain." In addition to the possible problems between mentors and their respective protégés, both persons have constellations of other role relationships which may conflict with the mentor-protégé relationship.

When a mentor takes on a protégé, imbalances in other role relationships are highly likely. Peers may feel that the protégé has acquired an advantage over them. Colleagues may not approve, for a variety of reasons, of a mentor's particular choice of protégé. Epstein (1970) notes that, especially in the case of a woman protégé and male mentor, significant others in each of the respective persons' role sets (spouses, colleagues) may be suspicious of the relationship.

Initially, the power relationship is imbalanced in favor of the mentor. However, due to the mentor's efforts the protégé's expertise, self-confidence, and influential contacts increase resulting in a rise in the protégé's status—both in the individual's eyes as well as in the eyes of the

professional world to which they both now belong. As Auster (1984, p. 146) notes, "At some point in the life of the relationship, it is likely (to apply Goode's terminology) that the 'role price' becomes too high for the protégé and the 'role bargain' no longer attractive" (1960, pp. 489–490).

George and Kummerow (1981) explain that other complications and difficulties may arise because the protégé may become overly dependent upon the mentor for assistance. In addition, mentors may become condescending or domineering toward their protégés.

Halcomb (1980) notes that the mentor relationship may have its pitfalls in the corporate world. The male mentor who is having a sexual relationship with his protégé may "instill in his protégé the notion that she cannot fulfill her talents without him. Or, consciously or not, she may not want to surpass her mentor or achieve autonomy" (Halcomb, 1980, p. 17).

In the most generic sense, problems with mentors can be summarized with the following quotation that one respondent made of her mentor, "It's very rare, I think, that another individual can know what's the best for you for very long" Halcomb (1980, p. 17).

METHODS

This chapter is based on data collected for a larger study. The population for the study consisted of attorneys in New York City (as identified by inclusion in the Martindale Hubbel Law Directory) who were between the ages of 32 and 39. This age range was selected because Levinson's study indicated that persons in the mid to late thirties are both old enough to be mentors and young enough to have recently had mentors.

A stratified random sample of 300 persons was drawn from the Martindale Hubbel Law Directory using a table of random numbers. Cases were sampled randomly until 150 men were included. The sampling then continued, selecting only women until 150 women had also been chosen. Subjects were sent a letter explaining the purpose of the study and requesting their cooperation, the questionnaire, and two follow-up letters requesting their cooperation. The research sample contained 115 usable responses; 69 were women and 46 were men.

In one part of the questionnaire, respondents were given a generalized definition of Levinson's concept of mentoring. They were then asked to describe, if applicable, a relationship with a mentor, a relationship with a protégé, a potential mentoring relationship that did not work out, and the nonexistence of a mentoring relationship.

The first two categories—relationship with mentor, and relationship with a protégé—are rather self-explanatory. With regard to the potential mentoring relationship that did not work out, respondents were told:

At some time you may have had a relationship which looked like it had the potential of becoming a mentoring relationship, but in fact did not work out in this way. Perhaps the other person was a teacher or boss who at first seemed to have a great deal to offer, but the promise never was realized: the relationship did not develop or developed in a hurtful way.

Correspondingly, when asked to discuss the possible nonexistence of a mentoring relationship, respondents were told that,

Many people never have a mentoring relationship. Perhaps there never was any opportunity; perhaps an opportunity that existed was deliberately passed up; perhaps there were other reasons.

FINDINGS

Fully developed mentoring experiences were described by 24 men (52%) and 32 women (46%). All men had male mentors. Ninety-four percent (23) of the women had a male mentor, while 6 percent (two females) had a female mentor.

Mentoring relationships that did not work out were reported by nine men (20%) and nine women (13%), either due to never being fully developed or developing in a negative (hurtful) manner. Eight men had male mentors and one man had a female mentor. Correspondingly, seven women had male mentors and two women had female mentors.

There is a good deal of literature that reviews and builds paradigms about mentoring, talks about gender differences, as well as relative access to mentoring. The specific literature with which we are concerned here are those that have implied that there is no (or very little) negative impact to having a mentor.

In the following discussion I will give examples that illustrate some of the possible negative consequences of having a mentor. These include betrayal, mentor's loss of power resulting in diminished career possibilities for the protégé, mentor's destructive personality, dependency and overdependency issues, traditional views of the mentor clashing with the protégé's newfound roles, exploitative relationships, encountering "the queen bee syndrome," and possible gender difficulties. Moreover, some women, in reading the literature that points out the advantages of mentoring, may not choose to take responsibility for themselves or their careers.

Halatin and Knots (1982) raise the issue of loyalty to the mentor, suggesting that it may be discarded when his or her support is no longer needed by the protégé.

Another danger inherent in a true mentoring relationship is that of losing a mentor's help due to his or her possible loss of power. This can be professionally as well as emotionally damaging.

Levinson et al. (1978, p. 253) say, "Another hazard is that the mentor is tempted to exploit the relationship, guiding the subject's work toward his own ends and using it for his own fame and fortune."

Fury (1979) indicates that another danger seldom discussed is the possibility of getting attached to a destructive or "bad" mentor.

Another important area to be considered in the discussion of the negative impact of mentoring is the idea of overdependency. Halatin and Knotts (1982, p. 28) state that, "Ordinarily it is the protégé who is guilty of excessive dependency on the mentor, but it is possible for the situation to be reversed."

In some situations, the mentoring relationship may benefit one person much more than the other. It is often a mixed blessing. One protégé was ready to move out into the world, but her mentor held much more traditional views as to what constituted appropriate role behavior for a woman of her station.

The queen bee syndrome has been suggested as a way of identifying women who are successful in spheres that typically exclude women. These women have "made it" in the professional world, and they do not choose to help other women or men to succeed.

I would now like to move on to a discussion of some of the ways gender differences can negatively impact mentoring relationships. There simply is not time to review properly the literature about gender differences and mentoring. It may be succinctly summarized by noting that men have more access than women to mentoring, that men more often mentor men, and that most women have male mentors.

In this study, as part of the guidelines for responding, subjects were told, "Mentoring relationships are influenced in different ways by the respective genders of the participants. In what ways did gender affect your mentoring relationship?"

Almost all of the men who had mentors said that gender had no effect. It will be remembered that their mentors were all men. Comments included "None that I'm aware of," "Not an issue," and so on. One man said that "Gender encouraged the father-son idea. His approval and acceptance of me was important to my wish for success in a 'man's world'." Another man said of his mentor, "Gender? I didn't think about it in those terms, but I can't imagine having developed the same degree of closeness in a working relationship with a woman."

Only one man spoke of a negative experience regarding the effect of gender upon his possible mentoring relationship. His choice of responding in the "potential which did not work out" category tells us a lot about the answer even before we read it.

In summation, men did not seem to regard gender as an issue in influ-

encing their respective relationships. This was not the case, however, for many of the women.

Almost all of the women had, it will be recalled, male mentors. It is interesting to note that many more women than men actually commented in response to the question about gender. Seven of the women who had male mentors characterized their relationships as "father-daughter" in nature. Several of the women commented about having had either a male or female mentor. One woman who had a male mentor said, "If *I* had been a man, possibly I would have had more of a choice of mentors." Another woman said that, "The fact that we are both women enhanced the relationship greatly—she was a role model, there was camaraderie, etc." Finally, a woman with a male mentor said, "I don't know what difference the fact that I was a woman and the judge was a man made to our relationship. I didn't have to prove more (or less) to gain his trust."

We must not overlook the negative aspects of not having any opportunity to be mentored. The literature has amply emphasized that women do have less access to mentors, and so at one level, just the lack of access negatively impacts careers.

Several women who did not have mentors raised the issue of gender while responding to the questions posed in the section where I discuss the nonexistence of a mentoring relationship.

One of the female respondents stated, "I don't really think that *anyone* was much interested in furthering the professional career of a woman when I was in college, or law school, or starting out in practice."

In reference to the influence of the respective genders of the participants, the issue of sexuality—when discussed—ranged from nonexistent to overt. Said one woman, "It was one of the few such relationships I have had where there was lots of warmth, maybe even love in some fashion, but no intrusion of sex. It was an almost older brother-sisterly relationship. Very comfortable." Another lady said that "There was a natural tendency for something more than professional."

Here, the potential for negative impact with regard to mentoring for women is rather obvious. One woman said, "In what ways did gender affect this relationship? Probably totally!! in that it might have continued if I were male. We ended . . . in a sexual clash."

Finally, another woman stated, "It turned almost immediately into a sexual relationship which lasted a year, until he left the city. It was fun . . . but it *interfered* with my scholastic success to a great extent."

CONCLUSIONS

In this chapter, I have tried to examine some aspects of the downside of mentoring—what happens when the phenomenon does not work out. Mentoring is most often presented in a most positive light. By trying to di-

minish the halo glowing about mentoring, perhaps a more balanced—and accurate—perspective may begin to emerge.

The positive aspects of mentoring have been overemphasized. There are, in fact, negative aspects with regard to the impact of mentoring, and while they have been given some attention, they certainly have not been accorded all the attention they need.

REFERENCES

Auster, D. (1984). Mentors and protégés: Power-dependent dyads. *Sociological Inquiry,* 54 (2), 142–153.

Bardwick, J., and Douvan, E. (1971). Ambivalence: The socialization of women. Gornick & Moran (Eds.). *Women in Sexist Society: Studies in Power and Powerlessness.* New York: Basic Books, 225–242.

Becker, H., and Carper, J. (1956). The development of identification with an occupation. *American Journal of Sociology,* 61, 289–298.

Becker, H., and Strauss, A. (1956). Careers, personality and adult socialization. *American Journal of Sociology,* 62, 253–263.

Bolton, B. (1980). A conceptual analysis of the mentor relationship in the career development of women. *Adult Education,* 30 (4), 195–207.

Bowers, A. (1985). Mentors and protégés in male-dominated cultures: The experience of top-level women executives. Ph. D. dissertation, California School of Professional Psychology, Los Angeles.

Clawson, J. (1985). Is mentoring necessary? *Training and Development Journal,* 39 (4), 195–207.

Collins, E., and Scott, P. (1978). Everyone who makes it has a mentor. *Harvard Business Review,* 56 (4), 89–101.

Cook, M. (1979). Is the mentor relationship primarily a male experience? *Personnel Administration,* 24 (11), 82–85.

Douvan, E. (1976). The role of models in women's professional development. *Psychology of Women Quarterly,* 1, 5–20.

Emerson, R. (1962). Power-dependence relations. *American Sociological Review,* 27 (1), 31–41.

Epstein, C. (1970). Encountering the male establishment: Sex-status limits on women's careers in the professions. *American Journal of Sociology* 75, 965–982.

_____. (1971). *Woman's Place: Options and Limits in Professional Careers.* Berkley: University of California Press.

_____. (1983). *Women in Law.* Garden City, New York: Anchor Press/ Doubleday.

Frey, B., and Noller, R. (1983). Mentoring: A legacy of success. *Journal of Creative Behavior,* 17 (1), 60–64.

Fury, K. (1979, December). Mentor mania. *Savvy,* 42–47.

Garfinkel, H. (1956). Conditions of successful degradation ceremonies. *American Journal of Sociology,* 61 (5), 420–424.

George, P., and Kummerow, J. (1981). Mentoring for career women. *Training HRD,* 44–49.

Gilligan, C. (1982). *In a Different Voice: Psychological Theory and Women's Development.* Cambridge, MA: Harvard University Press.

Goode, W. (1960a). Norm commitment and conformity to role-status obligations.
American Journal of Sociology, 66, 246–258.

————. (1960b). A theory of role strain. *American Sociological Review,* 25 (4),
483–496.

Halatin, T., and Knots, R. (1982). Becoming a mentor: Are the risks worth the rewards? *Supervisory Management,* 27 (2), 27–29.

Halcomb, R. (1980). Mentors and the successful women. *Across the Board,* 17,
13–17.

Henning, J. (1984). The lawyer as mentor and supervisor. *Legal Economics: Section
of Economics of Law Practice of the American Bar Association,* 10 (5), 20–25.

Hennig, M., and Jardim, A. (1977a). Women executives in the old-boy network.
Psychology Today, 1, 76–81.

————. (1977b). *the Managerial Woman.* Garden City, NY: Doubleday.

Kanter, R. (1977). *Men and Women of the Corporation.* New York: Basic Books.

Kemper, T. (1968). Reference groups, socialization and achievement. *American Sociological Review,* 33 (11), 31–45.

Levinson, D. (1959). Role, personality and social structure in the organizational
setting. *Journal of Abnormal and Social Psychology,* 58, 170–180.

Levinson, D., et al. (1978). *The Season's of a Man's Life.* New York: Knopf.

Lortie, D. (1959). Layman to layman: Law school, careers and professional socialization. *Harvard Educational Review,* 29 (4), 352–369.

Missirian, A. (1982). *The Corporate Connection: Why Executive Women Need Mentors
to Reach the Top.* Englewood Cliffs, NJ: Prentice Hall.

Neugarten, B., et al. (1965). Age norms, age constraints and adult socialization.
American Journal of Sociology, 70, 710–717.

Phillips, L. (1977). Mentors and protégés: A Study of the career development of
women managers and executives in business and industry. Ph.D. dissertation, University of California, Los Angeles.

Riley, S., and Wrench, D. (1985). Mentoring among women lawyers. *Journal of Applied Social Psychology,* 15 (4), 374–386.

Roche, G. (1979). Much ado about mentors. *Harvard Business Review,* 57 (1), 14–28.

Rosow, I. (1965). Forms and functions of adult socialization. *Social Forces,* 44
(1), 35–45.

Shapiro, E., et al. (1978). Moving up: Role Models, mentors and the patron system.
Sloan Management Review, 19 (3), 51–58.

Smigel, E. (1964). *The Wall Street Lawyer.* New York: Free Press.

Stuller, J. (May, 1983). Should you be a mentor? *Success,* 21–23.

Thompson, J. (1975). Patrons, rabbis, mentors—whatever you call them, women
need them, too. *MBA Magazine,* 10, 26–35.

20

An Exploration of Attributes Present in a Mentor/Protégé Relationship in Nursing Education Administration

Doreene Ward Alexander

As women have advanced in professional career endeavors they have identified several elements that have contributed to their success. These elements include the completion of higher education, appropriate work experience, and participation in a mentorship relationship. The mentorship relationship has been identified as one strategy which actively supports the professional development of one's career (Henning & Jardim, 1976; Levinson, Darrow, Klein, Levison & McKee, 1978; Spengler, 1982; Vance, 1977).

A mentorship relationship is comprised of two people, a mentor and a protégé, and is founded upon mutual trust, personal attraction, and professional admiration. Within this mentorship relationship, the less experienced individual can become more knowledgeable about the responsibilities, skills, and requirements of the mentor's position(s) (Collins, 1983; Hinshaw & Weinstein, 1983; Sheehy, 1976; Vance, 1977). The primary purpose of the mentorship relationship is the facilitation of the professional growth of the protégé to aid him/her in preparing for future career positions.

In the past, mentorship was often limited to male/male relationships enabling and facilitating the protégé's advancement up through the ranks of their organization to positions of leadership (Collins & Scott, 1978; Cunningham, 1984; Levinson et al., 1978; Lewin, 1979; Roche, 1979; Sheehy, 1976). Recently, career-oriented businesswomen have experienced

this type of mutually supportive relationship (Collins, 1983; Cunningham, 1984; Henning & Jardim, 1976; Missirian, 1982; Sheehy, 1976).

Nursing, a traditionally female-dominated profession, is continuously evolving and thus there is a need for strong and insightful leaders. Mentorship is one process that can be useful in the development of these future leaders. In 1984, Kelly stated that the key to nursing's future is the "commitment . . . of those in positions of influence to find, encourage, and nurture promising young nurses" (p. 1). It was the goal of this study to examine a group of nursing leaders, those in the decanal role in schools of nursing, to determine if they were ever involved in a mentorship relationship, and to seek information about the attributes that attracted them to their mentors. Additionally deans were asked to identify attributes that they believed contributed to the mentorship relationship and to provide information about their own experience, if any, as a mentor to others.

RESEARCH QUESTIONS

To gather these data five questions were asked:

Do deans who report having had mentors perceive themselves differently than deans who report not having had mentors?

What is the difference in the way deans who report having had mentors perceive themselves and the way they perceive their mentors?

What is the difference in the way deans who report having been mentors perceive themselves and the way they perceive their protégés?

What characteristics do deans, who report having had mentors, identify as contributing to the mentorship relationship in which they were protégés?

What characteristics do deans who report serving as mentors identify as contributing to the mentorship relationship?

For the purposes of this study it was important to define the following significant terms:

Mentorship relationship: an active process occurring between two individuals which is directed toward the professional advancement and personal growth of the less experienced individual.

Mentor: a person who willingly commits time, energy, and/or resources to assist another in professional development.

Protégé: a person who willingly accepts those efforts offered by a mentor to assist in professional development.

Attribute: a quality or characteristic of an individual that may be either positive or negative in nature.

A major goal of this descriptive study was the construction of a picture of the mentorship relationship as it existed in nursing educational administrations. Specific attention was directed to the initiation phase of this relationship—what attracted mentors and protégés to one another.

THEORETICAL FRAMEWORK

The theoretical framework that was utilized to examine the mentoring study was a combination of the framework of adult development as described by Levinson et al. (1978) and a refinement of interpersonal attraction derived from the writings of Duck (1973). The work of Levinson et al. (1978) identified specific phases of adulthood related to tasks and their accomplishment. Of these identified eras, the emphasis of this study was placed on the phase of early adulthood. For it is during this time that a mentor is of importance in the attainment of a professional career goal. The functions of the mentor were identified as teacher, sponsor, host and guide, exemplar, and counsel. The work of Duck (1973) further provided the basis from which to examine the initiation phase of the mentorship relationship. The available literature did not deal with this phase specifically.

SAMPLE

The sample for this study was drawn from the population of female deans of the 343 National League for Nursing accredited baccalaureate and higher degree programs in the United States. Of this number, 101 (65.5%) were actual participants in the study. Criteria for protection of human subjects were observed. Participants were asked to complete a questionnaire which included the demographic data form, and the Adjective Check List (ACL) developed by Gough and Heilbrun (1983).

FINDINGS

A description of the sample is as follows: Of the 101 participants, the majority of the participants held the title of dean ($n = 64$, 63%), had had six years of administrative experience ($n = 61$, 60%), held a Ph.D. ($n = 49$, 48.5%) and had areas of concentration in graduate education of either educational administration ($n = 26$, 25.7%) or medical/surgical nursing ($n = 26$, 25.7%). All nursing programs offered a baccalaureate program in nursing. Forty-two (41.6%) of the 101 stated that they had had mentors and 35 (34.6%) reported having protégés.

The first question to be evaluated was: "Do deans who report having had mentors perceive themselves differently than deans who report not having had mentors?" Deans were asked to complete the ACL to describe themselves and then statistical analysis was carried out on raw score data to de-

termine if significant differences existed on the 37 subscales of the instrument. The Hotelling's T^2 was utilized to determine if differences existed between the two groups. The Hotelling's $T^2 = 71.175$ ($df = 46, 48; p = 0.2388$). Based on the p value it can be concluded that there were no differences between the two groups.

Of the 101 respondents, 59 (58.4%) had not had mentors in their preparation for the decanal role whereas 42 (41.6%) had. Of the respondents in the sample, 77 (76.2%) were 45 years and older and thus had completed the phase of early adulthood as identified by Levinson et al. (1978). One of the tasks of early adulthood was the establishment of a mentorship relationship and approximately 40 percent of this sample had successfully completed this developmental task. Of note is the fact that the majority of this sample did not have mentors.

Possible explanations as to why the majority of the deans did not have mentors follow: The first reasons might be a lack of mentors for women in general (Sheehy, 1976) and in nursing and academia in particular (Moore, 1982). It is also speculated that women did not seek the decanal role and thus did not seek mentorship relationships. Collins (1983) found that women do not understand the mentoring concept and thus do not actively seek mentors.

It is also possible to conclude, based on the literature (Sheehy, 1976; Hamilton, 1981; Moore, 1982; and Kelly, 1984), that there were no mentors available at the time of their early career progression; thus participation in a mentorship relationship was not an option for career development. If the opportunity had existed, perhaps mentorship relationships would have been initiated.

Another consideration is that of the role of the secondary mentor as identified by Phillips (1977). The role of this type of mentor varies from that of the primary mentor in that the secondary mentor provides assistance in the attainment of specific goals or objectives. It is possible to speculate that nursing may have been at a stage of evolution that requires the successful completion of specific short-term activities as opposed to long-term career development.

The second question to be examined was: "What is the difference in the way deans who report having had mentors perceive themselves and the way they perceive their mentors?" Those 42 (41.6%) deans who stated that they had had mentors were asked to complete the ACL to describe first themselves and then their mentors. The deans' self-perceptions, as measured by the ACL, differed from their descriptions of their mentors. The multivariate Hotelling's T^2 was utilized to examine the raw data from each of the two groups' scores on the ACL. Results indicated a Hotelling's $T^2 = 129.3418$ ($df 34, 46; p = 0.0154$). Following this preliminary analysis further analysis was conducted using the procedure discriminant function analysis. The findings of the stepwise discriminant analysis indicated a canonical

correlation for the one discriminant function was .57, the chi-square 31.15 with 5 degrees of freedom and significance at the .0000 level. An examination of the standardized discriminant weights showed that five variables contributed to the derivation of the function and were achievement, creative personality, masculine attributes, A-2 and communality.

A picture of the differences between the deans' perceptions of themselves and their perceptions of their mentors evolved based on data analysis. The deans selected more adjectives to describe themselves, perceived themselves as more nurturing with greater self-control, were better adjusted, were affiliative with others to a greater degree than their mentors and were more respectful of others.

When describing their mentor, the deans used more negative adjectives. They perceived their mentors as displaying more forceful behaviors, taking greater risks, being more creative and avoiding conflict, but also being more autonomous. One possible explanation is that their mentors may have been "pioneers" in nursing rejecting the more acceptable image of the reserved, passive nurse and trailblazing the role of the "new" nursing leader.

Another potential explanation is that the deans, in describing their mentors, were influenced by the termination phase of the mentorship relationship. It is possible for one to speculate that they were disillusioned and this bias may be reflected in their descriptions (Phillips, 1977; Pilette, 1980; Missirian, 1982).

The third question to be considered was: "What is the difference in the way deans who report having been mentors perceive themselves and the way they perceive their mentees [protégés]?" Thirty-five (34.6%) deans identified that they were currently or had in the past served as mentors. Of this 35, 12 (34%) had had mentors and 22 (62.8%) had not had mentors. They were asked to describe their perceptions of their protégés using the ACL. Their descriptions of their protégés were compared with their self-ratings using the ACL. The Hotelling's $T^2 = 102.4158$ ($df = 37,32$; $p = 0.2245$). Based on the p value, it can be said that there were not statistically significant differences between deans' self-perceptions and their perceptions of their protégés.

As seen, the analysis of the ACL subscale scores supported a conclusion that the deans perceived no differences between themselves and their protégés. One possible reason for this is that deans selected, as protégés, individuals who were similar in personality, interests, likes, and dislikes. The majority responded that they believed they were indeed similar in personality to their protégés in another question of this study.

The fourth question to be examined was: What characteristics do deans, who report having had mentors, identify as contributing to the mentorship relationship in which they were mentees [protégés]?" Forty-two respondents reported having had mentors. The mean time of the mentorship relationship was five years with the mentor being between five to 15 years

older than the protégé ($n = 17$, 63%). The majority ($n = 25$, 59%) stated that they were dissimilar in personality to their mentor. The majority of the respondents stated that the mentorship relationship was mutual in initiation ($n = 30$, 71%). The respondents were asked to identify which elements contributed to the development of their mentorship relationships in which they were protégés. Those elements identified as occurring by 25 or more are identified in Table 20.1. Those ranked first in importance to mentees are identified in Table 20.2. Those elements identified as not contributing to the development of the mentorship relationship are shown in Table 20.3.

The final question to be considered was: "What characteristics do deans who reported serving as mentors identify as contributing to the mentorship

Table 20.1
Elements Contributing to Mentorship Development (Identified by 25 or more)

Elements	Number
Frequent, Informal discussions	36 (86%)
Well educated	33 (79%)
Friendly	30 (71%)
Expertise in area of interest	30 (71%)
Same geographic location	28 (67%)
Well-spoken, articulate	27 (64%)
Seeking my input and opinions	27 (64%)

Table 20.2
Elements Ranked First in Importance to Protégés

Elements	Number
Friendly	10
Well educated	7
Frequent, Informal discussions	7
Interacted well with others	6
Same geographic location	5

Table 20.3
Elements Not Contributing to Mentorship Development (Identified by 25 or more)

Element	Number
Style of dress	39 (93%)
Involved in research	36 (86%)
Involved in community activities	34 (81%)
Published	31 (74%)

relationship?" Thirty-five respondents reported having had protégés. Of this number 21 (60%) had had mentors while 14 (40%) had not. The majority ($n = 21$, 60%) stated that they were similar in personality to their protégés and that there was a 10-to-15-year age difference ($n = 17$, 48.5%) and that the relationship was mutual in its initiation ($n = 20$, 57%). The respondents were asked to identify which elements contributed to the development of their mentorship relationship in which they were mentor. Table 20.4 identifies those elements deemed as contributing to the mentorship relationship. The respondents then ranked the elements in terms of importance as seen in Table 20.5. Elements identified by the participants as not contributing to mentorship development are shown in Table 20.6.

Table 20.4
Elements Contributing to Mentorship Development (Identified by 24 or more)

Elements	Number
Seeking my input and opinions	28 (80%)
Friendly	25 (71%)
Well spoken, articulate	25 (71%)
Sensitive to needs of others	25 (71%)
Frequent, informal discussions	24 (69%)
Expertise in area of interest	24 (69%)

Table 20.5
Elements Ranked First in Importance to Mentors

Elements	Number
Well educated	9
Involvement in community activities	5
Expertise in area of interest	5
Sensitive to needs of others	5
Seeking my input and opinions	5

Table 20.6
Elements Not Contributing to Mentorship Development (Identified by 32 or more)

Element	Number
Style of dress	33 (94%)
Published	32 (91%)

SUMMARY

The purpose of this descriptive study was to examine the development of the mentorship relationship. Areas of exploration included the existence and frequency of the mentoring relationships experienced by deans of nursing programs; attributes of deans, mentors, and protégés and the identification of elements which supported the development of the mentoring relationships.

CONCLUSIONS

The conclusions drawn from this study about female deans of NLN accredited baccalaureate and higher degree programs follow:

1. There were no differences in perceived attributes between deans who had mentors and deans who did not have mentors.
2. There were differences in specific perceived attributes between deans who had mentors and their perceptions of their mentors.

3. There were not differences in perceived attributes between deans who were mentors and their perceptions of their protégés.

4. Specific elements contribute to and support the development of the mentorship relationship.

REFERENCES

American Psychological Association. (1983). *Publication Manual of the American Psychological Association*, 3rd ed. Washington, DC.

Chamings, P. A., and Brown, B. J. (1984). The dean as mentor. *Nursing and Health Care*, 5(2), 88–91.

Collins, E., and Scott, P. (1978). Everyone who makes it has a mentor. *Harvard Business Review*, 56(4), 89–101.

Collins, N. W. (1983). *Professional Women and Their Mentors*. Englewood Cliffs, NJ: Prentice-Hall.

Cunningham, M. (1984). *Powerplay: What Really Happened at Bendix*. New York: Linden Press.

Duck, S. W. (1973). *Personal Relationships and Personal Constructs: A Study of Friendship Formation*. New York: Wiley.

Gough, H. G., and Heilbrun, A. B. (1983). *The Adjective Check List*, 3rd ed. Palo Alto, CA: Consulting Psychologists Press, Inc.

Hamilton, M. S. (1981). Mentorhood: A key to nursing leadership. *Nursing Leadership*, 4(1), 4–13.

Hawken, P. L. (1980). Growing our own: A way to prepare deans. *Nursing Outlook*, 28(3), 170–172.

Henning, M., and Jardim, A. (1976). *The Managerial Woman*. New York: Pocket Books.

Hinshaw, A. S., and Weinstein, R. N. (1983). The mentoring relationship. *The Research Bridge*, 22(2), 1.

Kelly, L. Y. (1978). Power guide—the mentor relationship. *Nursing Outlook*, 26(5), 339.

———. (1984). Further reflections on mentoring. *Reflections*, 10, 1.

Levinson, D. J., Darrow, C. N., Klein, E. K., Levinson, M. H., and McKee, B. (1978). *The Seasons of a Man's Life*. New York: Ballantine Books.

Lewin, W. B. (1979). Mentoring: A concept for gaining management skills. *Magazine of Bank Administration*, 55, 6, 8, 55.

Missirian, A. K. (1982). *The Corporate Connection: Why Women Need Mentors to Reach the Top*. Englewood Cliffs, NJ: Prentice-Hall.

Moore, K. M. (1982). The role of mentors in developing leaders for academe. *Educational Record*, 63(1), 22–28.

Phillips, L. L. (1977). Mentors and proteges: A study of the career development of women managers and executives in business and industry. Unpublished doctoral dissertation, University of California at Los Angeles.

Pilette, P. C. (1980). Mentoring: An encounter of the leadership kind. *Nursing Leadership*, 3(2), 22–26.

Roche, G. R. (1979). Much ado about mentoring. *Harvard Business Review*, 57, 14–28.

Sheehy, G. (1976). The mentor connection. *New York Magazine*, April 5, 30–39.

_____. (1977). *Passages*. New York: Bantam Books.

Spengler, C. (1982). *Mentor-protégé relationships: A study of career development among female nurse doctorates*. Unpublished doctoral dissertation, University of Missouri at Columbia.

Vance, C. N. (1977). *A group profile of contemporary influentials in American nursing*. Unpublished doctoral dissertation, Teachers College, Columbia University, New York.

_____. (1982). The mentor connection. *Journal of Nursing Administration, 12*(4), 11–13.

21

The Mentor Relationship: Application of Theory to the Practice of Social Work

Patricia Aylward Farr

Discussion of the role of mentoring in social work modalities is notably absent in the professional literature. Yet, upon close examination of the subject in other professional domains, I have been led to believe that mentoring behavior is indigenous to social work practice.

The following theoretical perspectives are gleaned primarily from the fields of business (Kram, 1985; Zaleznik, 1977), nursing (Biordi, 1986; Vance, 1982), criminal justice (Whitehead, 1985), and psychology (Prisbell and Anderson, 1980). The methodological focus of this chapter is concerned with the potential mentoring role of the social work supervisor/educator, with both social work students and with new agency personnel. It is not suggested that mentoring is to be found only in the supervisor-supervisee relationship. Rather, future research endeavors will look at mentoring as a social work role with clients, as well as the mentor relationship between social work professors and university students.

The term *mentor* originated in Homer's *Odyssey*. The wise old man, Mentor, was King Odysseus' trusted friend, and he nurtured, protected and educated Odysseus' son, Telemachus. Mentor performed gatekeeping and sponsorship functions. As any good surrogate parent, Mentor was also instrumental in the socialization process.

In more contemporary literature, Levinson describes the mentor as a blend of parent and peer, whose functions include the following: teacher, sponsor, host, guide, exemplar, and counselor (Levinson, 1978, p. 97).

Levinson clearly states that the mentor is a transitional figure (Levinson, 1978, p. 98). More than one mentor relationship may exist in the space of one's professional lifetime.

Mentoring in the social work discipline is circumscribed by work parameters. Mentoring is by definition a relationship, and relationships at work are situated in an organizational context. Features of any organizational structure, including its culture, the reward system, task design, and performance management systems, affect relationships by shaping the behavior of individuals (Kram, 1985, p. 15). The social worker needs to know her organization's ecosystems in order to better understand and plan for specific mentoring relationship needs and functions.

Vance identifies the mentor relationship as "nurturing support systems . . . critical to a person's professional development, career success and satisfaction" (Vance, 1982, p. 6). Her mentor prototypes of "intellectual-guide, the visionary idealist, the socio-cultural role model, the promoter coach, and the peer-colleague" arise in response to the potentials and needs of the dyadic membership, the particular blend of characteristics present in the relationship, and the demands of the institutional setting (Vance, 1982 p. 11).

As social work continues to emphasize a broadbased generic approach, the social work professional is attuned to the acquisition of a variety of role skills. The roles most often listed are: enabler, teacher, broker, advocate, and activist (Zastrow, 1985, p. 15). I add mentor to this list. Furthermore, I suggest that social workers would be particularly adept at assuming any of the prototype mentor roles suggested by Kram, based on the nature of their training in human need assessment and problem solving.

Mentoring in social work can be formally appropriated by the profession without having to travel far from its theoretical base. Social work routinely deals with the development of relationships with a variety of system sets, in order to enable the fullest of joint problem solving and human growth and development. Communications theory has offered much to the predictive value of "continued human interaction and relationship development" (Prisbell and Anderson, 1980, p. 22). Maintenance and development of any continuous relationship is a result of communication exchange. This interaction decreases uncertainty levels of the dyad, and this in turn leads to more intimate communicative interactions. Self-disclosure is a component of intimacy, and as it escalates in the relationship, so does the relationship's development (Prisbell and Anderson, 1980, p. 23).

A major predictive variable of continuous interaction is "perceived homophily." Homophily is "the degree to which pairs of individuals who interact are similar with respect to certain attributes, such as belief, values, education, social status, and the like" (Prisbell and Anderson, 1980, p. 23). The National Association of Social Workers institutionally mandates the first two attributes, beliefs, and values. The Council on Social Work Educa-

tion sanctions both undergraduate and graduate programs of social work in U.S. colleges and universities, basing accreditation on standardized curriculum requirements. The majority of professional social workers ascribe to the Ethical Code of NASW, regardless of their age, sex, race, religion, ethnic background, or geographical locations. This professional ethic is most often acquired and enhanced in the supervisor-supervisee relationship.

To continue this line of reasoning, "perceived homophily not only leads to more frequent interaction, but also leads to more effective interaction. When source and receiver share common meanings, attitudes, and beliefs that are communicated through a mutual language, it follows that communication between them is likely to be more effective" (Prisbell and Anderson, 1980, p. 23).

When a social work supervisor and a student, or new employee, share in perceived homophily, all systems with which they come in contact will be benefited. And what may be lacking in shared beliefs may be rectified by empathetic understanding. Recognition of supervisee (or client) differences, either from oneself or from the ethnic, cultural, or socioeconomic group from which that person comes, avoids the assumption of similarity. Recognition of differences avoids ethnocentrisim, oppression, and the mistaken offering of sympathy (Simoni, 1986, p. 29). Those who share perceived homophily may also share empathetic feelings. If put into practice together, these two different concepts, homophily and empathy, can help transcend personal differences in the relationship dyad in a much more productive and functional manner.

Kram, in *Mentoring At Work*, describes four phases of the mentoring relationship: initiation, cultivation, separation, and redefinition (Kram, 1985). I use the first two of these phases in my remarks that follow.

The first phase, initiation, is routinely entered into by the supervisor and new supervisee in social work agency settings. Kram reports that during the first year of the relationship, (which in the social work profession is formally required for all professional training experiences), the dyad's "strong positive thoughts result in behavior which encourages an ongoing and significant relationship. While the formal role relationship varies . . . experiences during the initiation phase have much in common. Each individual gains valuable experiences through interaction with the other" (Kram, 1985, p. 512).

Tabbi astutely points out that student enrollment in most social work educational programs is moving toward part-time involvement, and because of this any sustained student-faculty contact will be depleted. Therefore, the student-field supervisor relationship, which has the potential for mentorship, will become even more important in the continuation of the culture of the profession. "Affirming the novice's sense of self, exploring professional aspirations, modeling, self-disclosing, recollecting, and being

accessible—all are elements in the supervisor's role as mentor" (Tabbi, 1983, p. 238).

Kram's second phase of mentor relationship is cultivation. As each member of the dyad continues to share with one another, "each individual discovers the real value of relating to the other. The range of career functions and psychosocial functions that characterize a mentor relationship peaks during this phase" (Kram, 1985, p. 53). An example from the social work profession often finds workers encouraged by their administrators to solicit social work graduate students to serve their field placements with them. Continued involvement as a field teacher with social work higher education is a given expectation for most social work professionals and they relate the positive value this tutorial relationship has for them, even though they rarely are monetarily reimbursed either by their agency, or the college or university.

Help with career functions (administrative choices and client treatment issues) emerges first as the supervisor provides assignments and work, coaching, protection, and exposure. As the relationship strengthens with time, psychosocial functions will emerge. The first ones are usually acceptance and confidence building, as well as role modeling. And counseling and friendship may also become strong components of the relationship. This stage of mentorship is especially beneficial to the mentor, as this is the point where she nurtures and supports, and in doing so "can note the extent to which she has influence in the organizational world. Not only can (she) open doors (for the supervisee), but she is also able to transmit values and skills that enhance that person's capabilities. These activities give rise to personal satisfaction and provide a unique avenue for expressing oneself through the next generation of (social workers)" (Kram, 1985. p. 55).

Most social work supervisors and administrators must perform a variety of work roles in their human service institutions and agencies, more so than the job expectations of their counterparts in business or corporate structures. But similarities still exist. Zaleznik's delineation of work roles in a corporate theory model is useful in elaborating these similarities.

Zaleznik dichotomizes leadership and managerial roles. He sees leaders as the visionaries of our society; managers are those who enable the realization of the visions (Zaleznik, 1977). I instead merge the two roles for the purpose of greater explication of social work mentoring. I see the social work supervisor overtly appropriating both managerial and leadership skills—and in turn transmitting these attributes to others in the mentor relationship.

A manager is first and foremost a problem solver. And social workers, by professional practice definition, exist within problem-solving domains. In social work the problem most often belongs to another, and, as Zaleznik quotes, "managers adopt impersonal attitudes towards goals. These goals arise out of institutional necessities, rather than (personal desires), and are

deeply embedded in the history and culture of the organization" (Zaleznik, 1977, p. 70). In human service organizations a primary task for the social worker is separating out her personal emotions from her expected professional response.

Yet, from a leadership position, it is the attitude of active problem solving, as opposed to a reactive posture, that promotes efficacy in innovative approaches to alleviation of dysfunction. The influence exerted by the use of leadership skills may set the tone for new directions in problem solving and this influence can effect the way people think about change. Issues involving change are most often a social worker's ultimate goal.

Having addressed how role skills differ in the human services versus the corporate, private enterprise sector, I now turn to a brief explication of career expectations and their implications for the mentoring relationship.

Numerous writers cite career advancement and success as invaluable products of a mentor connection (Vance, 1982; Zaleznik, 1977; Levinson, 1978). The model of career success generally adhered to is one that deifies upward mobility. Contrary to this schema, Lewin and Olesen (1980) advocate a modification of the concepts and assumptions that have traditionally defined achievement and success. Within this alternative framework, lateral work trajectories transform the definition of success to one in which "personal satisfaction and a sense of work well done become the central dimensions of ambition" (Lewis and Olesen, 1980, p. 624).

Notably absent from the literature on mentoring is the consideration of "lateralness as a viable and meaningful career pattern, challenging the long-standing equation of progress with ascent or upward mobility" (Lewin and Olesen, 1980, p. 626). Zaleznik notes (1977) that in the corporate setting, mentors assume a risk-taking posture with rising star protégés for the purpose of cultivating future leaders. The description of this process suggests an inherent quality of attractiveness between mentor and potential leader. This attractiveness is grounded in our cultural value investment and fascination for ascendant potentials in human behavior. The concept of laterality challenges the mentor to nonpejoratively view managers as worthy of, and entitled to, sponsorship in any organizational setting. As an extension to this consideration, the responsible mentor should actively promote lateral moves within the profession.

The assumption of leadership positions in the profession, and progression upward within an agency hierarchy are viable options for the social worker, and I do not suggest that they should be supplanted by the concept of laterality. Instead, I strongly espouse the complementarity of both professional trajectories and view the mentor relationship as providing opportunities for constructive experimentation with both.

In addition to facilitating professional development and contributing to career success, it has been noted that mentoring may also be instrumental in maximizing job satisfaction (Vance, 1982). A discussion of job satisfac-

tion necessitates consideration of "burnout potential." *Burnout* is "a syndrome of emotional exhaustion and cynicism that occurs frequently among individuals who do 'people-work' of some kind" (Maslach and Jackson, 1981 p. 100). The relevance of this phenomenon in social work is immediately apparent. For some previously dedicated workers, burnout may instigate occupational desertions. Disillusionment erodes loyalty and hope. For others, the job will not be deserted, but the quality of performance will be immensely compromised by feelings of cynicism and skepticism. In essence, as a result of burnout, the agency is left with either the loss of human potential, or the increased risk of harm to the client.

A relationship with a mentor may function as the appropriate intervention to prevent or ameliorate the debilitating effects of burnout. Of particular value are the psychosocial functions affirmation and support offered in the context of friendship and/or counseling. Furthermore, while utilizing the counseling modality, it is crucial for the mentor to remain cognizant of the concept of laterality as a professional option for the protégé. The occupational move from one position to another may provide the stimulation and rejuvenation essential for recovery from episodic burnout. From the institutional perspective, endorsement of laterality may help prevent a flood of burnout casualties flowing out of the social work profession.

I have endeavored to present a multifaceted discussion of mentorship as it directly applies to the social work supervisor-supervisee relationship. When viewed as a useful and cogent tool for supervisory effectiveness, its implementation becomes an expectation in social work agency function.

This presentation has demonstrated that mentoring is not a new word, or technique, in social work methodology. Mentoring is not reserved for business, academe, or politics. Most of us function as part of a mentor dyad—as students, supervisors, administrators, teachers, or new professionals in the social work field. We may be filling both roles in separate relationships. The better we understand and can discuss our roles in those relationships, the better we can utilize the strengths mentoring can offer us. And the ultimate outcome of this knowledge is the benefit it will bring to our clients.

REFERENCES

Biordi, C. (1986). Nursing service administrator: Marginality and the public person. *Nursing Clinics of North America,* 21(1), 173–183.

Gilbert, L. (1985). Dimensions of same gender student-faculty role-model relationships. *Sex Roles,* 12(1 & 2), 111–123.

Kram, K. (1985). *Mentoring at Work: Developmental Relationships in Organizational Life.* Glenville, IL: Scott, Foresman.

Lewin, E., and Olesen, V. (1980). Lateralness in women's work: New views on success. *Sex Roles,* 6(4), 619–629.

Levinson, D., et al. (1978). *The Seasons of a Man's Life.* New York: Knopf.

Maslach, C., and Jackson, S. (1981). The measurement of burnout. *Journal of Occupational Health, 2,* 99–113.

Prisbell, M., and Andersen, J. (1980). The importance of perceived homophily, level of uncertainty, feeling good, safety, and self-disclosure in interpersonal relationships. *Communication Quarterly,* Summer, 22–23.

Simoni, P. (1986). Role models, mentors and sponsors: The elusive concepts. *Signs,* 6(4), 692–712.

Tabbi, R. (1983). Supervisors as mentors. *Social Work, 28,* 3, 237–239.

Vance, C. (1982). The mentor connection. *Journal of Nursing Administration,* April, 7–13.

Whitehead, J. (1985). Job burnout in probation and parole: Its extent and intervention implications, *Criminal Justice and Behavior,* 12(1), 91–98.

Zaleznik, A. (1977). Managers and leaders: Are they different? *Harvard Business Review,* May–June, 67–78.

Zastrow, C. (1985). *The Practice of Social Work,* 2nd ed. Homewood, IL: Dorsey Press.

22

Mentoring Among Nurse-Faculty

Cesarina M. Thompson

Most of the behaviors we perform, such as reading, writing or functioning in various roles, are learned through the process of socialization. The types of skills we learn are dependent upon the environment in which we live. We could not function as we do unless others were able and willing to teach us the needed skills.

According to social learning theory, new behaviors are acquired through the processes of symbolic and verbal modeling. By observing others before performing new tasks, individuals can avoid making needless or costly errors. In addition, through abstract modeling, individuals can extrapolate the underlying rules and principles from the observed behaviors and apply these concepts to other situations. Thus, learning through modeling is wider in scope than learning by trial-and-error (Bandura, 1977).

Using social learning theory as a framework, it would follow that modeling is an invaluable concept in socializing individuals into occupational roles. In fact, the literature does describe the concept of mentoring as a means to help neophytes learn the roles and responsibilities of their profession.

As a newcomer to the profession of higher education, the writer is interested in the career development of women faculty, specifically nursing faculty. How do they advance through the academic ranks? Do they seek the advice and guidance of experienced colleagues, or do they struggle through their careers making needless mistakes? The purposes of this chapter there-

fore are: (1) to summarize selected literature on mentoring among professionals; (2) to review literature on mentoring in academia; and (3) to discuss implications for nurse educators.

THE CONCEPT OF MENTORING

Although the literature offers several definitions for the term *mentor,* agreement can be found about certain characteristics. A mentor is usually older than the protégé, has more experience and holds higher status in the profession. The mentor acts as a teacher, guide, sponsor, and generally helps the protégé achieve career goals (Sheehy, 1974; Levinson, 1978; Kanter, 1977; Phillips-Jones, 1982). Kanter describes three important functions of a "sponsor": to "fight" for the protégé when needed; to assist in "bypassing the hierarchy"; and to offer "reflected power" (Kanter, 1977).

MENTORING AMONG PROFESSIONALS

Mentoring is seen as a vital aspect of career development among business executives. In general, those who did have mentors report having a higher level of satisfaction with their careers, earning more money at a younger age, and having more opportunities for career advancement (Henning & Jardim, 1976; Collins & Scott, 1978; Roche, 1979).

Interestingly, the literature also shows that mentoring has played a greater role in the career development of males as compared to females. The shortage of female mentoring can be attributed to the few number of women traditionally found in the work force. As Levinson et al. (1978) explain, the few females who may act as mentors to younger women, are usually still struggling to make it in a man's work world. Thus, they have very limited, if any, time to devote to a newcomer. Similarly, Kanter (1977) agrees that there is a scarcity of "sponsors" for women because of the lack of women in top management positions. In addition, in her study of "Indsco" she found that top executives, mostly males, usually chose to sponsor subordinates most like themselves. Thus, women were automatically left out of this process (Kanter, 1977).

Among the few successful women in the business world, however, mentoring seems to have been a significant factor just as in the career development of men. In the Roche (1979) study of top business executives, it was found that women tended to have more mentors than men. On the average, women had three mentors, whereas the majority of men had one or two. Henning and Jardim (1976) found that each woman in their sample of top executives had a very close relationship with their boss during the first ten years of their career. Their boss promoted their career and "acted as a sales agent within and outside the company" (p. 130).

MENTORING IN ACADEMIA

The literature indicates that mentorship is a successful tool in the business world. Does mentoring exist in the academic environment to aid in the development of new faculty? If so, is it seen as a valuable process?

Hall and Sandler (1983) report that "in academe, as in the business world, success often depends not only on what you know but whom you know . . . " (p. 2). New faculty members can receive many benefits from having a mentor, including advice on how to fulfill the responsibilities of teaching, research and service, and support for promotion and tenure (Hall & Sandler, 1983). Interestingly, the authors note that women in academia are "least likely" to engage in mentoring relationships.

Similarly, in another survey, the process of "sponsorship" was reported to be a positive influence in the career development of 250 faculty members. Specifically this study looked at the relationship between "sponsorship": measured by financial, placement, publication, and personal supports, and four dependent variables: rate of publication, grants received, rate of collaboration, and professional associations/publishing network involvement. Each of the independent variables was found to be significantly correlated with at least one of the dependent variables. Working on sponsored research and publication support were significantly related to three dependent variables. The only difference related to sex of the faculty members was found in network involvement. Male faculty had developed a "significantly larger number of associations than females" (Cameron & Blackburn, 1981, p. 374).

Do women shy away from mentoring relationships? If so, why? As more women enter traditionally male-dominated professions, they are in great need of mentors. Two main ideas are reflected in the literature on mentoring among nurse-faculty: mentoring relationships are infrequently found among nurse-educators, however, the presence of a mentor is seen as a beneficial experience by those who have been mentored.

Mentorship is a vital factor in helping nurses develop the scholarly role (May, Meleis, & Winstead-Fry, 1982). According to the authors, mentorship includes role modeling, role clarification, and role rehearsal. They stress the importance of selecting a mentor who "practices what she preaches" (p. 26), and encourage the neophyte to seek out individuals who can specifically provide the needed guidance.

As a result of having a mentor, nurses may be more successful in their careers. Two studies of nursing leaders found that a mentor played a key role in the career development of these individuals. A survey (Vance, 1982) of 46 nursing leaders termed nursing influentials in the study showed that 83 percent reported having one or more mentors. Mentors most often provided the protégé with career advice, guidance, and aid in career promotion. Another frequent function of mentors was to serve as career model.

Vance agrees that mentoring among women has been scarce. She attributes this lack to women's poor self-image, to their defensive and competitive attitudes toward other women, and to the lack of women in top-level positions. Kinsey (1986), in a duplication of Vance's study, found that among 31 nursing leaders, 86 percent had mentors. These same individuals also reported acting as mentors to others.

Agreement is found in the literature that a planned socialization, which includes mentoring, may help new nurse-faculty succeed in the academic role (Conway & Glass, 1978; Barley & Redman, 1979; Beyer & Marshall, 1981; Mauksch, 1982). In addition, neophytes in nursing education may experience less role conflict and role strain by working with a senior faculty member (O'Shea, 1982). However, the use of mentoring is not the rule but the exception among nurse-faculty. What are the reasons for this?

The literature suggests that inadequate preparation for the faculty role contributes to the lack of mentoring among nurse-educators. Due to their recent arrival to the academic community, many faculty in schools of nursing are still in the early stages of faculty role development and have not become proficient in the areas of research and publication (Barley & Redman, 1979). Furthermore, unlike faculty in most other disciplines, beginning nursing faculty often do not hold doctorates. At the Master's level, nurse-faculty obtain teaching and advanced clinical skills, however, the research and scholarly skills are not as developed as they are at the doctoral level (Williamson, 1972; Beyer & Marshall, 1981; Megel, 1985).

Perhaps, these shortcomings stem from nursing's need to establish its independence and gain control over its activities. The medical profession and hospital administration had total control over nursing activities when nursing education was hospital based. As nursing education moved into the academic environment, it segregated itself from the rest of the university community in an attempt to be free of external controls. Thus, nursing departments were often found off the main campus, preventing students from interacting with the rest of the academic community (Williamson, 1972). As a consequence, nursing faculty did not feel obligated to fulfill traditional academic responsibilities: Few obtained doctoral degrees and engaged in scholarly activities. As a result of this traditional orientation to nursing education, conflict may arise between new faculty members who are motivated toward research and scholarship and the "old school" nursing leaders (Williamson, 1972). Therefore, new faculty may not have appropriate role models to emulate. Furthermore, a lack of interpersonal collegiality among nursing educators compounds the problem. Faculty who do not have a Ph.D., often new faculty members, are seen as "second class citizens." Thus, relationships are "less supportive, team efforts less cooperative, criticism less constructive and conflict can remain undiscussed and unresolved" (Beyer & Marshall, 1981, p. 664).

Incongruency between the faculty member's goals and the goals of the

institution may also contribute to his or her being poorly prepared for all facets of the role. Nurse-faculty may be torn between responsibility to the academic setting and responsibility to the practice arena. The faculty member who strongly believes in maintaining expertise in clinical skills may be devoting much time to clinical activities, while neglecting scholarly endeavors (Conway & Glass, 1978).

DISCUSSION AND SUMMARY

According to social learning theory, modeling is a valuable concept that can be utilized to teach new skills, rules, or principles. Sparing the learner from needless errors is a benefit of the modeling process. Mentoring, which includes role modeling, has been widely used in the business world to socialize newcomers and enhance their career development.

The review of the literature indicates that mentoring is a valuable means to socialize new faculty as well. The ability to work closely with a qualified senior faculty member guides the career development of the neophyte in a positive direction. It is hoped that as a result of such a relationship, the individual will be spared from making costly errors.

However, only a few women have benefited from mentoring relationships. The small percentage of women in the work force and the scarcity of women in top management positions have contributed to the lack of mentoring among professional women. Women in higher education are an example of this population.

It is theorized that a result of upbringing, women seek to establish and maintain affiliations with others, whereas men strive for independence (Gilligan, 1982). Thus, it was surprising to find a lack of mentoring among women. Vance (1982) suggests women adopt competitive and defensive attitudes in the workplace. Perhaps, these are coping mechanisms women utilize to survive in a strange environment which often fosters independence and achievement; the basis of male socialization. Women may avoid forming mentor-protégé relationships with another female as a result of their belief that all women lack the needed survival skills. Thus, rather than joining forces and combining resources, women may find themselves "fighting a losing battle." As a result, women are less successful than men in achieving their goals. In fact, in comparison to men, female college students experience a decrease in ambition during their college years and are less confident and less likely to apply to graduate school (Hall & Sandler, 1983).

What factors contribute to the lack of mentoring among nurse-educators? A major factor identified in the literature is inadequate preparation for the faculty role compounded by the recent arrival of nursing education to the academic setting.

Another recurring theme in the literature is the lack of collegiality among women. Nursing's need to be independent has greatly contributed to this problem. "Survival of the fittest" has become the motto among nurse-faculty. However, if women are to survive in a man's world, we need to learn how to play the game (Krueger, 1980). We need to have confidence in our skills and abilities. Rather than strive to be independent, we need to capitalize on our innate tendency to care and share. Men have learned this skill through the "old boy networks"; women have always possessed this skill. For nurse-faculty, the first step in learning to play the game is to learn the rules. Those who hold Ph.D.s should offer support and encouragement to younger faculty who are pursuing doctoral study, rather than treating them as second-class citizens, as suggested by Beyer and Marshall (1981). As more and more nursing educators become prepared at the doctoral level, their expertise in the research process and other scholarly activities will expand. They, in turn, will be more adequately prepared to mentor faculty lacking this knowledge. Lack of expertise and involvement in scholarly pursuits may explain why nurse-faculty devote much time to clinical endeavors: This is the area in which they feel most comfortable. Although clinical expertise is important in nursing education, nurse-faculty must decide which role they wish to fulfill—the educator or the clinician. If the role of educator is chosen, nurse-faculty must become familiar with the responsibilities of the role and prepare adequately to satisfy the requirements. As more nurse-faculty become prepared to mentor others, the process of mentoring will be understood. As a result, mentoring may be increasingly utilized to socialize neophytes.

The review of the literature presented poses additional questions for investigation. Vance (1982) and Kinsey (1986) report a high prevalence of mentoring relationships among nurse influentials. It would be interesting to survey nurse-educators in leadership positions, such as chairpersons, directors, and deans. If there is also a high prevalence of mentor-protégé relationships among these individuals, perhaps they would be best prepared to mentor others. These individuals may have certain qualities or may have acquired certain valuable skills that have enabled them to reach their positions of leadership. Their knowledge and experiences may greatly benefit younger faculty members. In addition, it would be interesting to gather data on the promotion and tenure records of nurse-faculty to explore whether a relationship exists between lack of mentoring and lack of career success in academia.

As Kelly (1978) states, women in the health care field are similar to women in business. Both groups are struggling to achieve positions previously denied to them. She emphasizes that women who are presently in top-level positions must act as mentors to younger nurses if nursing is to become influential in the health care delivery system.

REFERENCES

Bandura, A. (1977). *Social Learning Theory.* Englewood Cliffs, NJ: Prentice-Hall.

Barley, Z., and Redman, K. (1979). Faculty role development in university schools of nursing. *Journal of Nursing Administration,* 9, 43–47.

Beyer, J. E., and Marshall, J. (1981). The interpersonal dimension of collegiality. *Nursing Outlook,* 29, 662–665.

Cameron, S. W., and Blackburn, R. T. (1981). Sponsorship and academic career success. *Journal of Higher Education,* 52(4), 369–377.

Collins, E. G. C., and Scott, P. (1978). Everyone who makes it has a mentor. *Harvard Business Review,* 56, 89–101.

Conway, M. E., and Glass, L. K. (1978). Socialization for survival in the academic world. *Nursing Outlook,* 26, 424–429.

Gilligan, C. (1982). *In a Different Voice.* Cambridge, MA: Harvard University Press.

Hall, R., and Sandler, B. (1983). *Academic Mentoring for Women Students and Faculty: A New Look at an Old Way to Get Ahead.* Washington, DC: Association of American Colleges, Project on Status and Education of Women.

Henning, M., and Jardim, A. (1976). *The Managerial Woman.* New York: Anchor Press/Doubleday.

Kanter, R. M. (1977). *Men and Women of the Corporation.* New York: Basic Books, Inc.

Kelly, L. Y. (1978). Power guide—The mentor relationship, *Nursing Outlook,* 28, 374–378.

Kinsey, D. C. (1986). The new nurse influentials. *Nursing Outlook,* 34(5), 238–240.

Krueger, J. (1980). Women in management: An assessment. *Nursing Outlook,* 28, 374–378.

Levinson, D. J., et al. (1978). *The Seasons of a Man's Life.* New York: Alfred P. Knopf.

Mauksch, I. (1982). The socialization of nurse-faculty. *Nurse Educator,* 7, 7–10.

May, K. M., Meleis, A. I., and Winstead-Fry, P. (1982). Mentorship for scholarliness: Opportunities and dilemmas. *Nursing Outlook,* 30, 22–28.

Megel, M. (1985). New faculty in nursing: Socialization and the role of the mentor. *Journal of Nursing Education,* 24(7), 303–305.

O'Shea, H. (1982). Role orientation and role strain of clinical nurse faculty in baccalaureate programs. *Nursing Research,* 31(5), 306–310.

Phillips-Jones, L. (1982). *Mentors and Protégés.* New York: Arbor House.

Roche, G. (1979). Much ado about mentors. *Harvard Business Review,* 57, 14–17.

Shapiro, E. C., Haseltine, F. P., and Rowe, M. P. (1978). Moving up: Role models, mentors and the "patron system." *Sloan Management Review,* 19(3), 51–57.

Sheehy, G. (1974). *Passages.* Toronto: Clarke, Irwin and Co.

Vance, C. N. (1982). The mentor connection. *The Journal of Nursing Administration,* 12, 7–13.

Williamson, J. A. (1972). The conflict-producing role of the professionally socialized nurse-faculty member. *Nursing Forum,* 11(4), 356–367.

SECTION SIX

EQUITY ISSUES

*In this section equity issues such as criteria for promotion and ten-
ure, career productivity of women, and the additional challenges
faced by women who are also minorities are discussed.*

*Feldt studied the career paths of women who were successful in
achieving promotion and tenure at the University of Michigan. She
found that the relationship between tenure and potential and productivity varied considerably by discipline. Prior research and publication was a strong indicator for subsequent success as measured
by promotion or tenure.*

*Minority women and the additional barriers that they face in ad-
ministration in institutions of higher education are thoroughly discussed by Bassett. Attractiveness is detrimental to women in higher
education, particularly for minority women.*

*In a recent study of women in higher education, Maitland found
that there are still serious equity problems. She concludes that it is
not enough for universities to hire women; they must also see that
they receive equitable treatment in salaries, workload, and opportunities for promotion and tenure.*

*Burnaby and Missirian give personal examples of how women can
be successful in negotiating the barriers to success in higher education today. Strategies for everyday use are given, with their professional experiences as a framework for success.*

23

Potential, Productivity, and Payoff: An Analysis of the Careers of Nontenured Faculty Women

Barbara Feldt

This chapter addresses the problem of the low representation of females in the senior faculty ranks. Small numbers of female faculty are not just a problem at the University of Michigan. It is a national problem which, according to Clark and Corcoran (1986) "is especially acute in elite, research oriented institutions and in the ranks of tenured faculty." Although nationwide female faculty constitute 25 percent of total faculty, at the University of Michigan they are only 17 percent. Also, at this university 7.5 percent of all full professors are female, compared to 10 percent nationwide (Utah, 1986–87).

Vigorous efforts at the University of Michigan to improve the numbers and percentage of female faculty at all ranks have been only partially successful. From 1981 to 1987, the percentage of female full professors increased from 5.8 percent to 7.6 percent. The percentage of female associate professors decreased from 20.6 to 19.8 percent and assistant professors decreased from 31.4 to 30.8 percent.

Not only is a diverse faculty desirable for its own sake, but female and minority students need and deserve to have a larger number of such faculty for instructors, mentors, and role models. Student-faculty ratios for the university were 7:1 for males, 15:1 for minorities and 23:1 for females. Even though those ratios include the supplemental faculty in which there is a higher percentage of females than in the tenure track faculty, they are very disadvantageous for female students.

Because this university operates primarily on an internal promotion basis rather than hiring its senior faculty from other institutions, promotions rather than external hiring are the principal source of senior faculty. The time limits imposed on junior faculty status contribute to the danger that minorities and women will be recruited to assistant professor status but will not receive promotion and tenure and will therefore have to leave the university. If this happens, and additional women and minorities are hired into the junior ranks to replace them, the percentages of such individuals may remain high at the entry levels but rarely increase at the senior and total faculty levels. This is called "revolving door" phenomenon and would prevent the university from achieving its stated goal of increasing the percentages of minorities and females in all faculty ranks.

METHODOLOGY

The data presented in this study were collected as part of the Faculty Cohort Studies, an ongoing project of the Office of Affirmative Action at the University of Michigan. At the university there are 16 schools and colleges of varying sizes. The Faculty Cohort Studies were carried out in those which had sufficient minority or female junior faculty to provide meaningful comparisons to white males. Only two small, two medium-sized, and six or seven departments in each of the two largest schools were found to have enough such subjects for retention studies to be feasible. In other schools, colleges, and departments the lack of appointments are the major problem. This was not addressed by the cohort studies, although it is the subject of major efforts by the Affirmative Action Office.

After obtaining permission from the deans and department chairs in the appropriate units, a cohort of junior faculty members was identified who were appointed within a span of time when promotion criteria remained the same and which was far enough in the past for promotion decisions to have been made for most cohort members. The cohorts studied included junior faculty appointments made in the years 1972–1980.

Because the schools and departments chosen for inclusion in the studies were those few with sufficient minority or female junior faculty to permit meaningful comparisons, the women described in this report are situated in the most receptive units and do not represent the university as a whole.

Characteristics and accomplishments of males and females, minorities and nonminorities, were compared with their career outcomes to determine if the schools' stated promotion and tenure criteria were followed and whether they were followed consistently for subjects in different gender and race categories. Personal characteristics; teaching, scholarly, and service activities; and institutional variables were included in documenting qualifications at the time of appointment, productivity, and other factors related to success.

A total of 260 junior faculty were included in the cohort studies completed thus far. Of these, 71 were women. Because the results of the studies were for the confidential use of the deans and department chairs involved, the female subjects have been grouped by discipline, each involving subjects from two or more schools, to protect the identities of the units and individuals included.

FINDINGS OF THE STUDY

The intent of the analysis presented here is to compare the varying levels of productivity and different career outcomes of female junior faculty members. An attempt will be made to identify personal and institutional factors associated with the perceived differences in levels of productivity and rates of promotion.

Outcomes

The four possible outcomes described here include promotion to associate professor, departure, termination after a review, or continuation as assistant professor (the promotion decision has not yet been made). Of the 71 subjects included in this analysis, 33 (46.5%) were promoted, 22 (31.0%) departed, 14 (19.7%) were terminated, and 2 (2.8%) are still assistant professors.

Almost one-third of the subjects departed, and their reasons for doing so were unclear. Two-thirds of these departures occurred within three and one-half years of appointment, so it seems unlikely that they were positive moves into more desirable positions. Also, in comparing career outcomes for matched groups of 56 male and 56 female cohort study subjects, it was found that fewer males departed and a greater number were terminated compared to females. Personal interviews with departed subjects might have provided explanations for these departures. It would be especially interesting to compare male and female reasons and to know why some women left after such a short time. The departures occurred before the cohort studies began, however, and such interviews were not possible.

Outcomes and Accomplishments

Examining outcomes alone does not provide sufficient information to determine whether or not there was equity in the treatment of the subjects of this analysis. It is necessary to look also at the levels of accomplishment accompanying the outcomes. The accomplishments documented in the cohort studies included scholarly productivity measured by publications, receipt of research honors, and funding from sources outside the university; teaching quality and quantity measured by number of courses taught, stu-

dent and peer evaluations, receipt of teaching honors, and participation in doctoral committees; and service and administrative contributions described in correspondence from deans and department chairs.

The degree of relationship between teaching and outcomes varied from school to school. Teaching evaluations were available for less than half of the 71 subjects of this study and were not directly related to outcomes. On a scale of one to five, five being the highest, average teaching evaluations for promoted and terminated subjects were similar (4.18 and 4.12 respectively), but were lower for subjects who departed (3.70).

Scholarly productivity measured by publication, however, was related to outcomes in all the cohorts studied and will be the measure of accomplishments used in the following discussions. Level of productivity was determined within each school or department cohort by ranking individuals according to their output of the types of publications considered for promotion decisions in that school or department. Considerations of publication quality were incorporated into the determination of levels of productivity in several ways.

First, only articles appearing in peer-reviewed journals were included. Nonpeer-reviewed articles, papers delivered at conferences, project reports, reviews, and similar writings were excluded as were textbooks and other nonscholarly books.

Second, the research funding considered part of an individual's scholarly productivity in this report was awarded through a peer-review process. Internal grants from the department or the university, training grants, and first year seed grants were not included. Finally, career outcomes which appeared anomalous (promotion with apparent low productivity or termination with high productivity) were discussed with the deans or department chairs involved. They were able to point out cases where apparent high productivity was actually a matter of many low quality publications.

In each cohort, all subjects, male and female, were ranked by their productivity. The division into three levels—high, medium, or low—was made at observed breaks in the distributions rather than arbitrarily dividing each group into thirds. In this study percentages of women at the three levels were similar. There were 23 (32.4 percent) with high productivity, 22 (31.0 percent) with medium productivity, and 26 (36.6 percent) with low productivity.

This may not reflect a completely accurate picture of the situation at the time of this analysis because it includes seven women who were still assistant professors at the time data gathering was completed for their department cohorts. In the two years between the determination of their level of productivity and this report, that level may have changed. Since the level of productivity was determined by comparing all members of a cohort and some cohorts were quite large, it was not feasible to compute new levels of

productivity for those seven subjects. Five of them were in the medium category, one in the high, and one in the low.

Table 23.1 displays the levels of productivity associated with various career outcomes. It shows that the majority of subjects with high productivity (60.9%) or with medium productivity (59.1%) were promoted, while the majority of those with low productivity (61.5%) departed. Thus, productivity is demonstrated to be related to outcomes in most cases. However, six subjects with high productivity were terminated and six with low productivity were promoted. Possible explanations for these unexpected outcomes are provided in the following section.

Table 23.1
Outcomes and Accomplishments—Scholarly Productivity

	High Productivity		Medium Productivity		Low Productivity	
	No.	%	No.	%	No.	%
Promoted	14	60.9	13	59.1	6	23.1
Departed	2	8.7	4	18.2	16	61.5
Terminated	6	26.1	4	18.2	4	15.4
Still Ass't. Prof.	1	4.3	1	4.5	0	0
Total	23	100.0%	22	100.0%	26	100.0%

Factors Associated with Productivity and Promotion

Because there were variations among women who appeared qualified for appointments at this university, an attempt was made to identify personal and institutional factors associated with varying levels of productivity and rates of promotion.

Estimated Potential Related to Productivity

The first factor identified was estimated potential at the time of appointment. Closer examination showed that all candidates were not equally qualified when appointed. There were differences among appointees in academic preparation and in publication and employment experience prior to appointment. The extensive comparisons of qualifications and outcomes made in the faculty cohort studies demonstrated that these factors were so closely related to subsequent productivity that it was possible to use them as predictors to estimate the potential for success of each individual. This

was done by determining the total number of positive responses for the four factors:

1. The initial tenure track appointment was at the assistant professor level;
2. The doctoral level degree was completed prior to the beginning date of appointment;
3. The individual had research employment prior to the appointment; and
4. The individual had a high (one point) or medium (one-half point) level of publication prior to appointment compared to other appointees in the school or department cohort.

Those with a total of three to four positive responses were estimated to have a high potential, those with 1.5 to 2.5 to have medium potential, and those with none to have low potential.

Table 23.2 demonstrates the relationship between estimated potential at the time of appointment and subsequent levels of productivity. It shows that the largest percentage of those with high potential had high productivity (41.2%), those with medium potential had medium productivity (40.0%), and those with low potential had low productivity (66.7%).

Table 23.2
Potential and Productivity

	High Potential		Medium Potential		Low Potential	
	No.	%	No.	%	No.	%
High productivity	14	41.2	9	36.0	0	0
Medium productivity	8	23.5	10	40.0	4	33.3
Low productivity	12	35.3	6	24.0	12	66.7
Total	34	100.0%	25	100.0%	12	100.0%

At the time of appointment, ultimate success might have been predicted for all of the candidates with high estimated potential and most of those with medium potential. In fact, 24 of the 59 women in those two categories did achieve a level of productivity which equalled their estimated potential. In addition, nine women with medium potential achieved high levels of productivity and four women with low potential achieved medium productivity for a total of 13 whose levels of productivity exceeded their estimated

potential. Thus, in terms of productivity, there were 37 women whose experiences after appointment may be termed successful.

In contrast, there were 26 with high or medium potential whose subsequent productivity was lower than expected. Because these women had the potential to succeed when appointed but did not accomplish their expected levels of success, it is assumed that during the years after appointment they experienced factors which inhibited or failed to enhance their achievements. Thus, it seems appropriate in the following discussion of subjects who achieved at a level below their potential to adopt the medical term "failure to thrive," used elsewhere to describe infants who, through lack of appropriate stimulation and care, do not develop to their full potential.

Other Factors Related to Productivity

The search for reasons for lower than expected productivity among junior faculty members involves investigating other factors related to productivity by comparing subjects whose productivity exceeded or equalled their estimated potential to those who failed to thrive. The factors investigated were the discipline with which they were associated, race, marital status, parental status, source of candidacy, receipt of faculty development assistance, and collaboration with senior faculty in coauthoring publications.

Table 23.3 displays the percentage of women in each of the three success groups to which each of the seven factors pertain. Factors demonstrated to be associated with succeeding or failing to achieve one's potential are those which show a decrease in the percentages as one moves from the subjects whose productivity exceeded their potential, to those who succeeded in achieving their potential, to those who failed to thrive. The factor which demonstrates this relationship most strongly is receiving faculty development assistance. Table 23.3 shows that 53.8 percent of those who exceeded their potential received such assistance compared with 33.3 percent of those who succeeded and 23.1 percent of those who failed to thrive. The types of assistance included in this category were released time from teaching for one semester, research leaves funded from within or outside the department, and funding for travel and research assistants. Collaboration with senior faculty in coauthoring publications also shows a relationship to attaining one's potential. These two factors, in contrast to the personal factors described in Table 23.3, are amenable to change through improvements in policies and practices. Thus, demonstration of this positive relationship lends support to efforts to make such changes.

Being associated with the humanities and education disciplines, being white or Asian, and being married also demonstrated a relationship with success in terms of achieving one's estimated potential. Findings about increased productivity associated with being married corroborate the findings of studies such as Astin and Hirsh (1978). The positive effects of

Table 23.3
Factors Related to Productivity for Subjects Who Achieved or Exceeded Their Potential Compared to Those Who Failed to Thrive

	Exceeded Estimated Potential		Succeeded in Attaining Potential		Failed to thrive	
Discipline						
Basic Sciences	3	23.1%	8	33.3%	6	23.1%
Humanities and Education	5	38.5	5	20.8	4	15.4
Clinical Studies	4	30.8	3	12.5	6	23.1
Social Sciences	1	7.7	8	33.3	10	38.5
Personal Characteristics						
White or Asian	12	92.3%	21	87.5%	22	84.6%
Black	1	7.7	3	12.5	4	15.4
Married	10	76.9%	17	70.8%	15	57.7%
Not Married	3	23.1	6	25.0	10	38.5
Unknown	0	0	1	4.2	1	3.8
Children	6	46.2%	13	54.2%	11	42.3%
No Children	6	46.2	6	25.0	12	46.2
Unknown	1	7.6	5	20.8	3	11.5
Source of Candidacy						
External	7	53.8%	20	83.3%	18	69.2%
Internal	6	46.2	4	16.7	8	30.8
Collaboration with Senior Faculty						
Collaborated	4	30.8%	5	20.8%	4	15.4%
No Collaboration	9	69.2	19	79.2	22	84.6
Faculty Development Assistance						
Received Assistance	7	53.8%	8	33.3%	6	23.1%
No Assistance	1	7.7	5	20.8	7	26.9
Not Applicable	5	38.5	11	45.8	13	50.0
Number of cases	13		24		26	

association with humanities and education may be a result of the longer histories of participation with large numbers of women as colleagues in these disciplines. Such participation lessens some of the environmental factors which research has shown inhibit female productivity.

Relationships between Potential, Productivity and Outcomes

Although attaining one's predicted level of productivity may be considered a measure of success, real success must be defined as achieving promotion and tenure. Table 23.4 compares outcomes for the three groups, those who exceeded their potential, those who succeeded in achieving it, and those who failed to thrive. It shows that success or failure in achieving one's potential is not necessarily related to outcomes.

Table 23.4
Outcomes for Subjects Who Achieved or Exceeded Their Potential Compared to Those Who Failed to Thrive

	Exceeded		Succeeded		Failed to Thrive	
	No.	%	No.	%	No.	%
Promoted	6	46.1%	15	62.5%	12	46.1%
Departed	2	15.4	3	12.5	10	38.5
Terminated	4	30.8	5	20.8	4	15.4
Still Assistant	1	7.7	1	4.2	0	0
Total	13	100.0%	24	100.0%	26	100.0%

While 62.5 percent of women whose productivity equalled their potential were promoted, 46.1 percent of those whose productivity exceeded their potential and also of those who failed to thrive were promoted. It is interesting to note, however, that the largest percentage of women who were terminated (30.8%) were in the group whose productivity exceeded their estimated potential.

Clearly, there are factors other than productivity involved in the promotion and tenure decision. In attempting to explain outcomes that appeared anomalous (promotions with low productivity and departures and terminations with high or medium productivity), the first factor investigated was the discipline with which subjects were associated. Although there were no anomalous promotions for women in clinical studies and no departures for productive persons in the basic sciences, there was little relationship overall between discipline and unexpected outcomes.

It is therefore necessary to look at individual cases for possible explanations. Of the 22 apparently anomalous outcomes, there were explanations for all but three. Because these explanations were disclosed in written records or conversations with deans and department chairs, they may not be the reasons which the individuals involved would have provided. They do, however, suggest some valid grounds for apparently inequitable treatment. The possible explanations for *promotions with low productivity* were as follows:

Two occurred at an earlier time when promotion requirements were lower.

One was in the group described previously whose productivity may have changed in the two years between completion of data gathering and this analysis.

One was apparently based on publications prior to appointment.

One was a woman who was perceived as highly productive by the dean, but her records did not confirm this perception.

There was no explanation for one.

Departures of women with high or medium productivity were explained as follows:

Three were for personal reasons which did not appear to have an institutional basis.

One was due to unspecified difficulties with the school.

One was in order to accept a new position elsewhere with no indication of whether or not there were problems.

There was no explanation for one.

Explanations of *terminations for women with high or medium productivity* were explained as follows:

Three were recommended for promotion by their department chairs but were turned down by college executive committees.

Three were affiliated with programs that were discontinued in a reorganization of their school.

Two were transferred to the research scientist track because of alleged problems with teaching or lack of the required degree for a tenured position.

One was terminated for cause.

There was no explanation for one.

Summary of the Interrelationships Between Estimated Potential, Productivity and Outcomes

The question of equitable treatment has been demonstrated to involve a complex interaction of personal and institutional factors. A full understanding of the outcomes that occurred requires examining not only levels of productivity, but also estimated potential at the time of appointment. This is particularly true for women with low potential, two-thirds of whom have low productivity. All of those with low potential, even the four who achieved medium productivity, departed or were terminated.

Table 23.3 described some of the factors affecting productivity and promotions for women with medium or high potential. Factors found to be associated with increased productivity were affiliation with humanities and education, receiving faculty development assistance, collaborating with senior faculty in coauthoring publications, being married, and being white or Asian. The discussion of anomalous outcomes described factors such as program elimination and promotion recommendations turned down by

college executive committees which led to terminations of apparently qualified women.

Thus, the paths for women qualified for appointments at this university were not always straight. Figures 23.1a and 23.1b represent attempts to depict graphically these journeys for women in each of the four disciplines. It is apparent that the relationships between potential, productivity, and payoff are different within each discipline. For example, the social sciences have the most women with high potential (14) but fewer promotions (9) than the basic sciences (12) which have only ten subjects with high potential. In clinical studies there are few women with high potential or high productivity and the most departures (10). In the humanities and education are found the most women whose productivity has exceeded their potential.

Implication for Future Research

Assigning a level of estimated potential to each subject has proven fruitful in furthering our understanding of events that occur after a woman is appointed to a tenure track faculty position. It can explain the lack of success for those with low potential and it emphasizes the need to examine in depth the factors associated with lack of success in cases of subjects with medium and high potential. In one school included in the cohort studies, one such factor was lower financial support for the research of women in the initial appointment years than for men. The findings of other investigators suggest that additional factors include negative teaching evaluations by male students, less access to the wisdom and experience of senior colleagues (because they are male), lack of acceptance of research on women's issues, and more subtle issues of departmental climate. If further research into the effects of these factors could be combined with estimates of potential for success of the subjects involved, perhaps clearer and stronger relationships might be established.

In addition, although the methodology of the Faculty Cohort Studies did not include personal interviews, such interviews would undoubtedly uncover other instances of institutional factors which inhibit or fail to enhance productivity for female faculty.

REFERENCES

Astin, H. (1978). Factors affecting women's scholarly productivity. Astin, H. & Hirsh, W. (Eds.). *The Higher Education of Women: Essays in Honor of Rosemary Park*. New York: Praeger.

Clark, S., and Corcoran, M. (1986, January/February). Perspectives on the professional socialization of Women Faculty: A case of cumulative disadvantage. *The Journal of Higher Education*.

Utah System for Higher Education, State Board of Regents. (1986–87). *Women in Faculty Positions in the Utah System of Higher Education*. Salt Lake City, UT.

Figure 23.1a
Women in Basic Sciences

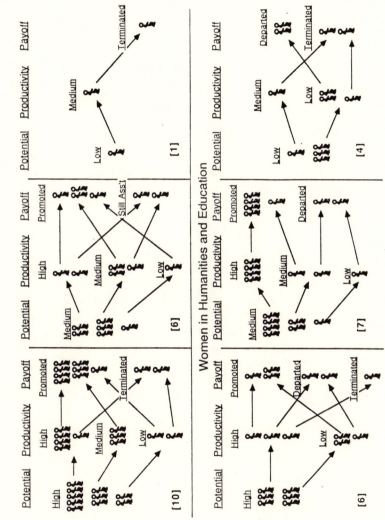

Women in Humanities and Education

Figure 23.1b
Women in Social Sciences

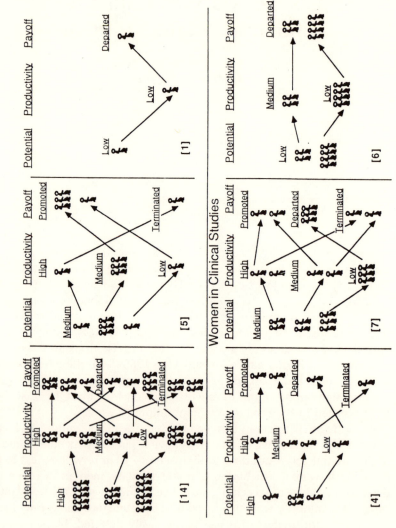

24

The Minority Female in Postsecondary Administration: Challenges and Strategies

Patricia Bassett

Minority female administrators on predominately white campuses are an endangered species (Mosley, 1980). They are still tokens in higher education. Minority women are often in positions peripheral to the decision-making core of the university. Mosley states, "often they feel overworked, underpaid, alienated, isolated, uncertain, and powerless." Minority women with doctorate degrees are a scarce commodity. There seems to be little, if any, change in higher education since the 1960s with the retention of minority women. Today, an array of entry-level opportunities exist. However, the retention opportunities have worsened considerably. Often backlashes have resulted in the removal of many minority women.

According to Bennett and Green (1983) the academic culture and federal law prohibit overt sexist and racist behavior. Thus, few people would dare to declare publicly—or admit to themselves—their unwillingness to work for a black woman. Furthermore, many scholars, men and women alike, deny the existence of race and gender bias in higher education. Despite the progress of minority women, a good deal of subtle race and gender bias yet remains. Unfortunately, this bias is not easily detected. Black women on predominately white campuses have reported that they often confront subtle gender and racial nuances from colleagues.

There is not an abundance of literature that addresses the unique experiences of black women in administration. The problems minority women face are complex. Often it is difficult to discern whether these difficulties

are a result of gender bias or racism. Some problems are the direct consequence of the insecurity of white colleagues. For example, colleague jealousy may precipitate overt and disparate treatment. Other kinds of difficulties result from poor communication and underdeveloped management skills of white colleagues and supervisors. Smith (1980) found that white administrators did not discuss evaluation procedures with minority employees until something was wrong.

Many minority women who work in higher education face double discrimination. Therefore, these women must first contend with the gender biases that all professional women experience. White males and females often feel uncomfortable dealing with minority women. Therefore, whites sometimes act from a variety of false assumptions. For example, many people presume white males to have intellectual competence and leadership ability valued in academic life. Hence the unintentional derogatory designation 'qualified minority woman' implies that most minority women do not meet qualifying standards. This illustration implies that qualified minority women are exceptions to their race and sex. Inevitably, they will have to face the perplexities caused by racial bias. Luckadoo's (1986) report confirms that minority women experience subtle race and gender discrimination from colleagues and students. Since their colleagues often are not aware that hidden biased attitudes shape their behavior, they may deny that they behave prejudicially.

The following information summarizes my personal experiences and the shared experiences of other minority females in administrative positions. Although there are many episodes to share, this chapter will concentrate on the primary sources of conflict for minority women. The twofold purpose of this chapter is to discuss distinctive obstacles confronting black female administrators, and provide strategies for success.

THE TOKENISM SYNDROME

The minority female in higher education, regardless of her qualifications, is often perceived as a 'token'. At times she may find herself disregarded or patronized, or she may meet open hostility. In part, competition for administrative positions in higher education exacerbates obstacles for minority women in predominately white institutions. Because of limited opportunities, minority females compete with white males and females and minority men for administrative positions. Although competition is the American way, it leads to jealousy, slander, and oppression for members of protected classes. Many times, resulting behaviors are subtle demonstrations of oppression. Being minority and female in college administration is often a curse rather than a blessing. Unfortunately, many people in higher education today believe black females have decided employment advantages.

The prevalent notion is curious since minority women are almost an extinct species in higher education.

One manifestation of hidden racial bias is the absurd belief that black women secure their position through gender and race. However, few leaders publicly acknowledge the intelligence and abilities of black females. Unlike white males and females, minority women must prove extraordinary qualifications for promotions. An unwise black woman will spend her time responding to these stereotypes—instead spend that precious time improving your skills. Many institutions seem to embrace mediocrity rather than excellence—do not get caught in that trap. Use your creative energy to improve skills and reach for excellence. At least once a week review these ideas and develop a strategy for improvement. Working harder is admirable. However, working smarter and harder is meritorious.

COPING WITH NEGROPHOBIA

Subconsciously many white office workers suffer from negrophobia. Negrophobia is a historical term which expresses the fear that many whites felt when slaves received their freedom. One year, my white supervisor talked with eight white secretaries to evaluate my performance. During my evaluation, he informed me that the secretaries feared me because none of them had ever worked for a black supervisor. He said, "I want you to know you have made a positive impression. One individual told me that you're not like other blacks." After this conversation, I remembered that I was different. This experience not only reminded me of the fears many whites yet experience, it helped me understand the office grapevine. My career could have had an unhappy ending if support staff had reported a more negative impression.

Minority professionals have to exhibit extraordinary patience when they hear racist language from their colleagues and support staff. They are often unjustly accused of overreacting if they respond to racial slurs. White colleagues exacerbate the problems by justifying their behaviors. For instance, on several occasions, I overheard a white female colleague call me a 'nigger'. Neither my supervisor, nor other colleagues made an attempt to correct her. Finally, I shared my hurt and frustration with one of my white colleagues. This colleague talked with the woman. He spoke with her primarily because he felt distressed that I had heard what she said. Since his conversation with her, I have not heard this offensive expression again.

Negrophobia causes stereotypical and irrational behaviors. For example, some people believe that minorities are inherently lazy. An easygoing minority member may reinforce that stereotype. On the other hand, ambitious and industrious minority women appear aggressive. When staff constantly scrutinize daily activities, it is easy to become offended. One day I returned from a workshop to hear my supervisor and his secretary dis-

cussing whether I had gone home early. After they noticed my presence, they seemed embarrassed. I calmly stated, "My appointment book shows that I had a presentation. If you want to know where I am, you may feel free to check the appointment book or ask my secretary."

Albey (1986) studied the effects that interracial communication training has on white supervisors' job performance ratings. She learned that supervisors who are unfamiliar with minority cultures may have problems communicating effectively with minority group employees. This failure to achieve adequate communication often results in adverse consequences for both supervisor and employees, but especially the employee. Unwittingly, a white male administrator may undermine the authority of the black female supervisor by publicly subjecting her to the scrutiny of subordinates. When this happens, meet with the department head. Explain to him how his behavior undermines your authority. However, don't become discouraged if he doesn't seem to understand. Supervisors may not understand the long-term detrimental impact of gender and race bias behavior. Supervisors who are oblivious to their own prejudices contribute to inaccurate performance evaluations of minority employees. To offset the possibility of this occurring, remember to keep accurate records of appointments and presentations. Above all, don't wear your feelings on your face.

The upwardly mobile minority female administrator will learn how to manage superiors whose professional skills are not as developed as her own. A white supervisor may experience increased anxiety the more capable a minority woman appears. This becomes especially critical if that supervisor comes into direct competition with her for a promotion that s/he wants. In unhealthy work environments, pursuing excellence invokes 'stoppers' from superiors and colleagues. *Stoppers* are attempts to sabotage the credibility and upward mobility of bright employees. To alleviate them, minority women must learn to recognize which battles to fight.

SURVIVING MICROSCOPIC EXPERIENCES

The sole minority female who works in a predominately white setting may feel that she's under a microscope. Sandler (1986) noted male administrators are more likely to question and scrutinize women's abilities while ignoring those of men. Because of the low margin of error allowed, mistakes stand out. Subordinates will notice even minor details. For example, office attire is especially scrutinized. Black women, in particular, report this as a prevalent idiosyncrasy in the workplace. When confronted with thoughtless remarks, avoid defensive responses. Continue to dress professionally and make every effort to respond graciously to tactless compliments and crude observations. Kindness goes a long way. Try not to respond defensively until you have accurate information.

However, be sure that your own perception is accurate. For example, dur-

ing a staff meeting, recently I notice three white female coworkers staring at me. I felt uncomfortable, but I chose not to react. Later in the day, each of them came to me in private. Each apologized for staring and explained her behavior by expressing admiration and complimenting me. Responding too quickly to circumstances can be disastrous.

While receiving compliments for beauty is a positive experience, good looks contribute to the problems black women face. In a recent study, Heilman et al. (1983) stated attractiveness was a positive attribute for men pursuing advancement. However, they found that attractiveness was detrimental to women. Attractive female executives achieved success resulting from luck and not ability. Many people believe unattractive women executives have more integrity and seem more capable. A close examination of this phenomenon reveals that attractive women appear more feminine than unattractive women. On the other hand, attractive men seem to be more masculine than unattractive men.

Thus, attractive women have an advantage in traditional female jobs. However, attractive women in traditional masculine positions appear to lack the necessary qualities required. Psychologists have confirmed that expected success results from internal motivation and ability. Attractive minority women seeking advancement suffer these same frustrations. For example, Taylor (1984) found that determination, ambition, and ability contributed to minority administrators gaining their positions. The innuendo of incompetence is one of the more insidious psychological pressures facing attractive minority women.

Attendance and promptness are important. Advise supervisors of unavoidable absence or tardiness. Remember that a pattern of absenteeism, though legitimate, can taint a career. Equally important, learn how to manage effectively allotted time. Upon completing an assignment, prepare for the next activity. Avoid the "she won't do a thing unless she's watched" image. The more you manage yourself, the more others won't feel compelled to do so.

Included in the microscopic experiences of black female administrators are feelings of isolation. Poussaint (1974) confirms that feelings of isolation are a consequence of working in an unfriendly atmosphere. These feelings become intense when colleagues presume black women to be race and gender relations experts. Furthermore, fighting race and gender battles alone intensify the feelings of isolation. Poussaint reported that black professionals described their jobs as window dressing for universities desiring to appear in tune with the times. There is an easy solution to this problem. Build a network with other professionals. Developing comradeship with colleagues will significantly reduce some of the feelings of isolation. The most important professional friendship I developed during the critical years in my profession was with a mature white male colleague. Dr. Henry (not his real name) sought me out and encouraged me. Because of his initiative, I

found courage and strength to endure some tough experiences. Unknowingly, Dr. Henry became my mentor.

Don't expect large numbers of people to flock to your office to introduce themselves. It is important for you to take the initiative to meet your colleagues. So, take the initiative. Identify and visit the people whose responsibilities influence your specific operation. Seek them out and meet them on their own turf. Greet everyone each day in a friendly manner regardless of how you feel. Concentrate on building bridges of mutual respect and cooperation essential to designing programs. It is important to realize that bureaucracies operate as much on collegiality—or politics—as they do on power and leverage.

UNDERMINED WRITING AND WORK EFFORTS

There are occasions when black administrators have their writing efforts deliberately undermined in distressing ways. For example, during an evaluation, my supervisor criticized my writing ability. Of course this disturbed me. All through my educational training, I had received excellent grades in writing. As I tried to determine what I needed to improve, I discovered my secretary had mailed several documents with blatant typing errors. I also discovered that the same secretary produced perfect copy for the white male department head.

I expected this secretary to produce the same quality of work for me as she did for my director. I met with her to discuss my concerns. She became defensive and responded negatively. We then met with the department head. I reaffirmed with both of them my expectations for the same standards of excellence. The department head did not respond. Later office reorganization resulted in a change of clerical help. My new secretary did not sabotage my work efforts. At the next evaluation, my supervisor told me my writing had improved 100 percent. I was never able to get the department head to understand the dynamics of the underlying problem. The first secretary simply did not want to work for a black administrator.

Do not become discouraged if subordinates, colleagues, or even a supervisor undermine your writing aspirations. Write anyway. Those who wish to develop a reputation in their field eventually acknowledge that they must write. Those who avoid writing must realize that they limit their professional reputation to the boundaries of the organization where they work. Correct writing deficiencies. Writing, like playing a musical instrument or involvement in sports, requires practice. Set aside time to read about job-related issues. Your written reaction to these issues can be in the form of professional articles or working papers for divisional consideration. If you need help, ask for it. Identify an experienced writer whose advice you can trust.

WORKING WITH WHITE MALE MENTORS

An ambitious professional needs a mentor. If your supervisor cannot fill that role, find someone else who can. A mentor can help you develop perspective, prevent you from overreacting, and keep you focused on what is important. Decisions based on whims, emotions, or biases will boomerang. Working with a mentor enables you to see how others work through a problem, analyze facts, and communicate decisions.

Request guidance from your supervisor on a regular basis. If you wait for your supervisor to take the initiative, conferences will get scheduled when something goes wrong. Therefore, the comments will likely be specific and more negative than positive, thus resulting in an unpleasant meeting for you and your supervisor. Try to arrange informal chats and ask for feedback. Balance these discussions by concentrating on what you should do to correct deficiencies. Such meetings are also an opportunity for brainstorming. If there is time remaining after such a discussion, ask questions about issues about your job. In other words, try to develop a set of guidelines for situations that might occur.

In these meetings, resist the temptation to talk about others in the division, or about how you compare with your predecessor. If your supervisor uses the performance of another as an example to illustrate a point, don't defend yourself. Just listen. Do not demean the character or work performance of colleagues. Being critical of one's colleagues and being defensive about your own shortcomings do little to contribute to your professional growth.

To conclude, black female administrators working at predominantly white campuses experience unique difficulties because of their race and gender. Small numbers of minority professionals heighten visibility. Therefore, their behavior seems to stand out and thus they are often subject to greater scrutiny. When few minority women work in a university, it is more likely that others will view them as tokens. Thus, stereotypes govern the relationships.

Universities who are serious about hiring and developing minority women need to evaluate the critical issues facing intelligent and capable minority women. Upper-division administrators help minority women create strategies that result in prolonged success and professional growth. For example, post-secondary executives must examine the biases and attitudes of the power base in the institution. Furthermore, administrators must recognize the manifestations of jealous behavior from colleagues and supervisors who attempt to obstruct the advancement of minority women.

Finally, minority women can become successful in white male systems. However, they must take responsibility for creating and communicating plans for their own growth and development in predominately white institutions. They must recognize that their growth and pursuit of excellence

may threaten insecure colleagues and superiors. Therefore, they must continually remind superiors how they can become winners in pursuing excellence. Finally, they must learn to evaluate which battles to fight and which to ignore.

REFERENCES

Albey, R. (1986, December). The effect of interracial communication training on Anglo supervisors' job performance ratings of minority employees. *Dissertation Abstracts International, 47,* 6.

Bennett, J., and Green, M. (1983). The subtler side of sexism. *Educational Record,* Winter.

Heilman, M. E., et al. (1983). Male and female assumptions about colleagues' views of their competence. *Psychology of Women Quarterly, 7,* 1, Summer.

Horton, E. (1985). No beauties in the executive suite. *Science Digest, 93,* 24.

Luckadoo, D. (1986). The status of black women faculty on predominately white college and university campuses in Georgia. Dissertation Abstracts International, 47, 6.

Mosley, M. (1980). Black women administrators in higher education: An endangered species. *Journal of Black Studies, 10,* 3.

Poussaint, A. (1974). The black administrator in the white university. *The Black Scholar,* September.

Revere, A. (1986). A description of black female school superintendents. Dissertation Abstracts International, 46, 11.

Sandler, B. (1986). *The Campus Climate Revisited: Chilly for Women Faculty, Administrators, and Graduate Students.* Washington, D.C.: Project on the Status and Education of Women, Association of American Colleges.

Smith, C. (1980). The peculiar status of black educational administrators in the university setting. *Journal of Black Studies, 10,* 3.

Taylor, C. (1984). The characteristics and experiences black administrators perceive as being relevant in acquiring their position in predominately white public four-year institutions of higher education in the state of Illinois. Dissertation Abstracts International, 45, 6.

25

The Inequitable Treatment of Women Faculty in Higher Education

Christine Maitland

Women have made gains in higher education in the last two decades—but is it enough? The professoriate has long been a male-dominated profession, especially in the senior ranks. Bowen and Schuster (1985) noted that between 1960 and 1981 the number of women increased rapidly from 25 to 34 percent of the faculty nationwide. During these two decades women in full-time positions increased from 17 to 27 percent and those in part-time positions increased from 23 to 36 percent. Much of this increase can be attributed to the civil rights movement and affirmative action laws. The American Council of Education reported that in the fall of 1983, of the 400,000 full-time faculty members, 27.3 percent were female, an increase from 22.3 percent in 1972 (Shavlik and Touchton, 1987).

These gains have led to a perception that there is no longer an affirmative action problem for women in higher education. However, the numbers are deceptive because there are still serious equity problems. A recent study conducted by Justus, Freitag, and Parker (1987) compared the University of California with research institutions nationwide, and concluded that women faculty tend to be grouped in the lower ranks and temporary positions, and are working at less prestigious community colleges, women's colleges, and small liberal arts colleges rather than in major research institutions. When they teach, women are paid less, receive tenure at lower rates, and rise through the academic ranks at a slower pace. Women are also concentrated in certain disciplines such as English, education, foreign

languages, nursing, home economics, fine arts, and library science, and are underrepresented in disciplines such as engineering, business, and the sciences.

Another recent study conducted in the Pennsylvania State University system reached similar conclusions. Women are underrepresented in executive, administrative, and faculty positions. Women were also underrepresented in the higher ranks. For example, women comprised 19 percent of the faculty but less than 6 percent were full professors (5.7%). The differences in rank of men and women faculty members contributed to a gender difference in salaries, and in addition there were also faculty differences in pay that were not attributable to rank, department, and other such factors (Report to the President and the Commission for Women, 1986).

The Pennsylvania (1986) study also found that the university employed almost 3700 part-time faculty members. Of this group 80 percent were classified as casual employees working less than 50 percent of a full-time schedule. "Many of these individuals were highly skilled, career-oriented members of the University workforce who make a significant and long-term contribution to Pennsylvania State." Yet they were not provided benefits and were paid at lower rates than full-time faculty members performing the same work. A majority of the part-time faculty members are women (58 percent).

The University of Virginia also conducted a recent study on the status of women. In the fall of 1986, women were 22 percent of all faculty members, but only 7.7 percent of the tenured faculty. With the exception of nursing and education, women comprised no more than 6.5 percent of the tenured faculty at any school at the university. The study found that the salaries of female faculty members were "noticeably lower than those of their male counterparts" in 34 of 68 categories (Preliminary Report of the Task Force on the Status of Women, May 1987).

In the academic year 1985–86, the U.S. Department of Education, Center for Education Statistics reported that the salary of male faculty members continued to exceed that of women faculty members in all ranks in both public and private institutions (see Table 25.1). In public four-year institutions the disparity was almost 25 percent when all ranks combined are compared with 31 percent in the private four-year institutions.

RECRUITMENT OF WOMEN FACULTY

Although many colleges and universities have affirmative action plans requiring that effort be made to recruit more women faculty, they are not making sufficient progress for several reasons. Search committees are dominated by men. The Penn State study found that only half the search committees had a female member and less than 10 percent had a female

Table 25.1
Faculty Salaries: Men's Pay Exceeds Women's

Average Salaries and Differences, by Level and Sex, and by Control and Academic Rank, 1985-86

Control and academic rank	4-year			2-year		
	Men	Women	Percent Difference	Men	Women	Percent Difference
Public						
All ranks combined	$35,800	$28,700	24.8	$30,800	$27,700	11.1
Professor	43,400	40,200	8.0	36,800	35,400	3.9
Associate Professor	33,000	31,500	4.7	31,200	29,900	4.4
Assistant Professor	27,800	25,800	7.7	26,800	25,400	5.3
Instructor	21,600	20,300	6.6	23,700	21,900	8.0
Lecturer	25,200	22,400	12.4	25,200	22,400	12.4
No academic rank	26,600	22,900	16.1	30,800	27,900	10.7

Private

All ranks combined	33,900	25,900	30.9	20,400	18,500	10.3
Professor	43,000	36,300	18.4	25,100	23,400	7.1
Associate Professor	31,200	28,500	9.5	22,400	22,100	1.7
Assistant Professor	25,900	23,500	10.5	19,900	18,900	5.0
Instructor	20,100	19,000	5.8	17,000	16,100	5.7
Lecturer	25,300	21,700	16.5	*	*	*
No academic rank	24,600	21,300	15.4	19,500	18,000	8.5

*Number of faculty reported in this category too small to yield reliable data.

Source: U.S. Department of Education, Center for Education Statistics, "Instructional Faculty Salaries for Academic Year 1985-86" (February, 1987).

chair. The task force also found job announcements did not tap women's networks, advertise in women's publications, and less than 10 percent specifically encouraged women to apply.

Justus et al. (1987) concluded that if traditional university hiring practices continue it will take more than 30 years to bring women proportionally into the ranks. A recent study by the Harvard Business School calculated that, based on current hiring practices, reaching a goal of 10 percent female faculty would take more than 50 years.

OBSTACLES FOR WOMEN IN HIGHER EDUCATION

The university has been a "traditionally male club" established and run by men. Rules pertaining to appointment, retention, promotion, and tenure are male-driven. "Male models are inappropriate when applied to women," and yet women continue to be evaluated according to male standards (Pearson, 1986). Astin and Bayer (1975) noted that:

Once on the faculty, women experience a second barrier to quality with men: the academic reward system is biased toward behaviors and activities exhibited more often by men than women. Indeed, the content of the academic reward system was established by men, so rewards go primarily to those women who accept and share men's criteria for academic rewards. Thus administration, research, and publications, which men engage into a greater extent than women, receive higher rewards than teaching, which women devote more time to than men. (p. 372, cited in Pearson, 1986)

Pearson (1986) conducted a national survey among associate and professional women in Speech Communication. Two of the questions asked the women for detailed information about the errors that women make which interfere with their ability to gain tenure and/or promotion and the advice these women would offer to others in the field. The common mistakes made by women in the field are summarized as "acquiescing to the traditional female role" by being too submissive, failure to do research, doing too much for too little gain, overly emphasizing the differences between women and men, and the discrimination that occurs in the university.

Justus et al. (1987) also noted five barriers faced by women in academia: the perceived lack of preparation, lack of sponsors, overt discrimination, competing obligations, and obstacles to productivity.

Barrier number one to women in academia is perceived as *lack of preparation*. Although women are attending college and graduate school in increasing numbers and studies show they make good grades, complete doctorates as fast as men in all fields, are successful at obtaining fellowships, and have a commitment to their fields, there is a common perception

that women are less prepared for an academic career and as a result they receive fewer rewards such as promotions and salary increases.

Barrier number two faced by women in higher education is *lack of sponsorship.* An academic career requires more than a degree and commitment; it also requires the assistance of influential people in the field to further obtain positions and grants. Women have difficulty gaining access to the "male club."

The third barrier women in academia face is *overt discrimination.* In addition to lower salaries, women sometimes receive negative recommendations for tenure and/or promotion that are discriminatory.

The fourth barrier facing women in academia is *competing obligations.* Women who work still assume an unequal share of responsibility for housework and child care. As an example, at one university in California a handbook issued for probationary faculty included the suggestion that women take leave without pay for child rearing so that it did not interfere with their research and publication. There was no such suggestion for the male faculty.

The final barrier facing women in higher education is *obstacles to productivity.* There is a perception that women do less research and publishing than men, in a career that makes high demands in these areas and there is some basis for this. Women tend to spend more time teaching and preparing for teaching, counselling students, serving on committees, and are assigned more undergraduate courses than men. Pearson (1986) also noted that women overextend themselves in the areas of counselling, advising, and committee work rather than spending time on the frequently rewarded publishing, researching, and administering.

WOMEN AS PART-TIME AND TEMPORARY FACULTY

The number of part-time temporary positions increased dramatically during the decade of the 1970s and into the late 1980s. In 1984, it is estimated that the full- and part-time temporary faculty (not including graduate teaching assistants) occupied 35 percent of the faculty positions nationwide and had increased by 22 percent since 1970 (Pierce, 1986). Temporary faculty receive less pay than their tenured counterparts and they seldom receive fringe benefits or retirement (Tuckman, Voglar and Caldwell, 1979; Maitland, 1987).

Tuckman et al. (1979) conducted a nationwide study of temporary faculty and concluded that most part-time faculty are male (61%). However, males tend to be grouped among the two-thirds that have full-time positions and moonlight as teachers. Among those who desired full-time positions, 52 percent were female, and those who chose part-time teaching because of family responsibilities were overwhelmingly female (97%).

Yang and Zak (1981) surveyed part-time faculty in public and private

four and two-year institutions in Ohio. Those who held other full-time positions were predominantly male. The majority of females (72%) either
taught only part-time or held a second part-time position compared to a
small portion of male faculty (2%) (cited in Wallace, 1984).

Yang and Zak also assessed job satisfaction among part-time faculty and
isolated factors that proved significant in predicting job satisfaction. They
found that part-time faculty seeking full-time employment expressed more
job dissatisfaction than others. Part-timers in the arts and humanities were
less satisfied than women teaching part-time if they had other employment, or if they were teaching part-time in business or education.

Universities hire large numbers of women for freshman composition and
writing programs. Business and humanities hire the largest numbers of
part-time faculty, with English being the subject that uses the highest number. Wallace (1984) concludes that the research confirms "that part-time
teaching in English (and frequently also in foreign languages) is primarily a
women's issue."

SOLUTIONS

Over the next 20 years institutions of higher education will be replacing
current faculty because of retirements. It is estimated that approximately
500,000 faculty will be needed nationwide to replace the large numbers of
faculty who will be retiring (Justus et al., 1987). These factors will change
the academic marketplace and many colleges and universities view the
turnover in faculty as an opportunity to improve the number of women
and minority faculty.

However, colleges and universities could immediately improve the status
and number of women faculty by promoting those women who are currently in temporary positions and in the lower ranks. Institutions should
also invest in programs to recruit women teaching in other segments of education just as they invest in programs to recruit and support athletes. Colleges could identify those with good teaching records who lack the
educational background to qualify for university positions. Programs of financial assistance such as tuition reimbursement, sabbaticals, or some
other form of support could be established to assist them in obtaining advanced degrees. Others need financial assistance for research and publication in order to qualify for positions. Child care is needed to allow parents
time for study and research. Some of those teaching part-time have full-
time careers in business or industry, and with financial incentives, colleges
could hire these individuals.

Collective bargaining is one way to address issues such as salary inequities and discrimination. The National Education Association (NEA) which
currently represents some 80,000 higher education members, believes that
salary and benefits are matters for collective bargaining. Salary schedules

should assure that initial placement and advancement on the salary schedule are nondiscriminatory. In addition, NEA endorses the concept of pay equity and comparable worth that establishes salary levels on the basis of skills, value, responsibility, and requirements of the job. Unions often negotiated grievance procedures with binding arbitration which offer faculty a speedy resolution of problems such as discriminatory treatment in tenure/promotion, pay discrimination, and sexual harassment. It may take five or six years to resolve a court case, while grievances can be resolved in six months or less.

Pearson's (1986) study included positive advice to women aspiring to become tenured professors. The suggestions fall into four major categories: (a) be androgynous or behaviorally flexible; (b) do your job, particularly in the area of research and writing; (c) be self-motivated or look to yourself for your success rather than others; and (d) gain the support of other people.

The study conducted by Justus et al. (1987) contained extensive discussion about the successful programs and procedures for hiring and retaining women as well as recommendations for institutions. Early identification of undergraduate and graduate students with a potential for academic careers combined with opportunities to do research while in college and financial support at each stage of the undergraduate and graduate work is necessary for their success. The support should be combined with training in research, scholarship, and teaching. Probationary faculty need to be fully informed about the expectations for tenure, reduced teaching, and committee loads, and access to colleagues in the fields.

It is not enough for institutions to hire women faculty; they must insure equitable treatment in salaries and workload, as well as opportunities for tenure and promotion.

REFERENCES

Bowen, Howard R., and Schuster, Jack H. (1985). *American Professors A National Resource Imperiled.* New York: Oxford University Press.

Justus, Joyce Bennet, Freitag, Sandoria B., and Parker, L. Leann. (1987). *The University of California in the Twenty-First Century: Successful Approaches to Faculty Diversity.* Unpublished paper.

Maitland, Christine. (1987, September). Collective Bargaining and Temporary Faculty. *The Journal of Collective Negotiations in the Public Sector,* 16(3), 233–257.

Pearson, Judy C. (1986). *Academic Women: How to Succeed in the University.* Paper presented at the 1986 Annual meeting of the Speech Communications Association, Chicago, Ill. (ERIC No. Ed 277076).

The Pennsylvania State University (1986). Report to the President and the Commission for Women. (Recommendation Package #1).

Pierce, Taeza. (1986, September 25). Gypsy Faculty Stirs Debate. *The Wall Street Journal.*

Shavlik, Donna, and Touchton, Judith G. (1987). Women in Higher Education. In
    Sara E. Rix (Ed.), *The American Woman 1987–88*, 237–242. New York: W. W.
    Norton and Co.

Tuckman, Howard, Vogler, William, and Caldwell, Jaime. (1979). *Part-time Faculty
    Series*. Washington, D.C.: American Association of the University
    Professors.

The University of Virginia (1987). *Preliminary Report of the Task Force on the Status
    of Women*.

U.S. Department of Education, Center for Education Statistics (February 1987). *In-
    structional Faculty Salaries for Academic Year 1985–86*.

Wallace, Elizabeth. (1984). *Part-Time Academic Employment in the Humanities*. New
    York: The Modern Language Association of America.

26

Two Fast-track Business Professors Tell the Secrets of Their Success

Priscilla Burnaby
Agnes K. Missirian

Women academics have to learn how to make the system work for them. It is a struggle; but rank, remuneration and the concomitant recognition are definitely worth the effort. The first section of this chapter will deal with the general characteristics of successful people and the three key elements that are the sine qua non of professional achievement. Next, a description of the personal career histories of two highly successful women in academe will be presented. The chapter concludes with strategies for career advancement.

CHARACTERISTICS OF SUCCESSFUL PEOPLE

While there are vast differences in the family backgrounds, personalities, and educational experiences of successful people, they have many characteristics in common. For the most part, they are bright—not geniuses—but intellectually agile. They are articulate both in their verbal and written expression. They are high-energy people with a strong self-image. Last but not least, they are people who have the desire to succeed.

There are lots of people who would like to be professionally successful, but just wishful thinking won't get them anywhere. Research based on the career histories of the top businesswomen in America suggests that there are three key elements that are essential on the road to success. These re-

quirements are a dream or a goal, plus the discipline, and the commitment to succeed.

The dream is the first step and probably the most important. If you cannot mentally visualize who and what you want to be five or ten years down the road, you cannot hope to match the image and achieve the goal. Once you have identified the goal, you must marshall the discipline to achieve it. If there are skills to be acquired, courses to be taken, additional experiences to be gained, you must be willing to make the sacrifices necessary to prepare yourself adequately to become a viable candidate for the career success to which you aspire. Last but not least, there is the issue of commitment. The famous comedian Eddie Cantor is credited with saying, "It takes 20 years to make an overnight success." Success takes preparation and time. Sometimes you feel as if you are moving forward apace. Sometimes it seems you are standing still, or even moving backward a step or two. The important thing is never to lose sight of the goal and never to lose heart. Those who do not make it are not necessarily those who do not have what it takes, but more likely they are those whose commitment waned. They gave up their dreams too soon.

As we become more adept at research, we find that we are becoming other people's mentors and advisers. The following section describes how we have conducted our own research and networking.

Tips for Research and Networking

In the past few years we have developed a plan of attack on how to succeed in the areas of research and publication. It takes a good two or three years of starting up projects and following through to develop a steady flow of publications. We have several suggestions for those of you who are interested in becoming successful researchers. First, work on several projects at a time. To find interesting questions to research, perform literature reviews on topics that interest you. We are currently working on over ten projects at various stages. Next, find several people with different skills with whom to work. Set agendas and deadlines for the work to be done. Do not be upset if you do more work than others on one project; it will be their turn another time. Offer to be the organizer, so that you can delegate the tasks to be performed and monitor progress.

Go to conventions to hear about new ideas. Offer your services to work at the conventions as a moderator, panel member, or presenter of a paper. Learn how to put together a good proposal. Send out as many proposals as you possibly can to present a paper or hold a panel at conventions. We usually spend September and October of each year writing proposals for conferences. We are rarely turned down if we submit a well thought out interesting proposal. You meet exciting people at conferences and get good ideas for additional research. You also find people to do additional research

with you. Join professional organizations and offer to work on committees. You will begin to increase your network from many of the above activities.

Improve your skills in the areas of writing, grammar, and proofreading. Learn to compose directly on a word processor. This will save you hours of writing and editing time. Have someone else read your work and use computer packages, such as Spell Check and Gramatic, to check your work. Start a research committee in your department that will foster a good environment for working together on projects. Hold colloquia to discuss each other's research or have brown bag lunches to keep in touch with what others are doing.

Networking is very important within your department, school, and in the professional community. Get to know the people in your department. If you have an idea you want to bring up at a departmental meeting, discuss it before the meeting with as many people in the department as possible. This will help you to better formulate your idea, get additional input, and hopefully win votes. Offer to work with others in your department. Even if this means that you do more than your fair share of the committee work. If possible become chair of key committees. By being an encourager, become a person people feel comfortable approaching for help. Always praise others for a job well done.

Career Advancement Strategies

If you want your vague aspirations to become realities, you must take responsibility for your own career advancement. Be prepared to do your own spade work because no one will do it for you. To be sure, there may be a sponsor or a mentor or colleagues who will offer their help and counsel. Welcome it, but don't expect it.

Learn to think big. Focus on positions that offer more dollars, more status, and greater access to power. The higher up you go, the more challenging the work becomes—and at times more exciting, but definitely not harder. Learn to negotiate hard for dollars and perks up front. Promises, however well intentioned, are hard to collect on after the fact.

Be willing to take risks. You're familiar with the old cliché, "Nothing ventured, nothing gained"? It has become a cliché because its truth is continually confirmed by experience. People who succeed—and those who want to succeed—are willing to take risks. They venture their time, their energies, and their reputations and they risk the stigma of failure on the assumption that they've got what it takes to make it.

Women are often reluctant to strike out on a new or untried venture. Some are even hesitant about accepting responsibility for directing activities for which they have experience and skills. They are plagued with doubt and fears of failure or somehow looking foolish. They want to be absolutely certain they have all the answers and that success is guaranteed.

Well, there is no such thing! Nobody has all the answers, and nothing is guaranteed. There are only questions to be answered and opportunities to be explored.

Make yourself visible and be prepared to do your own PR work. Women have been socialized to believe that it is somehow unladylike to call attention to one's self or to one's achievements in any overt way. One must wait to be noticed, to be recognized, to be asked. They seem to believe that if they are "good little girls" and do what they are told and perform exceptionally well, they will be recognized and rewarded. Well, that's a nice fairy tale that has little to do with the realities of organizational life.

People in decision-making positions of power must see you. They must hear about your good works, from you and from others. Learn to toot your own horn. This can be accomplished simply and effectively without earning you a reputation as a braggart. In your everyday discourse remember to communicate your achievements, aspirations and goals. Show interest and take pleasure in the achievements of others. Such activity is rewarding and comes under the category of intelligent self-interest. Remember, it's your career; and no one is more interested in it or has more to gain from your advancement than you do.

Accept the notion that discrimination exists. Be sensitive to the roadblocks, however subtle; but do not waste time or energy moaning or groaning about them. Find creative ways of overcoming those obstacles. Jump the hurdles, and go for it!

Bibliography

Bandura, A. (1977). *Social learning theory.* Englewood Cliffs, N.J.: Prentice Hall.

Bennis, W., & Nanus, B. (1985). Leaders: *The strategies for taking charge.* New York: Harper & Row.

Berryman, C. L., & Eman, V. (1980). *Communication, languages and sex-proceedings of the first annual conference.* Rowlely, MA: Newbury House.

Brille, J. (1987). *Woman to woman: From sabotage to support.* New York: Horizon.

Clance, P. (1985). *The imposter phenomenon.* Atlanta, GA: Peachtree.

Conway, C., & Andruski, A. (1983). *Administrative theory and practice.* Norwalk, CT.: Appleton-Century-Crofts.

Daly, M. (1973). *Beyond God the Father.* Boston: Beacon.

Eaton, J. (Ed.). (1984). *Emerging roles for community college administrators: New directions for community colleges.* San Francisco, CA: Jossey Bass.

Evans, N. (Ed.). (1985). *Facilitating the development of women.* Washington, DC: Jossey Bass.

Farley, J. (1981). *Sex discrimination in higher education.* Ithaca, NY: NY State School of Industrial Relations, Cornell University.

Farrant, P. (Ed.). (1986). *Strategies and attitudes: Women in educational administration.* Washington, DC: National Association for Women Deans, Administrators and Counselors.

Fisher, A. B. (1980). *Group decision making: Communication and the group process.* (2nd. ed.). New York: McGraw Hill.

Geeken, M., and Gove, W. (1983). *At home and at work: The family's allocation of labor.* Beverly Hills: Sage.

Gertzel, N., & Gross, H. (1984). *Commuter marriage: A study of work and family.* New York: Guilford.

Gilligan, C. (1982). *In a different voice: Psychological theory and women's development.* Cambridge, MA: Harvard.

Gordon, F. E., & Strober, M. H. (Eds.). (1975). *Bringing women into management.* New York: McGraw Hill.

Goss, B., & O'Hair, D. (1987). *Communications in interpersonal relationships.* New York: Macmillan.

Hall, R., & Sandler, G. (1983). *Academic mentoring for women students and faculty: A new look at an old way to get ahead.* Washington, DC: Association of American Colleges Project on the Status and education of women.

Harrigan, B. L. (1977). *Games mother never taught you: Corporate gamesmanship for women.* New York: Warner.

Hewlett, S. A. (1986). *A lesser life: The myth of women's liberation in America.* New York: William Morrow.

Highwater, J. (1978). *Dance: Rituals of experience.* New York: A & W.

Kamerman, S. B., et al. (1983). *Maternity policies and working women.* New York: Columbia University Press.

Kanter, R. M. (1977). *Men and women of the organization.* New York: Basic Books.

Kolb, D., et al. (Eds.). (1984). *Organizational Psychology's readings on human behavior in organizations.* Englewood Cliffs, N.J.: Prentice Hall.

Kram, K. E. (1985). *Mentoring at work: Developmental relationships in organizational life.* Glenview, IL: Scott Foresman.

Levinson, D. L., et al. (1978). *The seasons of a man's life.* New York: Knopf.

Loden, M. (1985). *Feminine leadership or how to succeed in business without becoming one of the boys.* New York: Time Books.

Miles, M. (1985). *Images and insights: Visual understanding in western Christianity and secular culture.* Boston, MA: Beacon.

Moore, N. L. (1986). *Not as far as you think: The realities of working women.* Lexington, MA: D. C. Heath.

Perun, P. (1982). *The undergraduate woman: Issues in educational equity.* Lexington, MA: D. C. Heath.

Peters, T., & Austin, N. (1985). *A passion for excellence.* New York: Random House.

Peters, T., & Waterman, R. (1982). *In search of excellence: Lessons from America's best run companies.* New York: Harper & Row.

Phillips-Jones, L. (1982). *Mentors and protégés.* New York: Arbor House.

Rip, S. (Ed.). (1987). *The American woman 1987–1988.* New York: Norton.

Schein, E. H. (1985). *Organizational culture.* San Francisco, CA: Jossey Bass.

Shakeshaft, C. (1987). *Women in educational administration.* Newbury Park, CA: Sage.

Sheehy, G. (1974). *Passages.* Toronto: Clarke, Irwin.

Stewart, L., et al. (1986). *Communication between the sexes: Sex differences and sex-role stereotypes.* Scottsdale, AZ: Gorsuch Scaribrick.

Stone, J., & Bachner, J. (1977). *Speaking up: A book for every woman who wants to speak effectively.* New York: McGraw-Hill.

Touchton, J., & Shavlik, D. (1984). *Senior women administrators in higher education: A decade of changes 1975–1983 preliminary report.* Washington, DC: Office of Women in Higher Education, American Council on Education.

Index

abortion, 54
academic administrators, team play by, 141–45
academic administrators, women: advancement by, 164; advice from, 156; attainment of positions by, 153–54, 157; characteristics of, 147; communication skills and, 167; experience of, 151; family life and, 169–70; job satisfaction and, 154, 155, 156; mentoring and, 153, 156, 157; mobility of, 151, 153, 158; motives of, 166; percentage of, 147, 150; personal background of, 154–55, 158; problems faced by, 167–69; racial bias and, 238–45; rank of, 148, 149, 155, 157, 164, 165; recommendations for aspiring, 158–59, 170–71; responsibilities of, 163; scholastic achievement and, 149, 151, 157; stress by, 177–78; success factors of, 155–57, 158; tracks of, 149, 151, 152, 158
academic careers: commuter marriages

in, 119, 120, 178; equity and promotion in, 233–35; failure factors for women with, 235; female percentage in, 225, 246, 247; fields of women with, 246–47; gender and salary differences in, 247, 248; housework sharing and, 75–82; income for women with, 73; male domination in, 163, 164–66, 225, 246–50; minority women with, 238–45; motherhood and, 4–5; obstacles for women with, 250–51; part-time, 251–52; productivity and promotion in, study of, 226–35; rank of women with, 73, 225–26, 246, 247, 249; solutions for women with, 252–53; speech and, 107; stress in, 5; success factors in, 231–32, 234; tenure for women with, 8–9, 246; variety in, 94. *See also* academic administrators
accountants, survey of male and female, 133–34
administrators. *See* academic

About the Editor and Contributors

LYNNE B. WELCH, Ed. D., is currently Director of Nursing Programs for the South Carolina Area Health Education Consortium. Her prior positions include: Dean and Professor, College of Nursing and Allied Health at the University of Texas at El Paso; Dean, School of Nursing, Southern Connecticut State University; Chairperson and Associate Professor, Baccalaureate Nursing, Pace University, Pleasantville; and Assistant Professor of Nursing, Western Connecticut State University. She received her doctorate from Teachers College, Columbia University, her master's degree from The Catholic University of America and her bachelor's degree from the University of Connecticut. She has served on a variety of professional and community boards and committees. She has published in a variety of journals, monographs, and symposia.

DOREENE WARD ALEXANDER is a Supervisor with the New Mexico Department of Health and an adjunct Professor of Nursing at The University of Texas at El Paso. Her research focuses in the area of mentor/protégé relationships.

ROBERTA T. ANDERSON is Vice-President for Academics at California State University at Stanislaus. She brings considerable experience as a female in higher education to her research about women in higher education.

PATRICIA BASSETT is Director of University Placement Services at Southern Illinois University at Carbondale. Her involvement in issues in higher education for ethnic minority women is extensive.

RONNIE BRAUN is a doctoral candidate in Sociology and Psychology at Yale University. Her area of research is mentoring as it relates to women.

PRISCILLA BURNABY is an Associate Professor of Business at Bentley College. She has a successful track record as a woman in management.

SUSAN SCHICK CASE is an Assistant Professor of Organizational Behavior in the Weatherhead School of Management at Case Western Reserve University. Her area of research is in communication and gender differences.

MAYA DURNOVO is Director of Women's Support Services at Houston Community College. Her research is focused on characteristics of women administrators.

PATRICIA AYLWARD FARR is Coordinator of the University of Texas at Austin Masters of Social Work program at the University of Texas, El Paso. Her research has centered on the mentor relationship.

BARBARA FELDT is in the Office of Affirmative Action at the University of Michigan. Her research focuses on the potential, productivity, and payoff for women in higher education.

DANNA FRANGIONE is Director of Dance in the Department of Theatre at Bucknell University. Her area of interest is women and dance.

NANCY HENSEL is Professor of Education at the University of Redlands. Her area of research is women's multiple roles.

SHARON HILEMAN is a professor at Sul Ross University. Her area of research is in female-determined relationships.

WILMA HOFFMAN is an Assistant Professor of Management at the University of Texas at El Paso. Her particular research area is that of Mexican and American cultural differences in attitudes toward managers.

ELAINE JARCHOW is Chairperson of the Department of Curriculum and Instruction at New Mexico State University. Her research focuses on the cost benefit of career advancement for women.

FEROZA JUSSAWALLA is an Assistant Professor of English at the University of Texas, El Paso. Her research area is the media and communication messages regarding women.

LINDA KUK is Vice President for Students at SUNY Cortland. Her area of research is the career potential of women upon graduation and then ten years later.

RITA LANDINO is counselor of students and Associate Professor of Education at Southern Connecticut State University. Her research focuses on self-efficacy.

CHRISTINE MAITLAND is a Higher Education Specialist with the National Education Association. Her area of research focuses on equity and women in higher education.

MARGARET MERRION is Acting Dean of the College of Fine Arts at Ball State University. Her research focuses on team playing techniques utilized by women.

PATRICIA R. MESSMER is a professor in the Department of Nursing and Human Development at Pennsylvania State University. Her research focuses on factors that affect the granting of tenure.

AGNES K. MISSIRIAN is a Professor of Business at Bentley College. She has published widely on mentoring, including her book *The Corporate Connection: Why Executive Women Need Mentors to Reach the Top.*

KAREN L. PATTON is Superintendent of Building Services in the Physical Plant at Ball State University. Her perspective as a woman in a traditionally male position is unique.

DEBORAH DIANE PAYNE is an Assistant Professor in the Department of Accounting at the University of Texas at El Paso. Her research has been in cultural aspects of attitudes toward management styles.

PAULINE RAMEY is an Associate Professor of Nursing at Morehead State University. Her particular area of research centers on development of women through administrative mentoring.

JOAN A. RANGE is an Associate Professor of Theology at St. Louis University. Her research focuses on the role of women in the Bible and Christian religions today.

JEAN SAUL RANNELLS is an Assistant Professor of Education at Texas Women's University. Her research centers on the empowerment of women through women's studies.

ANIL SAIGAL is a Professor in the Department of Mechanical Engineering at Tufts University. His research centers on the acceptance of women in the field of engineering.

RANJANI SAIGAL is a Professor in the Department of Engineering at Tufts University. Her research focuses on the lack of acceptance of women in the field of engineering.

IRMTRAUD STREKER SEEBORG is an Associate Professor of Management at Ball State University. Her area of research is in division of labor in two-career faculty households.

BARBARA SIMMONS is the Dean of the College of Education at New Mexico State University. Her research centers on women administrators and the relative costs and benefits of their pursuit of careers.

CESARINA M. THOMPSON is an Instructor in the School of Nursing at Southern Connecticut State University. Her research focuses on mentoring and adult learners.

DONNA THOMPSON is a Professor of Physical Education at the University of Northern Iowa. She has done extensive research about women's use of team play in work.

ALICE A. WALKER is an Associate Professor of Psychology at SUNY Cortland. Her research focuses on women's career choices and aspirations upon graduation and ten years later.